Lecture Notes in Artificial Intelligence 6532

Edited by R. Goebel, J. Siekmann, and W. Wahlster

Subseries of Lecture Notes in Computer Science

Tibor Bosse   Armando Geller
Catholijn M. Jonker (Eds.)

Multi-Agent-Based Simulation XI

International Workshop, MABS 2010
Toronto, Canada, May 11, 2010
Revised Selected Papers

 Springer

Series Editors

Randy Goebel, University of Alberta, Edmonton, Canada
Jörg Siekmann, University of Saarland, Saarbrücken, Germany
Wolfgang Wahlster, DFKI and University of Saarland, Saarbrücken, Germany

Volume Editors

Tibor Bosse
Vrije Universiteit Amsterdam, Faculty of Sciences
Department of Artificial Intelligence
De Boelelaan 1081, 1081 HV Amsterdam, The Netherlands
E-mail: tbosse@few.vu.nl

Armando Geller
George Mason University, Krasnow Institute for Advanced Study
Department of Computational Social Science
4400 University Drive, MS 6B2, Fairfax, VA 22030, USA
E-mail: ageller1@gmu.edu

Catholijn M. Jonker
Delft University of Technology, Faculty of Electrical Engineering
Mathematics and Computer Science, Department of Mediametics
Mekelweg 4, 2628 CD Delft, The Netherlands
E-mail: c.m.jonker@tudelft.nl

ISSN 0302-9743   e-ISSN 1611-3349
ISBN 978-3-642-18344-7   ISBN 978-3-642-18345-4 (eBook)
DOI 10.1007/978-3-642-18345-4
Springer Heidelberg Dordrecht London New York

Library of Congress Control Number: 2010942519

CR Subject Classification (1998): I.2, I.2.11, D.2, F.1, I.6, C.2.4

LNCS Sublibrary: SL 7 – Artificial Intelligence

Typesetting: Camera-ready by author, data conversion by Scientific Publishing Services, Chennai, India

Printed on acid-free paper

Springer is part of Springer Science+Business Media (www.springer.com)

Preface

This volume groups together the papers accepted for the 11th International Workshop on Multi-Agent-Based Simulation (MABS 2010), co-located with the 9th International Joint Conference on Autonomous Agents and Multiagent Systems (AAMAS 2010), which was held in Toronto, Canada, May 10-14, 2010. MABS 2010 was the 11th workshop of a series that started at ICMAS 1998 (Paris, France), and continued with ICMAS 2000 (Boston, USA), followed by nine editions of AAMAS (2002-2010). All information on the MABS Workshop Series can be found at http://www.pcs.usp.br/~mabs.

The MABS workshop offers a climate that enables cross-fertilization between social, economic and organizational sciences. Over the years this resulted in fruitful cooperation between these sciences, as can be seen from the articles in the MABS proceedings. The workshop has been an important source of inspiration for the body of knowledge that has been produced in the field of Multi-Agent Systems (MAS). As illustrated by this volume, the workshop continues to bring together researchers interested in MAS engineering with researchers focused on finding efficient ways to model complex social systems in social, economic, and organizational areas. In all these areas, agent theories, metaphors, models, analyses, experimental designs, empirical studies, and methodological principles all converge into simulation as a way of achieving explanations and predictions, exploring and testing hypotheses, and producing better designs and systems.

MABS 2010 attracted a total of 26 submissions from 16 different countries. Every paper was reviewed by three anonymous referees. In all, 11 papers were accepted for presentation, yielding an acceptance rate of 42.3%. We are very grateful to the participants who provided a lively atmosphere of debate during the presentation of the papers and during the general discussion on the challenges that the MABS field faces. Special thanks go to Dawn Parker from the University of Waterloo for the inspiring invited talk she gave about pressing issues in social simulation.

We are also very grateful to every author who submitted a paper, as well as to all the members of the Program Committee and the additional reviewers for their hard work. Thanks are also due to Kagan Tumer (AAMAS 2010 Workshop Chair), to Michael Luck and Sandip Sen (AAMAS 2010 General Chairs), to Wiebe van der Hoek and Gal Kaminka (AAMAS 2010 Program Chairs), and to Yves Lespérance (AAMAS 2010 Local Arrangements Chair). Finally, we wish to thank Jaime Simão Sichman and all members of the MABS Steering Committee for giving us the opportunity to organize this edition of the workshop.

November 2010

Tibor Bosse
Armando Geller
Catholijn M. Jonker

Organization

Workshop Chairs

Tibor Bosse   Vrije Universiteit Amsterdam, The Netherlands
Armando Geller   George Mason University, USA
Catholijn M. Jonker   Delft University of Technology, The Netherlands

Program Committee

Shah Jamal Alam   University of Michigan, USA
Frédéric Amblard   Université Toulouse 1, France
Luis Antunes   University of Lisbon, Portugal
João Balsa   University of Lisbon, Portugal
Shu-Heng Chen   National Chengchi University, Taiwan
Sung-Bae Cho   Yonsei University, Republic of Korea
Nuno David   Lisbon University Institute, ISCTE, Portugal
Paul Davidsson   Blekinge Institute of Technology, Sweden
Bruce Edmonds   Centre for Policy Modelling, UK
Joseph Giampapa   Carnegie Mellon Software Engineering Institute, USA
Nigel Gilbert   University of Surrey, UK
Nick Gotts   Macaulay Institute, Scotland, UK
Laszlo Gulyas   AITIA International Informatics Inc., Hungary
Rainer Hegselmann   University of Bayreuth, Germany
Mark Hoogendoorn   Vrije Universiteit Amsterdam, The Netherlands
Marco Janssen   Arizona State University, USA
Satoshi Kurihara   Osaka University, Japan
Maciej M. Łatek   George Mason University, USA
Jean-Pierre Muller   CIRAD, France
Emma Norling   Centre for Policy Modelling, UK
Paulo Novais   Universidade do Minho, Portugal
H. Van Dyke Parunak   NewVectors LLC, USA
Juan Pavón Mestras   Universidad Complutense Madrid, Spain
Juliette Rouchier   Greqam/CNRS, France
David L. Sallach   Argonne National Lab and University of
    Chicago, USA
Keith Sawyer   Washington University in St. Louis, USA
Jaime Simão Sichman   University of São Paulo, Brazil
Elizabeth Sklar   City University of New York, USA

Keiki Takadama	The University of Electro-Communications, Japan
Oswaldo Terán	University of Los Andes, Venezuela
Takao Terano	University of Tsukuba, Japan
Gennaro di Tosto	ISTC-CNR, Italy
Klaus Troitzsch	University of Koblenz, Germany
Maksim Tsvetovat	George Mason University, USA
Harko Verhagen	Stockholm University, Sweden

Additional Reviewers

| Bengt Carlsson | Inácio Guerberoff | Simon Parsons |
| Sara Casare | Johan Holmgren | Paulo Trigo |

Table of Contents

Models and Frameworks for MAS Development

Situational Programming: Agent Behavior Visual Programming for
MABS Novices 1
    Fabien Michel, Jacques Ferber, Pierre-Alain Laur, and
    Florian Aleman

IRM4MLS: The Influence Reaction Model for Multi-Level Simulation ... 16
    Gildas Morvan, Alexandre Veremme, and Daniel Dupont

Toward a Myers-Briggs Type Indicator Model of Agent Behavior in
Multiagent Teams 28
    Jordan Salvit and Elizabeth Sklar

Exploring MAS Behaviors

Pheromones, Probabilities, and Multiple Futures 44
    H. Van Dyke Parunak

Finding Forms of Flocking: Evolutionary Search in ABM
Parameter-Spaces 61
    Forrest Stonedahl and Uri Wilensky

Game Theory and Information Sharing

On the Profitability of Incompetence 76
    Eugen Staab and Martin Caminada

Mechanisms for the Self-organization of Peer Groups in Agent
Societies 93
    Sharmila Savarimuthu, Maryam Purvis, Martin Purvis, and
    Bastin Tony Roy Savarimuthu

Multigame Dynamics: Structures and Strategies 108
    David L. Sallach, Michael J. North, and Eric Tatara

MAS in Economics and Negotiation

Microstructure Dynamics and Agent-Based Financial Markets 121
    Shu-Heng Chen, Michael Kampouridis, and Edward Tsang

Computational Modeling of Culture's Consequences   136
    Gert Jan Hofstede, Catholijn M. Jonker, and Tim Verwaart

Agent-Based Simulation Modelling of Housing Choice and Urban
Regeneration Policy   152
    René Jordan, Mark Birkin, and Andrew Evans

Author Index   167

Situational Programming: Agent Behavior Visual Programming for MABS Novices

Fabien Michel[1], Jacques Ferber[1], Pierre-Alain Laur[2], and Florian Aleman[2]

[1] LIRMM Lab. d'Informatique, Robotique et Micro-électronique de Montpellier
CNRS - Université Montpellier II, 161 rue Ada 34392 Montpellier Cedex 5 - France
{fmichel,ferber}@lirmm.fr
[2] FEERIK, Inc. 91 rue Font Caude 34080 Montpellier - France
{pal,florian}@feerik.com

Abstract. This paper presents an agent-oriented visual programming approach which aims at providing MABS end-users with a means to easily elaborate artificial autonomous behaviors according to a targeted domain, namely *situational programming* (SP). More specifically, SP defines design principles which could be used to develop MABS visual programming toolkits suited for non developers and MABS novices. This paper presents SP and how it is used to build a MABS video game which can be played by MABS novices, that is any Internet user.

Keywords: MABS, Agent-Oriented Programming, Visual Programming, Situational Programming, Video Game.

1 Introduction

Multi-Agent Based Simulation (MABS) is used in various research and application domains such as social science, ecology, ethology, etc. Considering this interdisciplinary aspect, one crucial issue is that many MABS end-users are not professional programmers while most MABS toolkits require computer programming skills [1].

Many MABS toolkits tackle this issue by defining coding primitives that help to design autonomous behaviors with respect to a targeted domain (e.g. Cormas [2]). Still, even if such approaches may hide to some extent the complexity of high level programming concepts such as inheritance, one has still to be familiar with basic programming concepts such as conditional expressions (e.g. if-then-else statement), looping structures (e.g. for, while, etc.) and variable affectations. Additionally, a textual programming syntax remains to be learned in every case. Therefore, efforts have been done to provide MABS toolkits with visual programming (VP) features so that they require few or no programming knowledge. Indeed, even if VP is naturally not as flexible as textual programming, it represents a very interesting solution considering the use of MABS by non professional programmers.

This paper introduces and discusses a VP variant for designing artificial behaviors, namely *Situational Programming* (SP). The goal of SP is to focus on allowing artificial behavior programming without any programming skill nor MABS

T. Bosse, A. Geller, and C.M. Jonker (Eds.): MABS 2010, LNAI 6532, pp. 1–15, 2011.

modeling ability. To this end, SP does not intend to allow novice developers to build a MABS from scratch. SP rather defines design principles which could be used by programmers to develop MABS VP toolkits and graphical user interfaces (GUI) fulfilling this requirement. The outline of the paper are as follows. The next section discusses the motivations and advantages of VP approaches for MABS, presents some existing tools and then highlights the limitations of existing approaches. Section 3 presents the motivations and underlying ideas of SP. Section 4 details a SP case study which has been done in the scope of a MABS video game. Section 5 highlights the limitations of the proposed approach. Section 6 discusses some related research works and Sect. 7 concludes the paper.

2   Visual Behavior Programming for MABS

2.1   Motivations

VP enables MABS end-users to create behaviors by manipulating graphical programming elements which eventually represent textual programming blocks. In most cases, the graphical elements are connected by arrows representing relations such as actions ordering, condition statements, loops and so on. So, users have to build a diagram that will represent the agent behavior and do not have to know about the programming language which is used under the hood.

Another major interest of VP is to disentangle the user from the language syntax complexity and requirements. Indeed, users cannot do programming syntax errors since graphical elements represent only valid programming statements. Moreover, VP tools further help users as they usually embed a specific spatial grammar that does not permit invalid connections between graphical elements nor invalid states for the components.

The main advantages of VP tools are therefore twofold:

1. Knowing about the programming language which is used in the platform is not a requirement: Novice developers can thus use the simulation tool.
2. Syntax correctness could be ensured thanks to the grammar which could be embedded in the graphical elements and in the manner they could be defined, combined or connected.

2.2   Examples of Visual Programming for MABS

This section presents three examples of MABS platforms which have VP features: (1) AgentSheets, (2) SeSAm and (3) Repast Simphony.

AgentSheets Developed in the early nineties, the seminal idea of the end-user programming tool AgentSheets relied on building a new kind of computational media allowing casual computer users to design complex interactive simulation [3]. So, the philosophy of this environment is to hide as much as possible the complexity of simulation-authoring mechanisms, thus focusing on the idea that simulation could be fruitfully used as an interesting cognitive thinking tool in many domains. Especially, AgentSheets is mainly used for educational purposes.

The VP language of AgentSheets is called Visual AgenTalk (VAT). VAT is a rule-based language allowing users to express agent behavior as if-then rules containing conditions and actions. Additionally, VAT enables what is called *Tactile Programming* and adds interactivity on the program representation: Program fragments can be manipulated through drag and drop operations to compose behaviors and also help end-users to explore and test agent behaviors thanks to several operations obtained on mouse clicks. AgentSheets is today an on-going commercial tool[1] which has also been extended to a 3D version named AgentCubes [4].

SeSAm (Shell for Simulated Multi-Agent Systems) is a Java open source MABS tool which aims at providing a generic environment for modeling and simulating MABS [5]. SeSAm[2] embeds several VP tools that help for different tasks considering the modeling of agent behavioral processes.

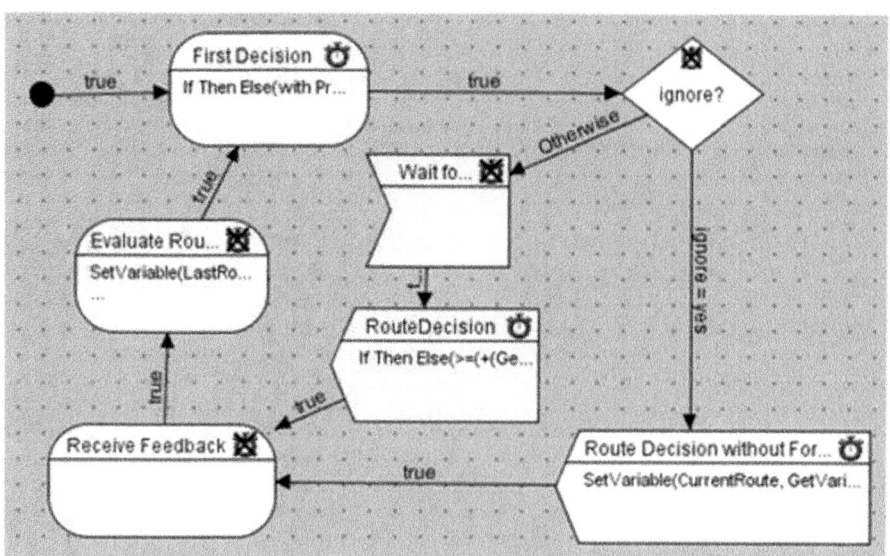

Fig. 1. Screenshot from the SeSAm implementation of a driver agent in [6]

For instance, interactive dialog elements enable to specify (potentially nested) primitive calls which could be used for specifying behavioral rules, creating initialization procedures, and so on. These interactive dialogs not only hide the use of Java but also dynamically check the underlying validity of the primitives (e.g. type-consistency). So, behaviors can be completely programmed without knowing the subtleties of an object oriented language such as Java. In SeSAm,

---

[1] http://www.agentsheets.com
[2] http://www.simsesam.de

VP is also used to visualize and specify the behavior of an agent using an activity diagram (Fig. 1): Activity nodes are linked with arrows describing transition rules between activities.

Repast Simphony (RS) is an open source generic MABS toolkit which is used in various application domains. RS extends the basic Repast[3] platform to provide advanced visual modeling and programming features for novice developers [7]. From a technical point of view, RS is a preconfigured Eclipse-based IDE (Integrated Development Environment) that notably uses the Flow4J[4] Eclipse plugin which enables to model process flows in a drag and drop manner.

As Fig. 2 shows, the Repast agent editor could be used to create a diagram using various block types (task, perceptions, condition evaluation, loop, etc.) which are connected by links defining the agent behavior logic.

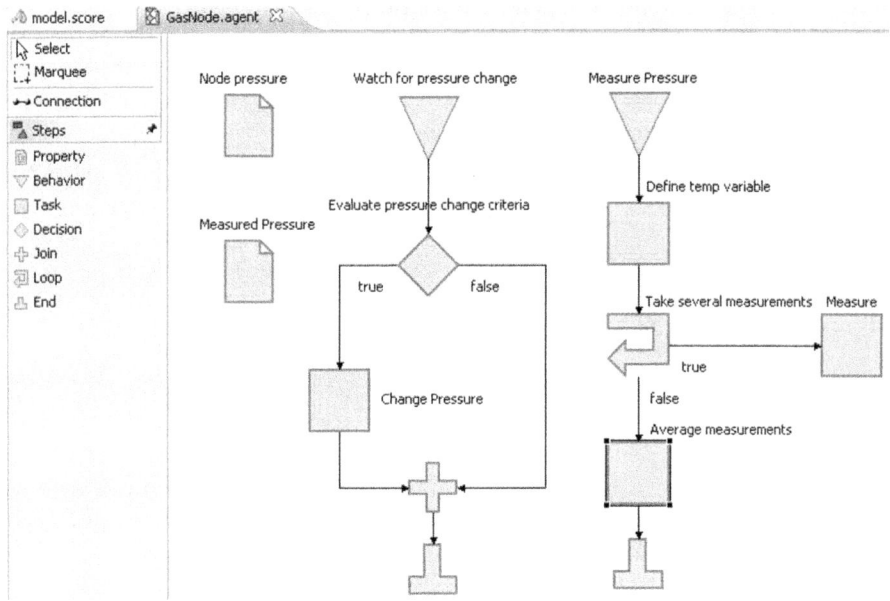

Fig. 2. The visual agent behavior editor of Repast Simphony

Thanks to this approach, the user does not need to write any line of code: When saved, the diagram is automatically translated in a traditional programming language and the behavior could be directly used within the simulation.

2.3   Limitations of Existing Approaches

Behavior Complexity. As remarked in [8], using existing MABS visual tools, building complex agents' cognitive models is clearly a tricky and painful task

---

[3] http://repast.sourceforge.net
[4] http://flow4jeclipse.sourceforge.net

because they usually allow to manipulate only basic concepts. To overcome this issue within the scope of social science, the authors have proposed a visual modeling language relying on the INGENIAS methodology [1]. This work allows to visually model complex behaviors based on intentional and organizational concepts. Still, the proposed modeling language is rather sophisticated as it intentionally targets MABS modeling experts, especially social scientists. Nonetheless, this work clearly highlights the complexity issue of existing MABS VP tools.

Behavior Graphical Representation. The difficulty of visually programming complex behaviors does not only come from the relative simplicity of the concepts usually used. Indeed, a critical issue which comes with existing MABS VP tools is to graphically represent complex behaviors. Obviously, a diagram containing more than about twenty graphical elements could not be really explicit nor intuitive and thus hardly understandable at first sight. Moreover, even if one can (1) reduce the size of each graphical element using explicit iconic symbols or (2) use nested components, the screen size will still be a limitation in itself. Therefore, it is crucial to provide end-users with behavioral graphical abstractions which enable simple and synthetic presentations of the behavior logic.

A Programmer's Mindset is Still Needed. Here, we want to emphasize on another issue which has been found crucial from our point of view: Even when a very high level of abstraction is considered, MABS VP tools still involve basic programming concepts. Especially, despite the intuitive aspects of MABS VP tools, the end-user has still to deal with concepts such as if-then-else statements, loops, variables usage and so on. In an educational context, this could be not a problem since the goal may be precisely to teach computer programming, or even agent-based programming concepts, to students. However, this remains a serious issue considering MABS end-users who are novice developers: Ultimately, they need to know and understand some fundamental computer programming concepts.

Therefore, we think that there is room for MABS VP tools that do not use any traditional programming concepts nor complex modeling features. The next section presents an approach which has such a goal, namely *Situational Programming* (SP).

3   Situational Programming

3.1   Objectives and Requirements

The main goal of SP is to provide non developers and MABS novices with a means to easily elaborate and test artificial behaviors with respect to a targeted domain. Obviously, such a goal requires to consider a VP approach. Additionally, we want our approach to overcome as much as possible the limitations discussed previously. Therefore, SP should also stick to the following requirements:

- End-users should not face any traditional programming concepts nor complex modeling tasks.
- The behavior logic representation should not take too much space on the screen and thus be as synthetic as possible.
- It should be still possible to define complex behavior logics.

So, even if we consider a VP-based approach, according to these requirements our focus is so that, contrary to the approaches we discussed, our current goal is not to provide a tool allowing non developers to build a MABS from scratch. The purpose of SP is rather to define agent-oriented programming principles which could be used to develop MABS VP tools which concretelly fulfill these requirements according to specific targeted domains.

3.2   Principle of the Approach

As we will now explain, inspirations for SP rely on observations and remarks about agent behavior programming in general, not only with respect to behavior VP. So, let us first consider a synthetic and traditional model of an agent behavioral process illustrated in Fig. 3: (1) perception, (2) deliberation, and then (3) action [9]. From a technical point of view, programming an agent behavior relies on (1) parsing perceptions, (2) using the obtained results in the deliberation, and (3) then take a particular decision based on deliberation, that is an action on the environment.

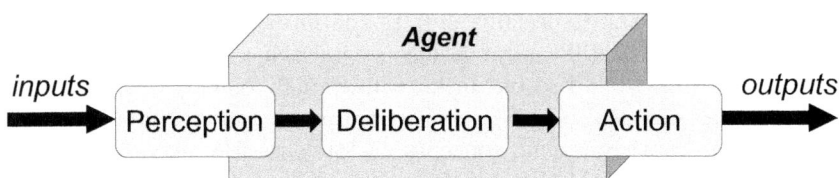

Fig. 3. The behavior of an agent: (1) Perception (2) Deliberation (3) Action

One has to remark that, considering a set of raw and basic percepts, it could be very difficult to programmatically define a relevant view of the world state. In other words, one has to first work on the percepts just to build structured data on which the deliberation could reason on. So, the programming complexity of this task rapidly grows according to the agent cognition level required. For instance, it is very difficult for a soccer robot to catch all the aspects of the current situation starting from its inputs [10].

Similarly, the same observation also holds about complex actions or plans: They are tricky to program starting from a set of basic actions manipulating only the effectors of the agent. So, in order to fulfill its objectives, SP is based on an approach wherein the perception and action phases are considered as too complex processes for MABS novices. Consequently, SP relies on preworking these phases so that end-users can focus on the deliberation part of the agent.

3.3   Very High Level Perceptions and Actions

The complexity of using raw percepts, and thus building relevant perceptions on which the agent could reason on, is very interestingly discussed in [11]. This work proposes a cognitive architecture composed by three layers: (1) *Reality*, (2) *Concept* and (3) *Mind*. The concept model layer is particularly of interest as it is in charge of mapping the physical environment reality to high level concepts which could be easily and efficiently used by the agent mind layer to deliberate. In other words, the goal of the concept layer is to allow agent minds to understand reality. The main idea underlying SP is related to such a conceptual philosophy.

The idea is to provide end-users with very high level percepts defining domain-oriented situations. By *situation*, we mean a combination of the possible states of high level percepts on which one has only to deliberate to choose an action: All the percepts compilation work is already done. For instance a percept could be *being under attack* or *dribbling the ball*, and the state within the situation *true, false*, or *ignored*. The end-user has thus only to select the state of each percept for defining situations.

The same philosophy is also used to define the actions that end-users will be able to select according to a particular situation. So, instead of basic actions, very high level plans are defined using a combination of easily tunable domain-oriented actions which are predefined. For instance, a plan could be *patrolling-an-area* (main plan) using a *sinusoidal move* (plan parameter). Figure 4 gives an abstract sketch of this approach.

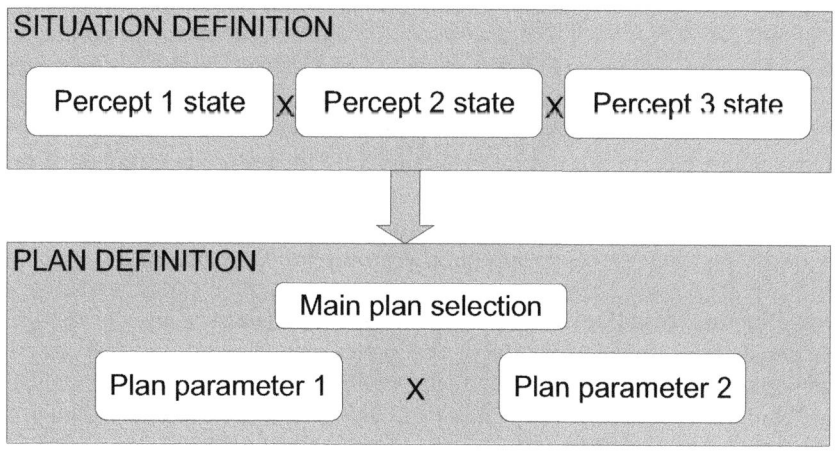

Fig. 4. Situational Programming Sketch

Of course, with respect to this approach, end-users should be able to define as many situations as they want. However, SP relies on the idea that it is very important for end-users to focus on defining *only one* situation/plan couple at a time. Following such a requirement disentangles the action selection part from the situation classification part. As we will see, this seriously reduces the complexity of both the end-user's work and the behavior graphical representation. Therefore, it is crucial to build the GUI with this requirement in mind. We will discuss how conflicts between situations are resolved by the user later on.

The basic work of the end-user is thus easy and straightforward: (1) tune the proposed percepts to define a particular situation and (2) then decide of a corresponding parameterizable plan. So, by defining several situation/plan couple matching, the end-user will define, and thus program, the agent behavior by reflecting his point of view and thus literally materializing his way of thinking.

3.4   Achieving Complex Behaviors without GUI Complexity

At first glance, the number of possible situation/plan combinations is the only factor of complexity. So, SP may look quite limited in terms of behavioral complexity since situations and plans are predefined. However, SP also includes additional design principles that allows behavioral complexity at a very low cost in terms of graphical user interface (GUI) complexity and understandability.

Situation Definition. As previously mentioned, the state of each percept contributes in defining a situation. The simplest percepts are related to the veracity of a particular fact and only have three states: (1) true, (2) false or (3) ignored (e.g. being under attack). State selection is done by single clicks that cycle through these three states.

Considering percepts related to a quantitative value such as *energy*, the state of the percept (e.g. *low energy* or *high energy*) must be defined according to a threshold (e.g. 50%). Such a threshold could be internally defined and not visible to the user. But, when explicitly presented, we give the user the opportunity of manually choosing this threshold using a usual graphical slider. We identified such percepts as *thresholded* and all others as *boolean*. So, when a thresholded percept is involved in a situation, this virtually increases the number of potential situations to infinity, thus introducing more behavior complexity without increasing GUI complexity. Also very important is the fact that this introduces singularity and heterogeneity among the programmed behaviors.

Plan Parameterization. Plans are defined from a very high level domain-oriented perspective. For instance, the plan *patrolling-an-area* may have two parameters: (1) the location and (2) the type of move (sinusoidal, straight lines, etc.). Much complexity could result from how plans are parameterizable. Still, this aspect is fully domain-oriented and not generalizable. However, we found an interesting parameter which could be applied in any domain. Indeed, one problem we found in the early stages of this research was that, in some cases, agents were constantly changing of selected plan: One situation may disappear and reappear in a very short period of time. To overcome this problem, we introduce an additional generic parameter to plans: *Stubbornness*. Stubbornness defines how much time the agent should stick to the selected plan without reconsidering situation. So, the stubbornness parameter solves the well know problem of persistence/commitment in action selection [12]. Stubbornness also introduces another level of complexity for the behaviors and increases their singularity, giving agents personality.

Situation/Plan Couples Priorities. An important aspect of SP which has not been discussed so far is that of situational conflicts. Indeed, it turns out that according to the way situations are defined by the user, several situations could simultaneously match the actual world state. Therefore it is important to provide end-users with a means of prioritizing situations against each other through a simple graphical presentation. In this respect, a column in which situations are ordered was found as the most appropriate solution. Moreover, such a presentation allows the user to prioritize the situations using a drag and drop approach. Once again, this introduces another behavioral complexity level without increasing the complexity of the GUI.

4   Applying SP: The Warbot Video Game

4.1   History and Objectives

Warbot[5] is a MABS game wherein teams of autonomous bots fight against each other. Historically, Warbot was designed ten years ago using the MadKit platform [13] to teach high school students agent-oriented programming through a competition: Students have to program the minds of Warbot agents whose bodies are predefined so that the best behaviors win the battle.

In collaboration with the Feerik[6] company, which is specialized in free-to-play on-line video games, we are developing a Warbot version that could be played by anyone, especially non programmers according to the Feerik's business model: A Feerik end-user could be any Internet user.

4.2   Warbot Domain-Oriented Percepts and Plans

As discussed in Sect. 3, to provide end-users with a SP-based MABS toolkit, developers have to first identify the related domain-oriented percepts and plans that will be used to program the behaviors.

Based on the experiences we had with the student version of Warbot, we identified a preliminary set of 5 high level percepts which were regularly programmed throughout the passed years:

- *Energy level.*
- *Number of detected enemies.*
- *Being under attack.*
- *Being helped by a teammate.*
- *Being asked for help by a teammate.*

---

[5] www.madkit.net/warbot
[6] www.feerik.com

Similarly, we identified 4 high level plans:

- *Go to point*
- *Patrol zone.*
- *Fight.*
- *Flee.*

Here, one may wonder why there is not a *help teammate* plan. In fact, it has been decided that this would be a parameter of all plans. That is, doing something, a bot can decide to take into account or not its teammates.

4.3 Warbot GUI

Figure 5 presents portions of the actual version of the Warbot behavior editor. The zone 1 presents the percepts which can be selected by the user to define a situation by dragging and dropping them in the zone 2. The zone 2 also permits to give a name to the current situation. In the third zone, the user can parametrize the plan which is associated with the current situation. The fourth zone summarizes the situations which have been already defined and also enables the user to prioritize them using drag and drop moves.

Figure 5 also shows that, defining situations in Warbot, it is possible to select different states of the same percept to associate a particular plan to several situations at once. In this example, the bot will fight whatever the number of enemies if it has more than 50% of energy.

The Warbot behavior programming GUI intentionally does not yet include all the Warbot domain-oriented percepts and plans discussed earlier. Indeed, it is planned to incrementally introduce each percept in the game in order to teach the end-users how to program complex behavior step by step: Simplicity at first glance is a major requirement for Feerik. Moreover, acquiring progressively new features is part of Feerik's business model.

Technically, the Warbot behavior GUI is made in Macromedia Flash. End-user's inputs are then compiled and used by the TurtleKit MABS platform [14] which in turn produces a game instance rendered by the Unity 3D web player in the user's web browser as shown in Fig. 6. Other web pages are used to define which bots compose the team and what are their equipment in terms of legs, arms, head, and weapon.

4.4 First Feedbacks and Remaining Work

Although game designers have not worked on the GUI design, first feedbacks from novice developers are very encouraging since they do easily find their way in developing artificial bot behaviors. Especially, they do appreciate that (1) situations can be defined by single mouse clicks and that (2) plans can be selected and parameterized using simple forms. Also, they find quite intuitive the use of a drag and drop approach to define priorities between situations.

The game-play is a major aspect of video game. So, one important work which remains to be done is to give the end-user statistical feedbacks about how his

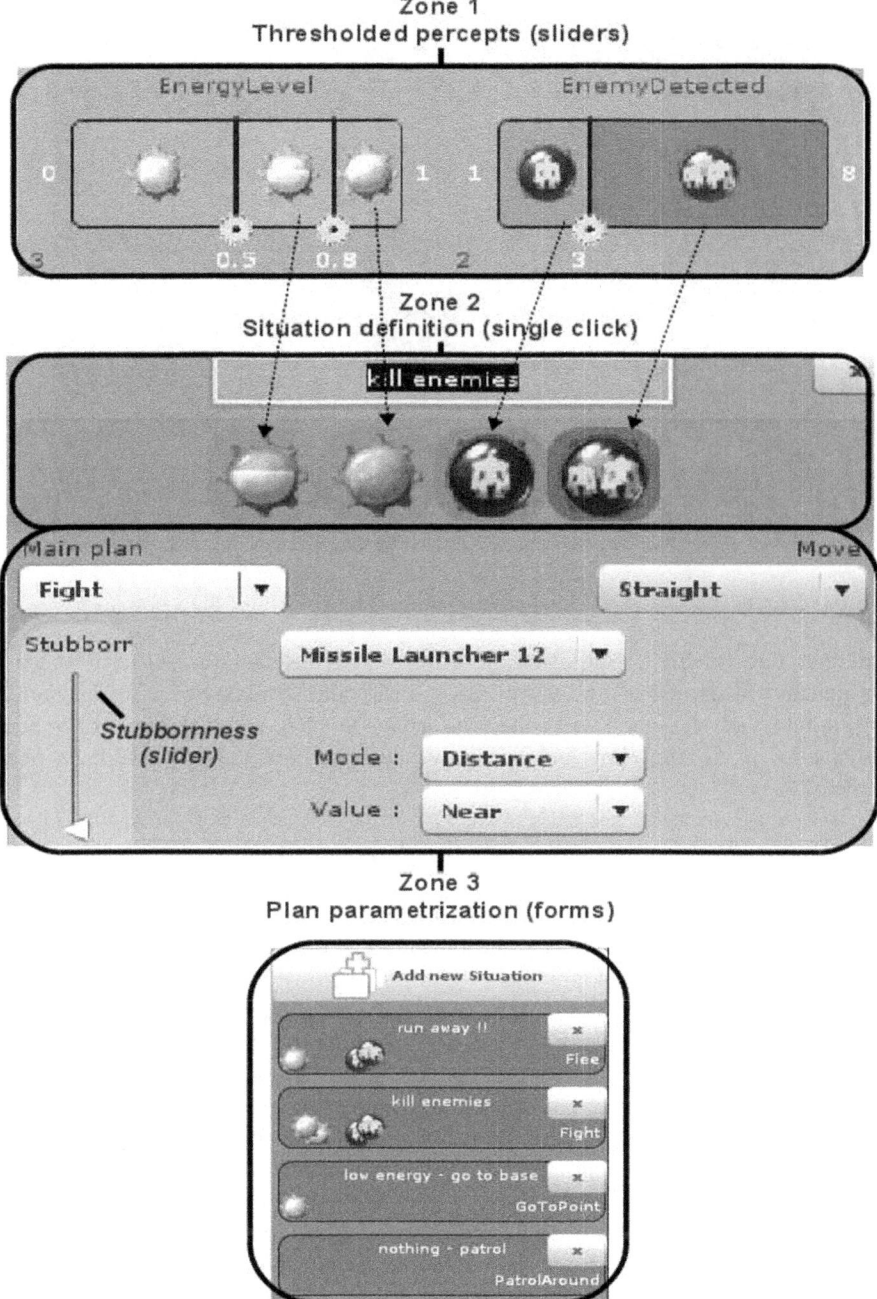

Fig. 5. Situational Programming with the Warbot GUI

Fig. 6. The Warbot video game rendered by the Unity 3D web player

bots behaved during a simulation, in order to provide the end-user with a means to identify the strengths and weaknesses of the defined behaviors. To this end, it is planned that the game will collect information such as which plans have been used, how much time, how much energy has been consumed during each plan, and so on.

5   Current Limitations of the Approach

As previously stated, SP does not intend to allow novice developers to build a MABS from scratch. Therefore, considering each targeted domain, SP of course requires that a true developer has programmed priorly all the different aspects of the corresponding SP-based MABS toolkit. Especially, this requires that the model be developed in close collaboration between the developers, on one hand, and researchers as well as householders, who know the real system, on the other hand. Still, one has to admit that this is true to some extent for any MABS platform. Moreover, we are actually tackling this issue at a software engineering level so that the underlying simulator software structure could be easily reused for new application domains.

Outside the scope of our current objectives, another limitation relies on the fact that end-users cannot add new percepts nor modify how they are defined. The same remark holds about plan structure. Still, we think that this is not a definitive limitation, at least considering percepts building. For instance, end-users may have access to another editor page which would consist in representing the characteristics of the environment. In such a page, the end-user could select some properties to define new usable percepts in just a limited number of clicks.

6   Related Works

Globally considering the issue of programming complex but efficient artificial behaviors, an interesting trend of research consists in tracking and learning how humans play a game in order to imitate their behaviors programmatically. For instance, in [10], considering the programming of Robosoccer agents, the authors track how a human controls a Robosoccer agent in order to model his behavior using machine learning techniques. SP could also be viewed as a means to take advantage of the human mind to build complex artificial behaviors. In this respect, a very interesting aspect of SP is that the reasoning of the human user has not to be programmed: It is entirely embedded in the resulting behaviors. For instance, with many players using the Warbot game, it will be possible to extract recurrent programming patterns which will be very interesting to study.

Obviously, there is an apparent conceptual link between participatory design of MABS (e.g. like in [15]) and SP since the behavior of the artificial agent partly remains inside the end-user's mind. So, both approaches strongly involve the end-user in the simulation design process as they both try to somehow capture and then compute his way of thinking. Still, these two are quite different, in terms of both objective and design work flow. Indeed, in a participatory mode, the user plays a role during the simulation, which is for instance incompatible with the game-play's objectives of Warbot. Moreover, while role-playing, the user does not program anything. In SP end-users have to program off-line all the behavior of the agent and thus cannot control its behavior while the simulation is in progress. Nonetheless, it is clear that SP and participatory design of MABS certainly share some common concerns which could be fruitfully exhibited.

The idea of using very high level concepts for simulation programming purposes is not new. For instance, in [16], the authors investigated the suitability of a very high level language (SETL [17]) for simulation. They said that such a language is one which incorporates complex structured data objects and global operations upon them. Obviously, SP relies on a similar philosophy. Therefore, it would be interesting to study how the design principles related with very high level language could be translated in our approach.

Finally, with respect to the idea of simplifying MABS programming, it would be interesting to study how SP could be coupled with the approach proposed in [18]. This approach, called *Interaction-Oriented Design of Agent simulations* (IODA), relies on defining a MABS as an interaction matrix specifying how the interactions between the agents take place. So, once a set of possible interactions is specified and programmed, defining the behavior of the agents simply consists in selecting, through a GUI representing the matrix, the interactions in which the agents could be involved. So, thanks to a visual interface that does not involve any programming concepts, this approach allows MABS novices to design and test numerous simulation models without any programming effort as end-users.

7   Conclusion

This paper has presented an agent-oriented programming approach which aims at providing MABS end-users with a means to easily elaborate artificial autonomous behaviors according to a targeted domain, namely *Situational Programming*. More specifically, SP defines design principles which could be used to develop MABS VP toolkits suited for non developers and MABS novices. So, following a MABS VP approach, one of the main interests of using a SP-based approach is to allow behavioral complexity with GUI simplicity.

We showed how SP is applied in the scope of a SP-based MABS online video game and, even if some work remains to be done on the Warbot GUI aesthetic, the first feedbacks we had are promising and showed us that SP is a concrete solution allowing any computer user to program artificial behaviors.

Among the related research perspectives we discussed in the previous section, collecting player data to study behavior programming patterns is of particular interest. Firstly, this will enable us to increase the game play of the Warbot game by rewarding the best players. Secondly, from a more general perspective, we think that SP could be a concrete alternative to participatory design or human imitation approaches for MABS. SP can be used as a means to *translate* human behaviors into computer programs. This in order to (1) study their characteristics in silico or (2) integrate realistic behaviors into MABS experiments.

References

1. Pavón, J., Sansores, C., Gómez-Sanz, J.J.: Modelling and simulation of social systems with INGENIAS. Int. J. Agent-Oriented Softw. Eng. 2(2), 196–221 (2008)
2. Bousquet, F., Bakam, I., Proton, H., Page, C.L.: Cormas: Common-pool resources and multi-agent systems. In: Proceedings of the 11th International Conference on Industrial and Engineering Applications of Artificial Intelligence and Expert Systems, pp. 826–837. Springer, Heidelberg (1998)
3. Repenning, A., Ioannidou, A., Zola, J.: AgentSheets: End-user programmable simulations. Journal of Artificial Societies and Social Simulation 3(3) (2000)
4. Ioannidou, A., Repenning, A., Webb, D.C.: AgentCubes: Incremental 3d end-user development. Journal of Visual Language & Computing 20(4), 236–251 (2009)
5. Klügl, F., Herrler, R., Fehler, M.: SeSAm: implementation of agent-based simulation using visual programming. In: AAMAS 2006: Proceedings of the Fifth International Joint Conference on Autonomous Agents and Multiagent Systems, pp. 1439–1440. ACM, New York (2006)
6. Klügl, F., Bazzan, A.L.C.: Route decision behaviour in a commuting scenario: Simple heuristics adaptation and effect of traffic forecast. JASSS, The Journal of Artificial Societies and Social Simulation 7(1) (2004)
7. North, M., Tatara, E., Collier, N., Ozik, J.: Visual agent-based model development with Repast Simphony. In: Agent 2007 Conference on Complex Interaction and Social Emergence, Argonne, IL, USA, Argonne National Laboratory, pp. 173–192 (November 2007)
8. Sansores, C., Pavón, J., Gómez-Sanz, J.J.: Visual modeling for complex agent-based simulation systems. In: Sichman, J.S., Antunes, L. (eds.) MABS 2005. LNCS (LNAI), vol. 3891, pp. 174–189. Springer, Heidelberg (2006)

9. Michel, F., Ferber, J., Drogoul, A.: Multi-Agent Systems and Simulation: a Survey From the Agents Community's Perspective. In: Weyns, D., Uhrmacher, A. (eds.) Multi-Agent Systems: Simulation and Applications. Computational Analysis, Synthesis, and Design of Dynamic Systems, pp. 3–52. CRC Press - Taylor & Francis (June 2009)
10. Aler, R., Valls, J.M., Camacho, D., Lopez, A.: Programming Robosoccer agents by modeling human behavior. Expert Systems with Applications 36(2, Part 1), 1850–1859 (2009)
11. Chang, P.H.M., Chen, K.T., Chien, Y.H., Kao, E.C.C., Soo, V.W.: From reality to mind: A cognitive middle layer of environment concepts for believable agents. In: Weyns, D., Van Dyke Parunak, H., Michel, F. (eds.) E4MAS 2004. LNCS (LNAI), vol. 3374, pp. 57–73. Springer, Heidelberg (2005)
12. Tyrrell, T.: The use of hierarchies for action selection. Adaptive Behavior 1(4), 387–420 (1993)
13. Ferber, J., Gutknecht, O., Michel, F.: From agents to organizations: an organizational view of multi-agent systems. In: Giorgini, P., Müller, J.P., Odell, J.J. (eds.) AOSE 2003. LNCS, vol. 2935, pp. 214–230. Springer, Heidelberg (2004)
14. Michel, F., Beurier, G., Ferber, J.: The TurtleKit simulation platform: Application to complex systems. In: Akono, A., Tonyé, E., Dipanda, A., Yétongnon, K. (eds.) Workshops Sessions, First International Conference on Signal & Image Technology and Internet-Based Systems SITIS 2005, pp. 122–128. IEEE, Los Alamitos (2005)
15. Guyot, P., Honiden, S.: Agent-based participatory simulations: Merging multi-agent systems and role-playing games. Journal of Artificial Societies and Social Simulation 9(4), 8 (2006)
16. Franta, W.R., Maly, K.: The suitability of a very high level language (setl) for simulation structuring and control. In: Robinet, B. (ed.) Programming Symposium. LNCS, vol. 19, pp. 156–169. Springer, Heidelberg (1974)
17. Schwartz, J.: Set Theory as a Language for Program Specification and Programming. Courant Institute of Mathematical Sciences, New York University (1970)
18. Kubera, Y., Mathieu, P., Picault, S.: Interaction-oriented agent simulations: From theory to implementation. In: Ghallab, M., Spyropoulos, C., Fakotakis, N., Avouris, N. (eds.) Proceedings of the 18th European Conference on Artificial Intelligence (ECAI 2008), pp. 383–387. IOS Press, Amsterdam (2008)

IRM4MLS: The Influence Reaction Model for Multi-Level Simulation

Gildas Morvan[1,2], Alexandre Veremme[1,2,3], and Daniel Dupont[1,3]

[1] Univ. Lille Nord de France, 1bis rue Georges Lefèvre 59044 Lille cedex, France
[2] LGI2A, U. Artois, Technoparc Futura 62400 Béthune, France
`firstname.surname@univ-artois.fr`
[3] HEI, 13 rue de Toul 59046 Lille Cedex, France
`firstname.surname@hei.fr`

Abstract. In this paper, a meta-model called IRM4MLS, that aims to be a generic ground to specify and execute multi-level agent-based models is presented. It relies on the influence/reaction principle and more specifically on IRM4S [13,14]. Simulation models for IRM4MLS are defined. The capabilities and possible extensions of the meta-model are discussed.

Keywords: multi-level simulation, influence/reaction model.

1 Introduction

The term "multi-level modeling" refers to the modeling of a system considered at various levels of organization. *E.g.*, a biological system can be considered at different levels:

$$... \rightarrow \text{molecule} \rightarrow \text{cell} \rightarrow \text{tissue} \rightarrow \text{organ} \rightarrow ... \,,$$

that basically correspond to the segmentation of biological research into specialized communities:

$$... \rightarrow \text{molecular biology} \rightarrow \text{cell biology} \rightarrow \text{histology} \rightarrow \text{physiology} \rightarrow ... \,.$$

Each research area has developed its own ontologies and models to describe the same reality observed at different levels. However, this reductionist approach fails when considering complex systems. *E.g.*, it has been shown that living systems are co-produced by processes at different levels of organization [12]. Therefore, an explanatory model of such systems should consider the interactions between levels. Agent-based modeling (ABM) is a paradigm of choice to study complex systems. But, while it seems more interesting to integrate knowledge from the different levels studied and their interactions in a single model, ABM often remains a pure bottom-up approach [4].

Thus, recently[1] various research projects have aimed at developing multi-level agent-based models (MAM) in various fields such as histology, ethology or

---

[1] It has to be noted that the eleven year old model RIVAGE pioneered the field of MAM [19].

T. Bosse, A. Geller, and C.M. Jonker (Eds.): MABS 2010, LNAI 6532, pp. 16–27, 2011.
© Springer-Verlag Berlin Heidelberg 2011

sociology [1,9,11,15,16,18,21]. A good analysis of some of these models, and the motivations of these works can be found in [8].

Various issues should be addressed when developing a MAM. For instance one major problem is the automatic detection of emergent phenomena that could influence other levels [2,3,17]. Another important problem is the temporal and spatial mappings of model levels and thus the scheduling of the simulations [10]. More exhaustive presentations of these issues can be found in [16,8].

In the models found in literature, these issues have been addressed according to the specificity of the problem. Indeed, they are based on *ad-hoc* meta-models and the transferability of ideas from one to another seems difficult.

In this paper, a meta-model that aims to be a generic ground to specify and execute MAM is presented. It is based on IRM4S (an Influence Reaction Model for Simulation) proposed in [13,14], itself based on IRM (Influences and Reaction model) originally presented in [7]. IRM4S is described in section 2 and its multi-level extension, called IRM4MLS (Influence Reaction Model for Multi-level Simulation), in section 3. Section 4 introduces two simulation models for IRM4MLS. The first one is very simple and similar to IRM4S but supposes that all levels have the same temporal dynamics while the second one has a more general scope but relies on temporal constraints and thus, is more complicated and time consuming.

2   The IRM4S Meta-Model

IRM was developed to address issues raised by the classical vision of action in Artificial Intelligence as *the transformation of a global state*: simultaneous actions cannot be easily handled, the result of an action depends on the agent that performs it but not on other actions and the autonomy of agents is not respected [7].

While IRM addresses these issues, its complexity makes it difficult to implement. IRM4S is an adaptation of IRM, dedicated to simulation, that clarifies some ambiguous points. It is described in the following.

Let $\delta(t) \in \Delta$ be the dynamic state of the system at time t:

$$\delta(t) =< \sigma(t), \gamma(t) >, \tag{1}$$

where $\sigma(t) \in \Sigma$ is the set of environmental properties and $\gamma(t) \in \Gamma$ the set of influences, representing system dynamics. The state of an agent $a \in A$ is characterized by:

- necessary, its physical state $\phi_a \in \Phi_a$ with $\Phi_a \in \Sigma$ (*e.g.*, its position),
- possibly, its internal state $s_a \in S_a$ (*e.g.*, its beliefs).

Thus, IRM4S distinguishes between the mind and the body of the agents.

The evolution of the system from t to $t + dt$ is a two-step process:

1. agents and environment produce a set of influences[2] $\gamma'(t) \in \Gamma'$:

$$\gamma'(t) = Influence(\delta(t)), \tag{2}$$

2. the reaction to influences produces the new dynamic state of the system:

$$\delta(t + dt) = Reaction(\sigma(t), \gamma'(t)). \tag{3}$$

As [14] notes, "the influences [produced by an agent] do not directly change the environment, but rather represent the desire of an agent to see it changed in some way". Thus, $Reaction$ computes the consequences of agent desires and environment dynamics.

An agent $a \in A$ produces influences through a function $Behavior_a : \Delta \mapsto \Gamma'$. This function is decomposed into three functions executed sequentially:

$$p_a(t) = Perception_a(\delta(t)), \tag{4}$$

$$s_a(t + dt) = Memorization_a(p_a(t), s_a(t)), \tag{5}$$

$$\gamma'_a(t) = Decision_a(s_a(t + dt)). \tag{6}$$

The environment produces influences through a function $Natural_\omega : \Delta \mapsto \Gamma'$:

$$\gamma'_\omega(t) = Natural_\omega(\delta(t)). \tag{7}$$

Then the set of influences produced in the system at t is:

$$\gamma'(t) = \{\gamma(t) \cup \gamma'_\omega(t) \cup \bigcup_{a \in A} \gamma'_a(t)\}. \tag{8}$$

After those influences have been produced, the new dynamic state of the system is computed by a function $Reaction : \Sigma \times \Gamma' \mapsto \Delta$ such as:

$$\delta(t + dt) = Reaction(\sigma(t), \gamma'(t)). \tag{9}$$

Strategies for computing $Reaction$ can be found in [14].

3   The Influence Reaction Model for Multi-Level Simulation (IRM4MLS)

3.1   Specification of the Levels and Their Interactions

A multi-level model is defined by a set of levels L and a specification of the relations between levels. Two kinds of relations are specified in IRM4MLS: an

---

[2] The sets of producible influence sets and influences produced at t are denoted respectively Γ' and $\gamma'(t)$ to point out that the latter is temporary and will be used to compute the dynamic state of the system at $t + dt$.

influence relation (agents in a level l are able to produce influences in a level $l' \neq l$) and a perception relation (agents in a level l are able to perceive the dynamic state of a level $l' \neq l$), represented by directed graphs denoted respectively $< L, E_I >$ and $< L, E_P >$, where E_I and E_P are two sets of edges, *i.e.*, ordered pairs of elements of L. Influence and perception relations in a level are systematic and thus not specified in E_I and E_P (cf. eq. 10 and 11).

E.g., $\forall l, l' \in L^2$, if $E_P = \{ll'\}$ then the agents of l are able to perceive the dynamic states of l and l' while the agents of l' are able to perceive the dynamic state of l'.

The perception relation represents the capability, for agents in a level, to be "conscious" of other levels, *e.g.*, human beings having knowledge in sociology are conscious of the social structures they are involved in. Thus, in a pure reactive agent simulation, $E_P = \emptyset$. E_P represents what agents are able to be conscious of, not what they actually are: this is handled by a perception function, proper to each agent.

The in and out neighborhood in $< L, E_I >$ (respectively $< L, E_P >$) are denoted N_I^- and N_I^+ (resp. N_P^- and N_P^+) and are defined as follows:

$$\forall l \in L, N_I^-(l) \text{ (resp. } N_P^-(l)) = \{l\} \cup \{l' \in L : l'l \in E_I \text{ (resp. } E_P)\}, \quad (10)$$

$$\forall l \in L, N_I^+(l) \text{ (resp. } N_P^-(l)) = \{l\} \cup \{l' \in L : ll' \in E_I \text{ (resp. } E_P)\}, \quad (11)$$

E.g., $\forall l, l' \in L^2$ if $l' \in N_I^+(l)$ then the environment and the agents of l are able to produce influences in the level l'; conversely we have $l \in N_I^-(l')$, *i.e.*, l' is influenced by l.

3.2   Agent Population and Environments

The set of agents in the system at time t is denoted $A(t)$. $\forall l \in L$, the set of agents belonging to l at t is denoted $A_l(t) \subseteq A(t)$. An agent belongs to a level iff a subset of its physical state ϕ_a belongs to the state of the level:

$$\forall a \in A(t), \forall l \in L, a \in A_l(t) \text{ iff } \exists \phi_a^l(t) \subseteq \phi_a(t) | \phi_a^l(t) \subseteq \sigma^l(t). \quad (12)$$

Thus, an agent belongs to zero, one, or more levels. An environment can also belong to different levels.

3.3   Influence Production

The dynamic state of a level $l \in L$ at time t, denoted $\delta^l(t) \in \Delta^l$, is a tuple $< \sigma^l(t), \gamma^l(t) >$, where $\sigma^l(t) \in \Sigma^l$ and $\gamma^l(t) \in \Gamma^l$ are the sets of environmental properties and influences of l.

The influence production step of IRM4S is modified to take into account the influence and perception relations between levels. Thus, the *Behavior*$_a^l$ function of an agent $a \in A_l$ is defined as:

$$\textit{Behavior}_a^l : \prod_{l_P \in N_P^+(l)} \Delta^{l_P} \mapsto \prod_{l_I \in N_I^+(l)} \Gamma^{l_I'}. \quad (13)$$

This function is described as a composition of functions. As two types of agents are considered (*tropistic* agents, *i.e.*, without memory and *hysteretic* agents, *i.e.*, with memory[3]), two types of behavior functions are defined [6].

An hysteretic agent ha in a level l acts according to its internal state. Thus, its behavior function is defined as:

$$Behavior_{ha}^l = Decision_{ha}^l \circ Memorization_{ha} \circ Perception_{ha}^l, \qquad (14)$$

with

$$Perception_{ha}^l : \prod_{l_P \in N_P^+(l)} \Delta^{l_P} \mapsto \prod_{l_P \in N_P^+(l)} P_{ha}^{l_P}, \qquad (15)$$

$$Memorization_{ha} : \prod_{l \in L | ha \in A_l} \prod_{l_P \in N_P^+(l)} P_{ha}^{l_P} \times S_{ha} \mapsto S_{ha}, \qquad (16)$$

$$Decision_{ha}^l : S_{ha} \mapsto \prod_{l_I \in N_I^+(l)} \Gamma^{l_I \prime}. \qquad (17)$$

There is no memorization function specific to a level. Like in other multi-agent system meta-models (*e.g.*, MASQ [20]), we consider that an agent can have multiple bodies but only one mind (*i.e.*, one internal state). Moreover, the coherence of the internal state of the agents would have been difficult to maintain with several memorization functions.

A tropistic agent ta in a level l acts according to its percepts:

$$Behavior_{ta}^l = Decision_{ta}^l \circ Perception_{ta}^l, \qquad (18)$$

with $Perception_{ta}^l$ following the definition of eq. 15 and

$$Decision_{ta}^l : \prod_{l_P \in N_P^+(l)} P_{ta}^{l_P} \mapsto \prod_{l_I \in N_I^+(l)} \Gamma^{l_I \prime}. \qquad (19)$$

The environment ω of a level l produces influences through a function:

$$Natural_\omega^l : \Delta^l \mapsto \prod_{l_I \in N_I^+(l)} \Gamma^{l_I \prime}. \qquad (20)$$

3.4 Reaction to Influences

Once influences have been produced, interactions between levels do not matter anymore. Thus, the reaction function defined in IRM4S can be re-used:

$$Reaction^l : \Sigma^l \times \Gamma^{l\prime} \mapsto \Delta^l, \qquad (21)$$

where $Reaction^l$ is the reaction function proper to each level.

---

[3] While the tropistic/hysteretic distinction is made in IRM, it does not appear clearly in IRM4S. However, in a multi-level context, it is important if multi-level agents are considered.

4   Simulation of IRM4MLS Models

In this section, two simulation models for IRM4MLS are proposed. The first one (section 4.1) is directly based on IRM4S. It supposes that all levels have the same temporal dynamics. The second one (section 4.2) has a more general scope but is also more complicated and time consuming. These models are compatible with the different classical time evolution methods (event-to-event or fixed time step) used in multi-agent simulation. In the following, t_0 and T denote the first and last simulation times.

4.1   A Simple Simulation Model

In this section, a model with single temporal dynamics is introduced. As there is no synchronization issue, it is very similar to the model of IRM4S. Eq. 22 to 28 describe this simple temporal model. $HA(t)$ and $TA(t)$ denote respectively the sets of hysteretic and tropistic agents in the system.

First, behavior sub-functions are executed for each agent:

$$\forall l \in L, p_a(t) = < Perception_a^l(< \delta^{l_P}(t) : l_P \in N_P^+(l) >) : a \in A_l(t) >, \quad (22)$$

$$\forall a \in HA(t), s_a(t + dt) = Memorization_a(p_a(t)), \quad (23)$$

$$\forall l \in L, \forall a \in HA_l(t), < \gamma_a^{l_I}{}'(t) : l_I \in N_I^+(l) > = Decision_a^l(s_a(t + dt)), \quad (24)$$

$$\forall l \in L, \forall a \in TA_l(t), < \gamma_a^{l_I}{}'(t) : l_I \in N_I^+(l) > = Decision_a^l(p_a(t)). \quad (25)$$

Then, environmental influences are produced:

$$\forall l \in L, < \gamma_\omega^{l_I}(t) : l_I \in N_I^+(l) > = Natural_\omega^l(\delta^l(t)). \quad (26)$$

The set of temporary influences in a level $l \in L$ at t is defined as:

$$\gamma^{l'}(t) = \{\gamma^l(t) \bigcup_{l_I \in N_I^-(l)} \gamma_\omega^{l_I}{}'(t) \bigcup_{a \in A_{l_I}} \gamma_a^{l_I}{}'(t)\}. \quad (27)$$

Finally, the new state of the system can be computed:

$$\forall l \in L, \delta^l(t + dt) = Reaction^l(\sigma^l(t), \gamma^{l'}(t)). \quad (28)$$

Algorithm 1 summarizes this simulation model.

4.2   A Simulation Model with Level-Dependent Temporal Dynamics

In this section, a simulation model with level-dependent temporal dynamics is introduced. In the following, t^l and $t^l + dt^l$ denote respectively the current and next simulation times of a level $l \in L$. Moreover $t = < t^l : l \in L >$ and $t + dt = < t^l + dt^l : l \in L >$ denote respectively the sets of current and next simulation times for all levels. It is mandatory to introduce rules that constraint perceptions, influence production and reaction computation. These rules rely primarily on the *causality principle*:

Algorithm 1: Simple simulation model of IRM4MLS

> **Input**: $< L, E_I, E_P >, A(t_0), \delta(t_0)$
> **Output**: $\delta(T)$

1   $t = t_0$;
2   **while** $t \leq T$ **do**
3   **foreach** $a \in A(t)$ **do**
4         $p_a(t) = < Perception_a^l(< \delta^{l_P}(t) : l_P \in N_P^+(l) >) : a \in A_l >$;
5   **if** $a \in HA(t)$ **then**
6            $s_a(t + dt) = Memorization_a(p_a(t))$;
7   **end**
8   **end**
9   **foreach** $l \in L$ **do**
10        $< \gamma_\omega^{l_I}{}'(t) : l_I \in N_I^+(l) > = Natural_\omega^l(\delta^l(t))$;
11   **foreach** $a \in HA_l(t)$ **do**
12           $< \gamma_a^{l_I}{}'(t) : l_I \in N_I^+(l) > = Decision_a^l(s_a(t + dt))$;
13   **end**
14   **foreach** $a \in TA_l(t)$ **do**
15           $< \gamma_a^{l_I}{}'(t) : l_I \in N_I^+(l) > = Decision_a^l(p_a(t))$;
16   **end**
17   **end**
18   **foreach** $l \in L$ **do**
19        $\gamma^{l}{}'(t) = \{\gamma^l(t) \bigcup_{l_I \in N_I^-(l)} \gamma_\omega^{l_I}{}'(t) \bigcup_{a \in A_{l_I}} \gamma_a^{l_I}{}'(t)\}$;
20        $\delta^l(t + dt) = Reaction^l(\sigma^l(t), \gamma^{l}{}'(t))$;
21   **end**
22      $t = t + dt$;
23 **end**

- an agent cannot perceive the future, *i.e.*,

$$\forall l \in L, l_P \in N_P^+(l) \text{ is perceptible from } l \text{ if } t^l \geq t^{l_P}, \qquad (29)$$

- an agent or an environment cannot influence the past, *i.e.*,

$$\forall l \in L, l_I \in N_I^+(l) \text{ can be influenced by } l \text{ if } t^l \leq t^{l_I}. \qquad (30)$$

However, the causality principle is not sufficient to ensure a good scheduling. A *coherence principle* should also guide the conception of the simulation model:

- an agent can only perceive the latest available dynamic states, *i.e.*,

$$\forall l \in L, l_P \in N_P^+(l) \text{ is perceptible from } l \text{ if } t^l < t^{l_P} + dt^{l_P}, \qquad (31)$$

- as a hysteretic agent can belong to more than one level, its internal state must be computed for the next simulation time at which it is considered, *i.e.*,

$$\forall l \in L, s_a(t_a + dt_a) = Memorization_a(p_a(t^l)), \qquad (32)$$

such as

$$t_a + dt_a = t^l + dt^l | \forall t^{l'} + dt^{l'}, t^l + dt^l \geq t^{l'} + dt^{l'}$$
$$\Rightarrow t^l + dt^l = t^{l'} + dt^{l'} \wedge a \in A_l, \tag{33}$$

– an agent or an environment can influence a level according to its latest state, i.e.,

$$\forall l \in L, l_I \in N_I^+(l) \text{ can be influenced by } l \text{ if } t^l + dt^l > t^{l_I}, \tag{34}$$

– reaction must be computed for the next simulation time, i.e.,

$$\forall l \in L, Reaction^l \text{ is computed if } t^l + dt^l \in min(t + dt). \tag{35}$$

Moreover, a *utility principle* should also be applied:

– perceptions should be computed at once, i.e.,

$$\forall l \in L, \forall a \in A_l, Perception_a^l \text{ is computed}$$
$$\text{if } \forall l_P \in N_P^+(l), t^l \geq t^{l_P}. \tag{36}$$

– as well as influences, i.e.,

$$\forall l \in L, Natural_\omega^l \text{ and } \forall a \in A_l, Decision_a^l \text{ are computed}$$
$$\text{if } \forall l_I \in N_I^+(l), t^l \leq t^{l_I} \vee t^l + dt^l < t^{l_I} + dt^{l_I}. \tag{37}$$

It is easy to show that the rule defined in eq. 36 subsums the rule defined in eq. 29. Moreover, the rule defined in eq. 35 implies the rule defined in eq. 31.

According to eq. 37, influences are not necessarily produced at each time from a level l to a level $l_I \in N_I^+(l)$. Thus, a function c_I, defines influence production from the rules defined by the eq. 34 and 36:

$$\forall l, \in L, \forall l_I \in N_I^+(l), c_I(l, l_I) = \begin{cases} \gamma^{l_I'}(t^{l_I}) \text{ if } & t^l \leq t^{l_I} \wedge t^l + dt^l > t^{l_I} \\ \emptyset & \text{else.} \end{cases} \tag{38}$$

The simulation model can then be defined as follows. First, if the condition defined in the eq. 36 is respected, agents construct their percepts and consecutively hysteretic agents compute their next internal state:

$\forall a \in A(t)$,

$$p_a(t^l) = < Perception_a^l(< \delta^{l_P}(t^{l_P}) : l_P \in N_P^+(l) >) : l \in L_P >, \tag{39}$$
$$s_a(t_a + dt_a) = Memorization_a(p_a(t^l)) \text{ if } a \in HA(t), \tag{40}$$

with $L_P = \{l \in L : a \in A_l(t) \wedge \forall l_P \in N_P^+(l), t^l \geq t^{l_P}\}$.

Then, if the condition defined in eq. 37 is respected, agents and environments produce influences:

$\forall l \in L_I$,

$$< c_I(l, l_I) : l_I \in N_I^+(l) > = Natural_\omega^l(\delta^l(t^l)), \tag{41}$$
$$\forall a \in HA_l, < c_I(l, l_I) : l_I \in N_I^+(l) > = Decision_a^l(s_a(t_a + dt_a)), \tag{42}$$
$$\forall a \in TA_l, < c_I(l, l_I) : l_I \in N_I^+(l) > = Decision_a^l(p_a(t^l)), \tag{43}$$

with $L_I = \{l \in L : \forall l_I \in N_I^+(l), t^l \leq t^{l_I} \vee t^l + dt^l < t^{l_I} + dt^{l_I}\}$.

The set of temporary influences in a level $l \in L$ at t^l is defined as:

$$\gamma^{l\prime}(t^l) = \{\gamma^l(t^l) \bigcup_{l_I \in N_I^-(l)} c_I(l_I, l)\}. \tag{44}$$

Finally, reactions are computed for levels that meet the condition defined in eq. 35:

$\forall l \in L_R,$

$$\delta^l(t^l + dt^l) = Reaction^l(\sigma^l(t^l), \gamma^{l\prime}(t^l)), \tag{45}$$

with $L_R = \{l \in L : t^l + dt^l \in min(t + dt)\}$.

The algorithm 2 summarizes this simulation model.

5   Discussion, Conclusion and Perspectives

In this paper, a meta-model of MAM, called IRM4MLS, is introduced. It is designed to handle many situations encountered in MAM: hierarchical or non-hierarchical multi-level systems with different spatial and temporal dynamics, multi-level agents or environments and agents that are dynamically introduced in levels. Moreover, IRM4MLS relies on a general simulation model contrary to the existing works published in literature. While this model is, in general, complicated, its implementation could be simplified to be more efficient in specific situations (single perception function, reactive simulation, etc.). Afterwards, examples of typical MAM situations as well as ideas to treat them in the context of IRM4MLS are presented.

In some models an agent can belong to different levels:

- in the model of bio-inspired automated guided vehicle (AGV) systems presented in [16], an AGV (a micro level agent) can become a conflict solver (a macro level agent) if a dead lock is detected in the system,
- in the SIMPOP3 multi-level model an agent representing a city plays the role of interface between two models and then is member of two levels [18].

The simulation of these models has been addressed using different strategies:

- in the first example (a control problem), a top-first approach is used: the higher level takes precedence over the lower one,
- in the second example (a simulation problem), levels are executed alternately.

These solutions are context-dependent and likely to generate bias. In IRM4MLS, the multi-level agent situation is handled by a single simulation model that generalizes the two previous ones without scheduling bias, thanks to the influence/reaction principle.

In many multi-level agent-based models, interactions between entities in a level affect the population of agents in another level. *E.g.*, in RIVAGE, a model

Algorithm 2: Simulation model of IRM4MLS with level-dependent temporal dynamics

    Input: $< L, E_I, E_P >, A(t_0), \delta(t_0)$
    Output: $\delta(T)$

1 **foreach** $l \in L$ **do**
2      $t^l = t_0$;
3 **end**
4 **while** $\exists t^l \leq T$ **do**
5   **foreach** $a \in A(t)$ **do**
6         $L_P = \{l \in L : a \in A_l(t) \wedge \forall l_P \in N_P^+(l), t^l \geq t^{l_P}\}$;
7         $p_a(t^l) = < Perception_a^l(< \delta^{l_P}(t^{l_P}) : l_P \in N_P^+(l) >) : l \in L_P >$;
8   **if** $a \in HA(t)$ **then**
9            $s_a(t_a + dt_a) = Memorization_a(p_a(t^l))$;
10   **end**
11   **end**
12     $L_I = \{l \in L : \forall l_I \in N_I^+(l), t^l \leq t^{l_I} \vee t^l + dt^l < t^{l_I} + dt^{l_I}\}$;
13   **foreach** $l \in L_I$ **do**
14         $< c_I(l, l_I) : l_I \in N_I^+(l) >= Natural_\omega^l(\delta^l(t^l))$;
15   **foreach** $a \in HA_l(t)$ **do**
16            $< c_I(l, l_I) : l_I \in N_I^+(l) >= Decision_a^l(s_a(t_a + dt_a))$;
17   **end**
18   **foreach** $a \in TA_l(t)$ **do**
19            $< c_I(l, l_I) : l_I \in N_I^+(l) >= Decision_a^l(p_a(t^l))$;
20   **end**
21   **end**
22     $L_R = \{l \in L : t^l + dt^l \in min(t + dt)\}$;
23   **foreach** $l \in L_R$ **do**
24         $\gamma^{l'}(t^l) = \{\gamma^l(t^l) \bigcup_{l_I \in N_I^-(l)} c_I(l_I, l)\}$;
25         $\delta^l(t^l + dt^l) = Reaction^l(\sigma^l(t^l), \gamma^{l'}(t^l))$;
26         $t^l = t^l + dt^l$;
27   **end**
28 **end**

of runoff dynamics, macro level agents (representing water ponds or ravines) emerge from micro level agents (representing water balls) when conditions are met [19]. Then, the quantity and the flow of water become properties of macro level agents: water balls are no longer considered as agents. Conversely, micro level agents can emerge from macro level agents. Similar situations can be found in hybrid modeling of traffic flows [5]. In IRM4MLS, the introduction of an agent a in a level l is performed by the reaction function of l that introduces environmental properties representing the physical state of a in $\sigma^l(t)$. Conversely, the reaction function can delete an agent from the level. An agent that does not belong to any level is inactive but can be reactivated later.

Finally, the definition of IRM4MLS is not closed in order to offer different possibilities of implementation or extension. *E.g.*, levels could be defined *a priori* or discovered during the simulation [8]. While this approach has never been used in any model so far, it seems particularly promising. In IRM4MLS, only the first possibility has been handled so far. It would be necessary to consider L and $< L, E_I >$ and $< L, E_P >$ as dynamic directed graphs.

The two main perspectives of this work are the design of a modeling and simulation language and a platform that comply to the specifications of IRM4MLS as well as the re-implementation of existing models to demonstrate the capabilities of the meta-model and its simulation models.

Acknowledgments

Authors would like to thank Javier Gil-Quijano (LIP6 – Université Paris VI, France), Fabien Michel (LIRMM – Université Montpellier 2, France), Daniel Jolly (LGI2A – Université d'Artois, France) and Luce Desmidt (HEI – France) for their help and support.

References

1. An, G.: Introduction of an agent-based multi-scale modular architecture for dynamic knowledge representation of acute inflammation. Theoretical Biology and Medical Modelling 5(11) (2008)
2. Chen, C.C., Clack, C., Nagl, S.: Identifying multi-level emergent behaviors in agent-directed simulations using complex event type specifications. Simulation (2009)
3. David, D., Courdier, R.: See emergence as a metaknowledge. a way to reify emergent phenomena in multiagent simulations? In: Proceedings of ICAART 2009, Porto, Portugal, pp. 564–569 (2009)
4. Drogoul, A., Vanbergue, D., Meurisse, T.: Multi-agent based simulation: Where are the agents? In: Sichman, J.S., Bousquet, F., Davidsson, P. (eds.) MABS 2002. LNCS (LNAI), vol. 2581, pp. 89–104. Springer, Heidelberg (2003)
5. El hmam, M., Abouaissa, H., Jolly, D., Benasser, A.: Macro-micro simulation of traffic flow. In: Proceedings of the12th IFAC Symposium on Information Control Problems in Manufacturing (INCOM 2006), pp. 351–356. Saint Etienne, France (2006)
6. Ferber, J.: Multi-Agent Systems: An Introduction to Distributed Artificial Intelligence. Addison-Wesley Longman Publishing Co., Amsterdam (1999)
7. Ferber, J., Müller, J.-P.: Influences and reaction: a model of situated multiagent systems. In: 2nd International Conference on Multi-agent systems (ICMAS 1996), pp. 72–79 (1996)
8. Gil Quijano, J., Hutzler, G., Louail, T.: De la cellule biologique à la cellule urbaine: retour sur trois expériences de modélisation multi-échelles à base d'agents. Actes des 17èmes Journées Francophones sur les Systèmes Multi-Agents, JFSMA 2009 (2009)
9. Gil Quijano, J., Piron, M., Drogoul, A.: Mechanisms of Automated Formation and Evolution of Social-Groups: A Multi-Agent System to Model the Intra-Urban Mobilities of Bogota City. In: Social Simulation: Technologies, Advances and New Discoveries, IGI Global (2008)

10. Hoekstra, A., Lorenz, E., Falcone, J.L., Chopard, B.: Towards a complex automata framework for multi-scale modeling: Formalism and the scale separation map. In: Shi, Y., van Albada, G.D., Dongarra, J., Sloot, P.M.A. (eds.) ICCS 2007. LNCS, vol. 4487, pp. 922–930. Springer, Heidelberg (2007)
11. Lepagnot, J., Hutzler, G.: A multiscale agent-based model for the simulation of avascular tumour growth. Journal of Biological Physics and Chemistry 9(1), 17–25 (2009)
12. Maturana, H.R., Varela, F.J.: Autopoiesis and Cognition The Realization of the Living. Boston Studies in the Philosophy of Science, vol. 42. Springer, Heidelberg (1980)
13. Michel, F.: The irm4s model: the influence/reaction principle for multiagent based simulation. In: AAMAS 2007: Proceedings of the 6th International Joint Conference on Autonomous Agents and Multiagent Systems, pp. 1–3. ACM, New York (2007)
14. Michel, F.: Le modèle irm4s. de l'utilisation des notions d'influence et de réaction pour la simulation de systèmes multi-agents. Revue d'Intelligence Artificielle 21, 757–779 (2007)
15. Morvan, G., Jolly, D., Veremme, A., Dupont, D., Charabidze, D.: Vers une méthode de modélisation multi-niveaux. In: Actes de la 7ème Conférence de Modélisation et Simulation MOSIM, Paris, France, vol. 1, pp. 167–174 (2008)
16. Morvan, G., Veremme, A., Dupont, D., Jolly, D.: Modélisation et conception multi-niveau de systèmes complexes : stratégie d'agentification des organisations. Journal Européen des Systèmes Automatisés 43, 381–406 (2009)
17. Prévost, G., Bertelle, C.: Detection and Reification of Emerging Dynamical Ecosystems from Interaction Networks. In: Complex Systems and Self-organization Modelling, pp. 139–161. Springer, Heidelberg (2009)
18. Pumain, D., Sanders, L., Bretagnolle, A., Glisse, B., Mathian, H.: Complexity Perspectives in Innovation and Social Change, Methodos. In: The Future of Urban Systems: Exploratory Models, pp. 331–360. Springer, Netherlands (2009)
19. Servat, D., Perrier, E., Treuil, J.P., Drogoul, A.: When Agents Emerge from Agents: Introducing Multi-scale Viewpoints in Multi-agent Simulations. In: Sichman, J.S., Conte, R., Gilbert, N. (eds.) MABS 1998. LNCS (LNAI), vol. 1534, pp. 183–198. Springer, Heidelberg (1998)
20. Stratulat, T., Ferber, J., Tranier, J.: Masq: towards an integral approach to interaction. In: AAMAS 2009: Proceedings of The 8th International Conference on Autonomous Agents and Multiagent Systems, Budapest, Hungary, pp. 813–820. International Foundation for Autonomous Agents and Multiagent Systems, Richland (2009)
21. Zhang, L., Wang, Z., Sagotsky, J., Deisboeck, T.: Multiscale agent-based cancer modeling. Journal of Mathematical Biology 48(4-5), 545–559 (2009)

Toward a Myers-Briggs Type Indicator Model of Agent Behavior in Multiagent Teams

Jordan Salvit[1] and Elizabeth Sklar[1,2]

[1] Brooklyn College, City University of New York, Brooklyn NY 11210 USA
jordan@jordansalvit.com
[2] The Graduate Center, City University of New York, New York NY 10016 USA
sklar@sci.brooklyn.cuny.edu

Abstract. This paper explores the use of the Myers-Briggs Type Indicator (MBTI) as the basis for defining the *personality* of an agent. The MBTI is a well-known psychological theory of human personality. In the MBTI model, four axes are defined to explain how humans perceive their environment, how they interact with others and how they make decisions based on these traits. The work described here presents a preliminary model of agent behavior in which two of the axes are implemented, combining to reflect four distinct agent personality types. Experiments were conducted under three environmental conditions: single agent setting, homogeneous multiagent team, and heterogeneous multiagent team. Results are presented for each condition and are analyzed in comparison with the other conditions, as well as within the context of the expected MBTI behaviors given each environment and the simulated task. It is demonstrated that agents of each personality type produce very different results, distinct for and characteristic of each MBTI personality type.

1   Introduction

We explore the use of the Myers-Briggs Type Indicator (MBTI) as the basis for defining the *personality* of an agent. The MBTI is a well-known psychological theory of human personality developed in the mid 1900's by Katharine Myers and Isabel Briggs Myers [1], based on an earlier theory developed by Carl Jung [2]. Four axes are defined to explain how humans perceive their environment, how they interact with others and how they make decisions based on these traits.

Jung's theory states that human mental activity essentially involves receiving information and processing that information to make decisions. The input of information ("perceiving", according to Jung) can be handled in one of two ways, either by overtly *sensing* or by using *intuition*. The process of making decisions ("judging", according to Jung) can be driven by logical *thinking* or by emotional *feelings*. Some people derive their energy for these processes from the influences of the external world around them (*extroversion*), while others rely on internal mechanisms such as thoughts or memories (*introversion*). Briggs and Myers expanded on these three dichotomies by adding a fourth "lifestyle" axis which distinguishes between people whose personalities rely more on either perception or judging.

T. Bosse, A. Geller, and C.M. Jonker (Eds.): MABS 2010, LNAI 6532, pp. 28–43, 2011.

Typical results of MBTI tests label individuals using one-character abbreviations for each pole on each axis, as follows:

- *Extraversion* (E) versus *Introversion* (I)
- *Sensing* (S) versus *iNtuition* (N)
- *Thinking* (T) versus *Feeling* (F)
- *Judging* (J) versus *Perceiving* (P)

So, for example, an individual whose personality is labeled ENTJ is someone who gets their energy from interacting with others, who makes decisions based on observations of their environment, who solves problems using logical reasoning and is organized and methodical about what they do. An ENTJ individual makes a commitment to complete a certain task in a certain way and sticks with their plan until the task is complete. In contrast, an individual whose personality is labeled ISFP is someone who gets their energy from inside, who learns from experience and focuses on facts, and lets emotions influence their decision-making. An ISFP individual commits to a task, but constantly re-evaluates to decide if there is a better way to complete the task or a better task to address.

The Meyers-Briggs hypothesis is that all combinations of $4^2 = 16$ personality types exist in humans, and knowledge of which personality type corresponds to an individual can help that individual make life and career decisions. For example, certain personality types tend to be well-suited to particular types of jobs; certain pairings of personality types tend to work better than others for business or life partners. People use the MBTI model to influence decisions or explain how decisions they have made in the past or actions they have taken have been driven.

We are interested in applying MBTI to agent-based systems by implementing agents with different personality types. Although there exist in the literature a range of frameworks and some widely accepted methodologies for agent modeling (e.g., [3,4]), most models abstractly describe how an agent processes inputs and executes outputs, leaving the details to the discretion of the developer. We speculate that it may be the case that a developer will, subconsciously, encode in the agents her own personality type. The work presented here demonstrates that each personality type performs differently, even on a simple task in a simplified environment. The resulting observation in our simulated environment is that some personality types are better suited to the task—the same observation that psychologists make about humans. The implication in the agent modeling and agent-based simulation communities is that the success or failure of an experiment could be affected by the agents' inherent personality types, rather than (necessarily or exclusively) the underlying theory driving the experiment. Thus the need for a concise model of personality type arises.

In the long term, we envision an additional step in agent modeling in which *personality type* plays a factor. When constructing a system, after selecting an agent's behavioral model, the agent's environment, its tasks and goals, the developer can determine experimentally which (set of) personality type(s) would best be suited to accomplish those goals. MBTI is generally used to help develop people's understanding of each other and how differences are not flaws but features, when recognized as such. MBTI is a tool to help people, organizations and/or teams learn how best to leverage each other's personality preferences to accomplish their goals together. Our aim is to bring these ideas, in the context of agent design, to the agent modeling and agent-based simulation fields. We believe that MBTI can provide a clear methodology for expressing and applying agent personality types.

The work described here presents a preliminary model of agent behavior where the MBTI personality types are employed as the basis for defining different agent personalities. As a first step, we focus here on the two axes that do not look at other agents, namely: sensing (S) versus intuition (N) and judging (J) versus perceiving (P). We implement agents exhibiting each of the $2^2 = 4$ personality types: SJ, SP, NJ and NP. The agents are deployed in a simple environment and given simple tasks to complete. The results show marked differences in the way agents of each personality type address the given task.

The remainder of the paper is organized as follows. Section 2 outlines our approach, describing the simulated environment used for experimentation and explaining how each of the four personality types are implemented within this environment. Section 3 presents experiments in which agents of each personality type perform tasks in the simulated environment and produce very different results, distinct for each personality type. Section 4 describes some related work in the literature. Finally, we close with a summary and discussion of future work.

2   Approach

This section introduces our simulated environment and describes how each of the personality types are exhibited within that context. The implementation details for each of the two personality preference axes studied here are explained.

Our methodology first considers how each personality preference axis (S versus N and J versus P) applies within the given environment. Then a set of rules is defined for each axis that modulates the interpretation of input and the production of output, according to the characteristic personality preferences of the two extremes along that axis. Rather than engineering four separate rule sets, one for each of the four personality types (i.e., SJ, SP, NJ and NP), instead two separate rule sets are composed: one that distinguishes between S and N, and one that distinguishes between J and P. Each agent invokes task-dependent functions at run-time, and the behavior of each function is affected by the combined influence of the agents' two separate personality preference rule sets. Details are discussed below, within the context of our simulated environment.

Our environment is based on an existing model from the artificial life community in which termites are simulated [5]. The termites' task is to gather food from their environment and place it in piles. We modify the baseline termite model by using pre-determined locations (instead of allowing the number and locations of piles to emerge as the simulation runs) in order to help illustrate the distinguishing characteristics of the different agent personality types. The environment is represented as a two-dimensional grid, where each (x, y) location in the grid is referred to as a "patch". The differences between the personalities should be revealed quantitatively in terms of the amount of food gathered and delivered to a pile, the number of different patches visited, and the time interval between gathering a food particle and delivering it to a pile.

The basic agent behavior employs a classic *sense-plan-act* model [6,7]. At each time step in the simulation, an agent senses its environment, then decides what to do, and then does it. The agents can sense the following properties:

- am I holding food?
- am I "at" food (i.e., on the same patch as a piece of food)?
- distance to food
- distance to pile

They can sense the world around them within a specified radius. Their sensing function sorts the detected locations of food according to the agents' priority system and returns the coordinates of a single patch. A sensing (S) agent returns the closest patch whereas an intuitive (N) agent returns the patch with the largest surrounding cluster of nearby patches containing food. The agents can perform the following actions:

- move forward
- turn
- pick up food
- drop off food
- wiggle (turn randomly and move forward)

Personality preference axis: S versus N. An agent with a sensing (S) personality preference is concrete. It looks at proximity and focuses on what is closest. For example, it will move toward the closest food pile, even if it is small. This agent also looks at the past. It has a short-term (1 timestep) memory of what it saw in the past. In contrast, an agent with an intuitive (N) personality preference is more abstract. It looks at density and focuses on what is largest. For example, it will move toward the largest food pile, even if it is far away. This agent does not have any memory of the past.

Personality preference axis: J versus P. An agent with a judging (J) personality preference makes a decision about where to go and commits to its decision until it reaches its target location. It does not attempt to sense (perceive) the world again until the target is reached. In contrast, an agent with a perceiving (P) personality preference makes a decision about where to go and commits to it, but only for one timestep. After moving toward the target for one timestep, it perceives the world again and potentially changes its target if conditions dictate.

Pseudo code. The simulation is controlled by a main loop that iterates over a fixed number of timesteps[1]. Each iteration consists of calls to `sense()`, `plan()`

---

[1] Note that the number of timesteps was fixed only for experimental purposes. Other termination conditions could be used.

and act() functions, one for each of the agents in the simulation. The differences between agent personality types are evident in the sense() and plan() functions, as detailed below. The plan() function generates a plan and the act() function executes the plan. The act() function is the same for all agents.

Figure 1 illustrates the perception functionality of the agents. Note that the term "perception" is used in the classic sense of agent-based or robotic systems, meaning that its execution causes the agent to use its sensors to evaluate its environment. For example, a robot might use its sonar to detect distance to obstacles. The sense() function correlates very well to N versus S. The intuitive agent looks at every piece of food in its radius of vision and calculates which patch is surrounded by the most food. The patch with the largest cluster is sent to the plan() function. On the opposite spectrum, the sensing agent calculates the distance between itself and each patch of food in its radius of vision. The closest patch to the agent is sent to the plan() function. The only time the J and P preferences affect the sensing function is when a decision has been committed to and is not yet complete. This is the case when an agent with a judging preference has already set a path in motion and completely bypasses the sense() function until it reaches its destination.

```
function sense() {
  if ( not J ) or ( J and plan is empty ) {
    holdingFood <- am I holding food?
    atFood <- am I at food?
    if ( S ) {
      locFood <- location of closest food source
      locPile <- location of closest pile
    }
    else { // N
      locFood <- location of largest food source
      locPile <- location of largest pile
    }
  }
}
```

Fig. 1. Pseudo code for agents' perception functionality

Figure 2 illustrates the planning functionality of the agents. The plan() function takes the inputs from the sense() function and decides how to proceed. The biggest difference in the plan() function is that if sensing agents are looking for either food or a pile and cannot see one, they rely on their memory to lead them backwards to where they came from. Intuitive agents do exactly the opposite: they try to explore new territory. This distinction emphasizes the *exploitation* versus *exploration* trade-off frequently discussed in the evolutionary computation and artificial life communities. Similar to the sense() function, if a judging agent has already made a decision and has yet to complete the task at hand, the decision step is completely bypassed. On the other hand, perceiving agents always re-evaluate their decisions.

```
function plan() {
  if ( not J ) or ( J and plan is empty ) {
    if ( holdingFood )
      if ( distance to locPile = 0 )
        plan <- put food down
      else // not at pile
        plan <- go toward locPile
    else // not holding food
      if ( atFood )
        plan <- pick up food
      else
        if ( I can see food )
          plan <- go toward locFood
        else
          if ( S )
            plan <- go toward last location where food was found
          else // N
            plan <- go toward a new (unexplored) location
}
```

Fig. 2. Pseudo code for agents' planning functionality

3   Results

Our experimental system was implemented as a prototype in NetLogo [8]. An illustration of the "termite world" is shown in Figure 3. The small dots represent particles of food. The large circles represent food piles. A single agent is shown near the center, a very rough visual approximation of an insect. Experiments were run with different sets of agent populations consisting of five different personality types: SJ, SP, NJ, NP, and random (for comparison). Each experimental condition was run for 1000 timesteps. To illustrate the model and set a baseline for multiagent sets, Section 3.1 shows the results for experiments in which one agent of each type was simulated. These results were discussed in detail in [9]. Section 3.2 describes the new results, for homogeneous teams of agents, and Section 3.3 presents the new results for heterogeneous teams.

3.1   Single Agent Results

The first set of experiments replicated the results from [9] and are shown here as the basis for comparison with the new results presented in the rest of this section. The agents' world is a 200×200 patch arena. Five scenarios were run, each with one agent of each type. The agent started each run in the center of the arena.

Table 1 contains average values and standard deviation (in parenthesis), over 4 experimental runs. The first data column shows the average number of food

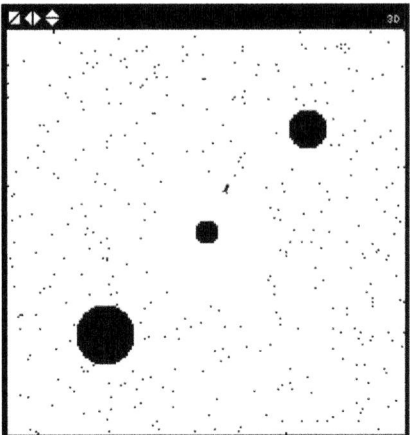

Fig. 3. Sample screen shot of "termite world"

Table 1. Single agent, 200x200 world

	food delivered	path length	path efficiency	team size	team efficiency
SJ	**23.25** (2.22)	764.25 (22.87)	32.87	1	**23.25**
SP	12.00 (2.00)	309.50 (3.70)	**25.79**	1	12.00
NJ	11.75 (0.96)	**880.50** (9.57)	74.94	1	11.75
NP	2.25 (1.50)	329.25 (3.20)	146.33	1	2.25
random	0.25 (0.50)	332.50 (1.00)	1330.00	1	0.25

particles collected and deposited in piles. A higher number is better. The SJ agent delivered the most food particles. The second data column shows the length of the path traveled. A lower number means that the agent did not explore much territory, whereas a larger number means that the agent explored more. The larger number is better, because it shows that the agent covered more of its environment; since the food particles do not move during the simulation (unless the agent moves them), the agent will only be able to gather more food particles if it also explores more area. The NJ agent traveled the furthest. The third data column shows the agent's "path efficiency". This divides the length of the path traveled by the number of food particles delivered, producing a value that indicates how much the agent was able to accomplish given its effort expended. Lower values are better. THIS SHOULD REALLY BE THE INVERSE: AMOUNT OF FOOD DELIVERED DIVIDED BY PATH LENGTH. HIGHER NUMBER IS BETTER. The SP agent is the most efficient. This is because it goes to the closest food location from its current position, so it does not spend a lot of time wandering around. The fourth data column contains the team size, i.e., the number of members on the team. In the case of these single agent baseline runs, the size of the team is, of course, 1; but the table format is used throughout this section, so this columns is included for consistency.

The final data column shows the "team efficiency". This is an indication of how efficiently the team members perform as a group. It is calculated as the total amount of food delivered by the team divided by the number of team members. For example, if a team of 4 agents can deliver 100 particles of food in the same time that a larger team of 10 agents delivers the same amount of food, then the first team is considered more efficient; i.e., $(100/4 = 25) > (100/10 = 10)$. Higher values are better. In the case of a single-agent team, the team efficiency is the same as the amount of food delivered (shown here in the first data column); but again, the table format is used for consistency, to enable easy comparison with the tables that appear later in this section.

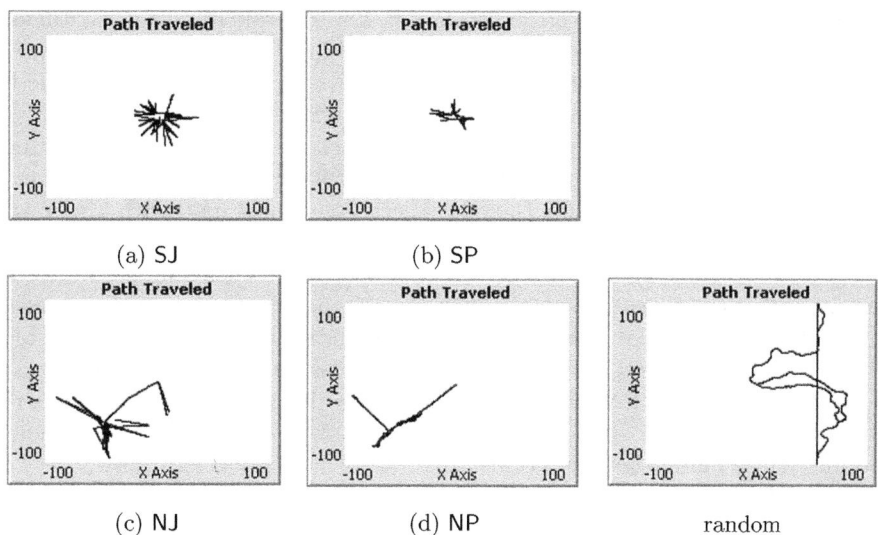

Fig. 4. Typical paths taken by each agent personality. Different path shapes and lengths reflect different decisions about where to go.

Figure 4 shows the paths each agent in a single agent experiment takes while collecting food and bringing it back to the piles. The agents' actions create straight or squiggly lines, depending on their approach and commitment. This figure illustrates where each agent's focus lies. For both sensing agents, SJ and SP, Figure 4b and 4c, respectively, their paths are short and they do not stray far from their starting point. The graphs illustrate how the focus of sensing types is based on proximity and that they prefer to concentrate on the details in front of them. On the other hand, intuitive types tend to focus on the bigger picture and try to look for patterns or clusters. Their paths are typically longer because they are willing to travel further out to find the largest cluster of food. Notice how both the NJ and the NP do not stay near their starting points for long. They are quickly pulled towards the largest pile. This again illustrates how the N's focus is not defined by proximity, but cluster size.

Looking at both the NJ's and NP's paths side by side and the SJ's and SP's paths side by side, it is also clear that aside from the length of their paths, there are other differences between the types. The other differences can be attributed to the judging and perceiving function. As explained in Section 1, judging types prefer to make a decision and commit to it. Perceiving types prefer to continue researching and are not committed to their decisions. Looking at the NJ's and NP's paths, we can see that the NJ's paths taken are all straight, whereas the NP's paths are mixed with both straight and squiggly lines. This shows how the NJ senses for food, is able to find the largest cluster of food within its line of sight and makes a decision of where to go. The agent continues in a straight line till arriving at its destination. On the other hand, the NP re-evaluates its path at every step. Since moving forward may bring new information about the largest cluster, the old decision is no longer valid. The re-evaluation and continuous research is illustrated by the squiggly path. To think of it a little differently, the NP first tries to find the largest cluster that exists in its environment. The NJ looks for the local maximum, where "local" is defined by its line of sight.

Having explained the differences between each of the types, it is not only understandable but expected that each agent type should perform differently. According to our experiments, the SJs collected the most food with SPs in second place, NJs in third, NPs in fourth and the random agent coming in last. Regardless of which agent came in first and which last, their functions are consistent with their types. Assuming they can see food, both agents with judging preferences have regular intervals between each return trip to the pile. The SP's time between trips gets increasingly longer as it is forced to travel farther and sense the world more frequently. Since the NP is always looking for clusters the interval is dictated by how far it has to travel between each cluster and when it decides it has found the largest cluster.

Table 2 shows baseline results with the new system, modified from [9] to accommodate multi agent teams. These baseline results are, as above, for single agents; the data is averaged over 16 runs. The agents' world is smaller, 100×100 patches. Each agents' visual radius is also smaller, 30 patches long (as opposed to 50 patches in the original model). This allows the agents to collect nearly all the food in the environment within the alloted time and illustrates the Sensing type's memory and the Intuitive type's interest in undiscovered territory. Two starting conditions were simulated for each agent type: first, starting the agent at the origin and second, starting the agent at a random location in its world. The first line in each pair for each agent type is the first condition; the second line is the second condition. The data shown is averaged over 16 runs for each starting condition and each agent type. The differences between the two starting conditions are negligable.

The results are consistent with the original experiment: the SJs collected the most food, and the NP and random agents collected the least. The SP and NJ agents collect similar amounts of food, with the former slightly edging out the latter in the original experiments, and the order reversed in the replicated experiments. The difference in the size of the world and the smaller vision radius

Table 2. Single agent, 100x100 world

	food delivered		path length		path efficiency	team size	team efficiency
SJ	**28.25**	(1.53)	713.50	(15.77)	25.26	1	**28.25**
	26.81	(5.09)	673.50	(72.62)	25.12	1	26.81
SP	14.75	(0.86)	304.00	(1.93)	**20.61**	1	14.75
	13.56	(2.00)	306.38	(4.18)	22.59	1	13.56
NJ	18.25	(1.53)	**812.25**	(13.92)	44.51	1	18.25
	15.94	(6.38)	740.50	(151.54)	46.46	1	15.94
NP	3.25	(1.53)	327.00	(3.18)	100.62	1	3.25
	3.13	(1.09)	327.56	(2.25)	104.82	1	3.13
random	0.56	(0.51)	332.19	(1.22)	590.56	1	0.56
	0.69	(0.79)	332.00	(1.21)	482.91	1	0.69

accounts for these differences. The NJ agent travels the furthest. The SP agent has the best path efficiency, while the SJ agent displays the best team efficiency.

3.2 Multiagent Experimental Results, Homogeneous Teams

Table 3 contains results from multi agent simulations. Each simulation contains a homogeneous team of 5 members. Runs were conducted using the same two starting conditions, as above: starting at the origin and starting in a random location. The first line in each pair for each agent type is the first condition; the second line is the second condition. The data shown is averaged over 16 runs for each starting condition and each agent type. Other than the agent starting positions, the 16 runs also differed by the locations of food patches in the environment. The differences between the two starting conditions are negligible.

Although the results between starting at the origin and random positions are negligible on average, the differences illustrate the competitiveness of the environment and agents. For example, by placing five SJ agents at the origin at the same time, they will all view the exact same starting world and focus on the same piece of food. As we explained in Section 2, the Judging preference

Table 3. Multi agent, homogeneous, starting at origin, 100x100 world

	food delivered		path length		path efficiency	team size	team efficiency
SJ	15.60	(1.65)	684.85	(44.54)	43.90	5	3.12
	15.71	(1.45)	669.98	(30.61)	42.64	5	**3.14**
SP	9.80	(0.53)	311.20	(1.20)	31.76	5	1.96
	10.18	(0.54)	312.96	(1.19)	**30.76**	5	2.04
NJ	12.90	(1.00)	**711.60**	(31.88)	55.16	5	2.58
	12.95	(1.32)	702.04	(36.72)	54.21	5	2.59
NP	2.00	(0.57)	329.20	(1.01)	164.60	5	0.40
	2.21	(0.44)	329.28	(1.02)	148.82	5	0.44
random	0.68	(0.23)	331.99	(0.46)	491.83	5	0.14
	0.64	(0.28)	332.09	(0.51)	520.92	5	0.13

means that each agent will set a plan and not sense again until it reaches its destination. In other words, each of the agents will target the same exact piece of food, but only one agent will actually get it. The second agent will realize there is nothing to pick up and will sense the world again.

Table 3 shows the results of five different experiments. Each experiment has 5 agents of the same personality type. Notice that the results are similar to our findings for the single agent environment. SJs still collect the most food, and SPs are the most efficient for each step they take. As we explained in Section 3.1, this makes sense even with the competition of a multiagent system. Since SJs are committed to their plan, they only sense the world and make decisions when they do not have a target. Although they compete with other like agents, once they are far enough away from the other agents in the space, they do not miss many opportunities. SPs remain the most efficient because as soon as the environment changes they are aware of those changes. This means that in a very competitive space, they immediately see the change and update their target accordingly.

Although homogenous sets of agents collect a lot of food, it is interesting to see how each agent type on average collects less, compared to the single agent environment; this difference is reflected in the disparate values for "team efficiency" in Table 3 as compared to Table 2. This is because a single SJ agent can focus on what it does best, without any distractions and without the environment changing. In a competitive space, like agents start by focusing on similar targets; e.g., all 5 SJs try to collect nearby food first. When the 5 agents deplete nearby food, they are forced to look farther out; and they now operate like an NJ does, traveling longer distances before picking up food. Although one might think that starting at random positions would lessen the impact on the mean, in practice, it does not. The reason is that our environment drives agents back to a nest once they have collected food, resetting the gains made by starting at a random position.

3.3   Multiagent Experimental Results, Heterogeneous Teams

As we described in Section 3.2, homogenous sets of agents are extremely competitive, thereby diminishing the overall productivity of the team. In this section we explore different combinations of agent types working in teams, to try and maximize the amount of food collected by a team of agents and the team effectiveness. To demonstrate that not all agents are competitive, Table 4 shows that in an environment with only two agents, one SJ and one NJ, since their foci are different, their overall perfomance is similar to that of a single agent environment.

If we extend this idea, we see that diverse teams of agents are able to collect more food per agent than homogenous teams. In the above example, a single SJ and NJ on the board produces a total team efficiency of 22. Over the 231 different heterogenous experiments we ran, the five groupings that distributed the work of collecting food the most efficiently are shown in Table 5. Notice that the groupings with the highest team efficiencies do not always collect the most food.

Instead if we focus on the most food collected, Table 6 shows the top 5 heterogenous sets of agent populations. As discussed earlier, the competitiveness

Table 4. Multi agent, heterogenous (1 SJ, 1 NJ)

	individual				team	
	food delivered	path length	path efficiency	size	efficiency
SJ	27.00 (1.93)	726.00 (17.57)	26.89	2	22.88
	25.75 (3.92)	699.38 (52.45)	27.16	2	21.16
NJ	18.75 (1.13)	796.50 (15.21)	42.48	2	22.88
	16.56 (2.53)	790.56 (51.17)	47.74	2	21.16

Table 5. Top 5 team efficiency

SJ	SP	NJ	NP	random	food collected	team size	path efficiency	team efficiency
1	0	1	0	0	45.75	2	33.28	22.88
1	1	0	0	0	37.50	2	27.63	18.75
1	1	1	0	0	49.75	3	35.89	16.58
0	1	1	0	0	33.00	2	33.68	16.50
1	0	1	1	0	48.00	3	38.71	16.00

of each similar agent brings the team efficiency down. As is the ultimate question in many projects when deciding if more resources are necessary or more time, we show here that putting more agents to the task does not boost the overall performance. In this environment we might have simply collected more food by extending the time limit instead of adding more that one agent of each personality type.

Table 6. Top 5 food collection

SJ	SP	NJ	NP	random	food collected	team size	path efficiency	team efficiency
5	5	5	5	0	94.50	20	91.58	4.73
5	5	5	0	0	94.25	15	74.75	6.28
5	5	5	1	0	94.00	16	79.59	5.88
5	5	5	5	1	93.63	21	95.24	4.46
5	5	5	0	1	92.81	16	80.07	5.80

Finally, we examine path efficiency, to determine which groupings produce agents that explore the space effectively. Table 7 lists the five groupings with the best (lowest) path efficiency. It is interesting to see that these teams have reasonable team efficiency values, including the most efficient team with a value of 22.88; however, these teams are in the bottom third in terms of the amount of food collected. These results highlight the conclusion that agents with different personality types can be shown to behave differently in a simulated environment. Future work involves categorizing heterogeneous groupings of agents according to their ability to accomplish particular tasks.

Table 7. Top 5 path efficiency

SJ	SP	NJ	NP	random	food collected	team size	path efficiency	team efficiency
1	1	0	0	0	37.50	2	27.63	18.75
1	1	0	1	0	41.50	3	32.80	13.83
1	0	1	0	0	45.75	2	33.28	22.88
1	0	0	1	0	31.25	2	33.30	15.63
0	1	1	0	0	33.00	2	33.68	16.50

4   Related Work

There is a limited amount of research into the use of personality types in agent-based systems. Most approaches focus in one of two directions. The first, more prevalent focus is on creating personalities for agents that interact with human users in social environments. In these cases, the research involves encoding personality type or temperament to increase social acceptance. Dryer [10] explains that personality types can be used to enhance human-machine interaction. Lin and McLeod [11] introduce personality into their work, but instead of incorporating type as the part of the mechanism underlying agents' actions, they train their engine to recognize temperaments and information associated with each temperament. They use this training to filter results more effectively and provide better recommendations. Allbeck and Badler [12] use the "Big Five" theory to embody personality traits and make the motions of each agent flow more realistically and believably.

Lisetti [13] defines a taxonomy for socially intelligent agents, stressing *emotion* as a strong component of personality. She describes state machines that illustrate how an agent can shift from one emotion, such as "happy", to another emotion, such as "concerned". These shifts can occur for different reasons in agents with different personality types. For example, a "determined" agent that is "frustrated" may shift into an "angry" state and use that anger to work itself back into a "happy" state; whereas a "meek" agent may shift from "frustrated" to "discouraged" and never return to "happy".

The second focus is on modeling complex interactions between agents and their environment and describing variations in agent behaviors as personalities. Castelfranchi *et al.* [14] present a simulation framework called "GOLEM" in which agents of different personality traits are modeled. GOLEM provides an experimental framework for exploring the effect of personality traits on social actions, such as delegation. Agents develop models of each other, labeled as personality traits, and use these models to motivate their interactions. Talman *et al* [15] model personality along two axes: "cooperation" and "reliability". These different traits are implemented in a logical framework where agents play a game and reason about each others' "helpfulness", or lack thereof. Agents can recognize different personality types and respond effectively, customizing their actions appropriately for different personalities. Drupinar et al. employ the

OCEAN personality model [16] to an agent-based visualization of crowds [16]. They employ a crowd simulation system and assign to individuals in the crowd personality traits that correspond to the OCEAN model. They associate particular behavioral characteristics, such as willingness to wait or walking speed, are with specific personality traits, e.g., agreeableness or extraversion, respectively.

Both of these last two examples use the notion of personality as a means for agents to model each other and make decisions about how to effect (or not) cooperative activity with others. Another approach is given in [17] where personality is closely tied to emotion, as with the first type of focus listed above. In this work, agents' internal decision-making processes are guided by personality types. Agents are deployed in a simulated military combat scenario in which factors such as "cowardice" and "irritability" are modeled and act as motivators for certain types of actions. For example, an agent labeled as cowardly may be driven by fear and run away from threats when attacked; whereas an agent driven by anger might move forward and face the enemy.

All of the work discussed above is highly context dependent: personality traits are designed in tandem with the environment in which agents are simulated and the tasks that agents are addressing. The advantage of the MBTI model is that it is generic and can, in theory, be adapted to any environment and task. While the instantiation details of agents' personalities will necessarily be tailored to a particular environment, the abstract definition of the personality traits themselves is not specific.

Campos *et al.* [18] is the most closely aligned with our work, mainly because of their use of the MBTI model to leverage personality type and test agent performance in the same environment with different personalities. Similarly, the authors also started with two axes to illustrate personality, though they chose the S-N and T-F dichotomies. Even with our implementation of the S-N function we differ. Campos *et al.* implemented the dichotomy as a mechanism for developing a plan, a hybrid between the S-N and J-P dichotomies. We instead use the S-N function to weight inputs and allow the J-P function to develop the plan.

5   Summary

In the work presented here, we have shown how each personality type functions, illustrating the differences between them and explaining the factors that drive the differences. Since our goal was to see which personality type collected the most food within a given timeframe, we were able to conclude that the SJ personality type is the "winner". In proving that one personality type outshined the others, we are able to conclude that different personality types are in fact better for different tasks—at least in this highly simplified example.

Our next step is to enhance the agent model to include all four MBTI axes, producing a total of 16 personality types. As mentioned in Section 1, here we only looked at the two preferences that did not require other agents. Once we include the extroverted (E) and introverted (I) preferences, we aim to demonstrate how some personality types are better suited to working alone and others are better suited to working with others. Including the thinking (T) and feeling (F) preferences should illustrate how certain agents are more empathetic than others and may be better suited for missions that involve helping others, such as robot-assisted search and rescue (e.g., [19]).

Once the model is expanded to simulate all sixteen types, different and more complex environments and tasks will be explored in order to illustrate the differences between personality preferences. Group dynamics will also be examined, where the interactions of agents with different personality types can be shown to bring complexity to coordination even in groups that have previously been seen as homogeneous—because personality types were not implemented. We will then be able to test different combinations of heterogeneous agent groupings to see which groups work most efficiently together for which types of tasks.

References

1. Myers, I.B., Myers, P.B.: Gifts Differing. Consulting Psychologists Press (1980)
2. Jung, C.: Psychological types. In: The collected works of C. G. Jung, vol. 6. Princeton University Press, Princeton (1971) (originally 1921)
3. Bratman, M.E., Israel, D.J., Pollack, M.E.: Plans and resource-bounded practical reasoning. Computational Intelligence 4(4), 349–355 (1988)
4. Kinny, D., Georgeff, M.: Modelling and design of multi-agent systems. In: Jennings, N.R., Wooldridge, M.J., Müller, J.P. (eds.) ECAI-WS 1996 and ATAL 1996. LNCS, vol. 1193, pp. 1–20. Springer, Heidelberg (1997)
5. Resnick, M.: Turtles, Termites and Traffic Jams: Explorations in Massively Parallel Microworlds. MIT Press, Cambridge (1994)
6. Nilsson, N.J.: Technical note no. 323. Technical report, SRI International, Menlo Park, CA (1984); This is a collection of papers and technical notes, some previously unpublished, from the late 1960s and early 1970s
7. Brooks, R.A.: New approaches to robotics. Science 253(5025), 1227–1232 (1991)
8. Wilensky, U.: NetLogo (1999), http://ccl.northwestern.edu/netlogo/
9. Salvit, J., Sklar, E.: Toward a Myers-Briggs Type Indicator Model of Agent Behavior in Multiagent Teams. In: Bosse, T., Geller, A., Jonker, C.M. (eds.) MABS 2010. LNCS (LNAI), vol. 6532, pp. 28–43. Springer, Heidelberg (2011)
10. Dryer, D.C.: Getting personal with computers: how to design personalities for agents. Applied Artificial Intelligence 13, 273–295 (1999)
11. Lin, C.-H., McLeod, D.: Temperament-based information filtering: A human factors approach to information recommendation. In: Proceedings of the IEEE International Conference on Multimedia & Exposition, New York (2000)
12. Allbeck, J., Badler, N.: Toward representing agent behaviors modified by personality and emotion. In: Proceedings of the Workshop on Embodied Conversational Agents at the 1st International Conference on Autonomous Agents and Multiagent Systems (AAMAS), Bologna (2002)
13. Lisetti, C.L.: Personality, Affect and Emotion Taxonomy for Socially Intelligent Agents. In: Proceedings of the 15th International Florida Artificial Intelligence Research Society Conference (FLAIRS 2002). AAAI Press, Menlo Park (2002)
14. Castelfranchi, C., de Rosis, F., Falcone, R., Pizzutilo, S.: A Testbed for investigating personality-based multiagent cooperation. In: Proceedings of the Symposium on Logical Approaches to Agent Modeling and Design (1997)

15. Talman, S., Gal, Y., Hadad, M., Kraus, S.: Adapting to Agents' Personalities in Negotiation. In: Proceedings of the International Joint Conference on Autonomous Agents and Multiagent Systems (AAMAS). ACM, New York (2005)
16. Durupinar, F., Allbeck, J., Pelechano, N., Badler, N.: Creating Crowd Variation with OCEAN Personality Model. In: Proceedings of the 7th International Conference on Autonomous Agents and Multiagent Systems (AAMAS), pp. 1217–1220 (2008)
17. Parunak, H.V.D., Bisson, R., Brueckner, S., Matthews, R., Sauter, J.: A Model of Emotions for Situated Agents. In: Proceedings of the International Joint Conference on Autonomous Agents and Multiagent Systems (AAMAS). ACM, New York (2006)
18. Campos, A., Dignum, F., Dignum, V., Signoretti, A., Mag'aly, A., Fialho, S.: A process-oriented approach to model agent personality. In: Proceedings of the 8th International Conference on Autonomous Agents and Multiagent Systems (AAMAS), Budapest, pp. 1141–1142 (2009)
19. Kitano, H., Tadokoro, S.: RoboCup Rescue: A Grand Challenge for Multiagent and Intelligent Systems. AI Magazine 22(1) (2001)

Pheromones, Probabilities, and Multiple Futures

H. Van Dyke Parunak

Vector Research Center of Jacobs Technology
3520 Green Court, Suite 250
Ann Arbor, MI 48105 USA
van.parunak@jacobs.com

Abstract. Most agent-based modeling techniques generate only a single trajectory in each run, greatly undersampling the space of possible trajectories. Swarming agents can explore many alternative futures in parallel, particularly when they interact through digital pheromone fields. This paper shows how these fields and other artifacts developed by such a model can be interpreted as conditional probabilities estimated by sampling a very large number of possible trajectories. This interpretation offers several benefits. It supports theoretical insight into the behavior of swarming models by mapping them onto more traditional probabilistic models such as Markov decision processes, it allows us to derive more information from them than swarming models usually yield, and it facilitates integrating them with probability-based AI mechanisms such as HMM's or Bayesian networks.

Keywords: Polyagent, swarming, probability distributions, agent-based modeling, Markov decision process, Monte Carlo tree search.

1 Introduction

Agent-based models are widely used for planning and forecasting, as attested by the ten-year history of the MABS workshop and the rich literature on the subject at AA-MAS and other venues. Such models offer important benefits over other modeling techniques, not the least of which is that they can capture nonlinear effects dependent on differences between agents, effects that are hidden when population averages are used in equation-based models (EBMs) [23, 26]. However, their relatively slow execution places them at a disadvantage in highly nonlinear domains, since it is costly to sample the space of alternative futures that such a domain supports.

One family of agent-based modeling constructs, known variously as polyagents [14] or delegate MAS [25] and generically as EPU systems [18], uses multiple swarming agents to represent each domain entity. Each agent explores a different future of its entity concurrently. When these agents interact, not directly but through shared quantitative markers that they deposit in the environment, they allow an explosion in the space of alternative futures explored, far greater than simply the number of agents per entity. If the system is modeling e entities with g agents per entity, the number of futures sampled is on the order of g^e. Analysis of these futures can yield probability distributions over a variety of propositions of interest. The wide

T. Bosse, A. Geller, and C.M. Jonker (Eds.): MABS 2010, LNAI 6532, pp. 44–60, 2011.

use of such distributions in machine reasoning systems (including HMM's, Bayesian networks, and fluent graphs) allows the integration of agent-based simulation with these techniques. In addition, the probabilistic perspective on a polyagent system allows an insightful comparison with more traditional probabilistic models such as Markov decision processes.

This paper discusses the problem of multiple futures and how it is addressed in previous modeling technologies (Section 2). Then it summarizes the polyagent construct, shows how pheromones can be interpreted as probabilities, and presents a mapping of polyagent reasoning to the Monte Carlo tree search approach to Markov decision processes (Section 3). Section 4 estimates the number of futures actually sampled. Section 5 explains how to analyze the artifacts generated by polyagents to yield distributions of interest, and illustrates these methods with data from a simulated combat model. Section 6 concludes.

2 The Problem of Multiple Futures

2.1 Source of the Problem

Imagine $n + 1$ entities in discrete time. At each step, each entity interacts with one of the other n. Thus at time t its interaction history $h(t)$ is a string in n^t. Its behavior is a function of $h(t)$. This toy model generalizes many domains, including predator-prey, combat, innovation, diffusion of ideas, and disease propagation.

It would be convenient if a few runs of such a system told us all we need to know, but this is not likely to be the case.

- We may have imperfect knowledge of the agents' internal states or details of the environment. If we change our assumptions about these unknown details, we can expect the agents' behaviors to change.
- The agents may behave non-deterministically, either because of noise in their perceptions, or because they use a stochastic decision algorithm.
- Even if agents' reasoning and interactions are deterministic and we have accurate knowledge of all state variables, nonlinear decision mechanisms or interactions can result in overall dynamics that are formally chaotic, so that tiny differences in individual state variables can lead to arbitrarily large divergences in agent behavior. A nonlinearity can be as simple as a predator's hunger threshold for eating a prey or a prey's energy threshold for mating.

An EBM typically deals with aggregate observables across the population. In the predator-prey example, such observables might be predator population, prey population, average predator energy level, or average prey energy level, all as functions of time. No attempt is made to model the trajectory of an individual entity.

An ABM describes the trajectory of each agent. In a given run of a predator-prey model, predator 23 and prey 14 may or may not meet at time 354. If they do meet and predator 23 eats prey 14, predator 52 cannot later encounter prey 14, but if they do not meet, predator 52 and prey 14 might meet later. If predator 23 meets prey 21 immediately after eating prey 14, it will not be hungry, and so will not eat prey 21, but if it did not first meet prey 14, it will consume prey 21. And so forth. A single run of the model can capture only one set of many possible interactions among the agents.

In our toy model, during a run of length τ, each entity will experience one of n^{τ} possible histories. This estimate is of course worst case, since domain constraints may make many of these histories inaccessible. But we must sample the system to know which regions of trajectory space are accessible and which are not. The population of $n + 1$ entities will sample $n + 1$ of these possible histories. It is often the case that the length of a run is orders of magnitude larger than the number of modeled entities ($\tau \gg n$).

Multiple runs with different random seeds is only a partial solution. Each run only samples one set of possible interactions. For large populations and scenarios that permit multiple interactions by each agent, the number of runs needed to sample the possible alternative interactions thoroughly can become prohibitive. In one recent application, $n \sim 50$ and $\tau \sim 10,000$, so the proportion of possible entity histories actually sampled by a single run, or even by a thousand runs, is vanishingly small.

2.2 Multiple Futures in Conventional Modeling

For given inputs, a deterministic simulation sees only one future. A stochastic simulation can sample alternative futures by repeating the entire simulation with different random seeds. This ensemble approach faces several challenges.

- Replication is a very inefficient way to sample a trajectory space with a size on the order of n^{τ}.
- This approach considers only alternatives that result from incorrect information, and ignores the far richer set of alternatives generated by chaotic interactions of the entities as a scenario unfolds.
- To be useful in estimating the probabilities of alternative futures, each of the random starting conditions must lie on the manifold defined by the system's dynamics. If this manifold is sparse in the space from which replications are drawn (as is the case with a chaotic system), most replications will not satisfy this condition, and as a result probabilities computed from their trajectories will be misleading [24].

With an EBM, stochastic differential equations can propagate uncertainty through the model. However, such approaches are subject to the recognized weaknesses of EBM's resulting from the use of aggregated population characteristics.

One approach to multi-trajectory simulation [7] evaluates possible outcomes at each branch point stochastically, selects a few of the most likely alternatives, and propagates them. This selection is required by the high cost of following multiple paths, but avoiding low-probability paths violates the model's ergodicity and compromises accuracy [8], and random sampling does not satisfy the requirement of choosing an ensemble from the system's attractor [24].

3 Pheromones and Probabilities

3.1 The Polyagent Construct

In the polyagent modeling construct [15], a persistent *avatar* manages a stream of transient *ghosts*, each of which explores one alternative future for the entity. As the ghosts of different avatars interact, they explore alternative futures for their individual entities, complete with the full range of possible interactions that might result from the alternative futures of other entities. These futures are executed in one or more virtual *environments*, such as a book of temporally successive geospatial maps or a task network, whose topology reflects that of the problem domain. To ensure that the ensemble of ghosts actually fall on the behavioral manifold of the entities being modeled [24], we either embed that behavior explicitly in the ghosts when we construct them, or evolve their parameters against observed behavior of the entity [16].

Ghosts are tropistic. Their behavior responds to a set of fields ("digital pheromones") in their environment. Each field associates a scalar value with each cell of the environment. Some fields are emitted by objects of interest (such as roads or buildings). Others are deposited by the ghosts as they move about. A ghost's behavior is determined by a weighted sum of the pheromones it senses in its vicinity, where the weights define the ghost's personality and can be either manually coded or learned by observation of the entity that the ghost represents.

In the real world, one entity's behavior can depend on the presence or absence of another entity. A ghost's behavior depends on the fields of other entities, and thus reflects an average response across all of the locations of the other entities that their ghosts have explored.

Each ghost has a strength, which changes to reflect its interaction with the environment (such as combat in a battlefield model). The ghost's strength can be interpreted as its degree of health, or more abstractly as the probability that the entity that it represents would be at full strength at the ghost's time and place. A history of each ghost's strength as a function of time is an additional resource, alongside the pheromone fields deposited by the ghost, for deriving probabilities. An entity's avatar can estimate the strength of its entity by taking the average of the strengths of its ghosts.

Each ghost increments the field corresponding to the entity it represents as it moves (Fig. 1). The strength of this particular field at a location represents how frequently ghosts of that entity visit that location. The amount of the deposit depends on the ghost's strength, so its field takes into account the effects of attrition. A ghost can increment multiple fields. For example, one might correspond to its own avatar, one to the entire team to which its avatar belongs, and one to a unit within the team. A field modulated by strength yields an estimate of the probability of encountering a unit of force at each location. Fields can also be modulated by a ghost characteristic other than strength, such as current preference for a given course of action, yielding a field with different semantics that may be useful in some applications.

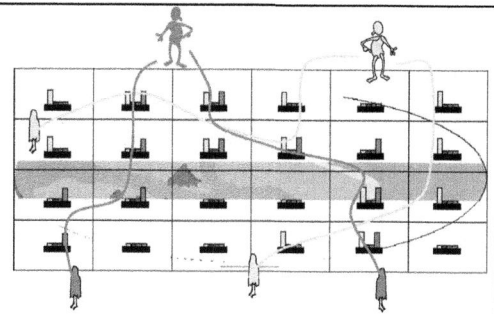

Fig. 1. Ghosts deposit pheromones reflecting their presence, and sense the presence of ghosts of other entities through their pheromones

Field strength depends not only on entity type and location, but also on time. In forecasting applications, we maintain a set of field maps, one for each successive time step from a specified time in the past (the "insertion horizon") to a specified time in the future (the "forecast horizon"). Each page covers the entire area of interest (AOI). This set of maps is called the "book of maps." The number of pages is fixed, and as real time advances, we drop the oldest page and add a new page one time step further into the future. Pages are indexed by τ. $\tau = 0$ corresponds to "now." $\tau < 0$ indexes pages in the past (used to train the ghosts by evolution against observations [16]), and $\tau > 0$ indexes pages in the future. Thus if the current real time is t, the real time represented on a given page with index τ is $\tau + t$.

Polyagents execute on two time scales.

At the coarsest time scale, avatars dispatch their ghosts, use the results to select a course of action, and take that action, advancing the pages in the book of pheromones as outlined above.

At a shorter time interval, each avatar's ghosts move from one page to the next through the book of pheromones. At each step, each ghost

- Evaluates the fields on its current page;
- Increments the fields at its location on its current page;
- Chooses an action based on the field strengths in step 1;
- Executes the action while moving to the next page.

Map pages for which $\tau \geq 0$ have real fields only for relatively persistent environmental features such as topography or clan territories. Otherwise, the fields to which ghosts respond on these pages are built up by the ghosts themselves as they traverse them. The first ghosts to visit each page do not see any ghost-generated fields, and their behavior is constrained only by persistent features. To enable ghosts to respond to one another, avatars release them in *shifts*. In one application, each avatar releases a total of 200 ghosts over 100 shifts, two per shift. The ghosts in each shift respond to the state of the fields as modified by the previous shifts. This mechanism is analogous to recursive rationality planning models [6, 11], where the number of shifts corresponds to the depth of the recursion: the nth shift makes its decision based on the system's estimate of the decisions of the previous $n - 1$ shifts.

Ghosts in early shifts do not have well-defined fields to which to respond, so their movements are not as reliable an estimator of entity movement as those in later shifts, when the fields have converged. To accommodate this increase in accuracy over time, at each simulation step the field strengths on each page are attenuated by a constant factor E (a process inspired by pheromone evaporation in insect systems). The effect is to weight deposits by later shifts more strongly than those by earlier ones.

The polyagent model has been applied successfully to manufacturing scheduling and control [2], control of robotic vehicles [21, 22], forecasting of urban combat [16], and reasoning over hierarchical task networks [3, 20], among other problems. For example, in battle forecasting, ghosts are evolved against observations of enemy forces, then run into the future to estimate where the adversary may move.

3.2 Pheromone Fields Are Probabilities

Up to a normalizing constant, the pheromone field incremented by the ghosts of a given entity on a given page of the book of maps is the conditional probability $P(e|x,y,t)$[1] of encountering entity e at location (x,y)[2] and time t, estimated over all possible futures explored by that entity's ghosts. This claim is supported by the dynamics of pheromone field strength. The strength of the field in a cell is 0 before any ghosts visit it, and is augmented by a constant deposit D each time a ghost visits the cell, and decremented by a constant fraction E each time step. The strength $\varphi(t)$ for a single cell with a single ghost has dynamics.

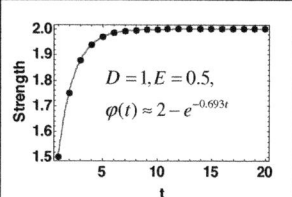

Fig. 2. Exponential convergence of pheromone field under constant deposit

$$\varphi(0) = 0; \varphi(t) = E\varphi(t-1) + D = D\sum_{i=0}^{t-1} E^i = D\frac{1-E^t}{1-E} \qquad (1)$$

In the continuous time limit, $\varphi(t)$ converges exponentially to $\frac{D}{1-E}$. Fig. 2 shows the excellent agreement of this limit model even with discrete data. This result has two important consequences.

First, the field converges if enough shifts of ghosts visit a page. We determine experimentally how many shifts are needed in each application.

Second, because the evaporation rate E does not change over time, the converged strength of a pheromone field is proportional to the amount of deposit, even in the presence of evaporation. If multiple ghosts visit a cell over time and deposit the same pheromone flavor, the converged strength of the field in the cell is proportional to the average number of deposits experienced by the cell per unit time. In other words, pheromone strength measures ghost traffic through a cell.

To compute the appropriate normalization, observe that all ghosts representing an avatar must pass through some cell on a given page as they move through the time interval represented by the page. The proportion of the ghosts that visit a given cell is equal to the ratio between their pheromone in that cell, and

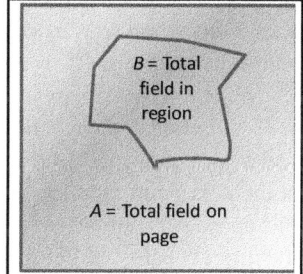

Fig. 3. Computing probability that an entity is in a region

the total amount of pheromone deposited on the entire page. But this ratio is just the probability that the avatar will visit that cell.

We can use the field to estimate the probability that the entity is in a given region of the page. Let A be the total amount of the entity's pheromone on the entire page, and B the amount in a region of interest (Fig. 3). Then B/A estimates the probability

---

[1] x,y,t is shorthand for the event of making an observation at the specified location and time.

[2] For simplicity of exposition, we imagine that the polyagents are restricted to a Cartesian lattice. The location could have more dimensions, or even be relative to a non-Cartesian topology [20].

that the entity is in the limited region. The entity's most likely location is given by the center of mass of the field.

Often we are interested not in the location of an individual entity, but in the distribution of a group of entities (for example, all members of a team). In this case, all ghosts of entities on the same team increment the same field, which now reflects the probability of encountering any team entity over the area of interest.

In interpreting these probabilities, we must understand that ghosts' movements are constrained by environmental influences on earlier pages (represented as pheromones of other flavors). The probability that they estimate is thus not simply $P(e|x, y, t)$, but $P(e|x, y, t,$ other conditions at $t' < t)$. That is, the movements of individual ghosts are not independent of one another. They are all subject to the same conditions. However, *given* those conditions, the ghosts' locations (and thus the pheromone field that they generate) *can* be treated as independent samples of the avatar's location in space-time.

3.3 Polyagents, Monte Carlo Tree Search, and Markov Decision Processes

Recognizing the isomorphism between digital pheromone fields and probabilities reveals a deep and useful connection between the polyagent modeling construct and other planning formalisms that are cast explicitly in terms of probabilities. Consider Markov decision processes (MDPs), and one recent development in addressing them, Monte Carlo Tree Search (MCTS).

A MDP consists of a set of states S, a set of actions A, a mapping $P_{sa}(s')$ from a specific state s and action a to the probability of transitioning to a specified new state s', a distribution $R(s, a)$ over the reward expected for performing action a in state s, and a discount $\gamma \in [0, 1]$ applied at each time step to devalue more remote rewards. The objective is a policy $\pi: S \rightarrow A$ that maximizes the expected reward.

Conventional approaches to solving MDPs are based on the Bellman equation, a recursive definition of the value of the state at one point in time in terms of the value at the next point, applied through dynamic programming. While theoretically elegant, this approach stumbles over the large $|S|$ and $|A|$ encountered in realistic problems, and the impracticality of defining the transition and reward distributions for every combination of states and actions.

A major step forward is based on the realization that explicit definition of the transition and reward distributions can be replaced with a black-box simulator that maps a given s and a to a successor s' and reward r [9]. The simulator can be, in the worst case, a random process. The decision tree is played out to any desired horizon a fixed number of times, and the distribution over outcomes used to decide the best choice for the next move. This approach has come to be called "Monte Carlo tree search" (MCTS).

This algorithm has running time independent of $|S|$. Still, it is very slow. The next step in the Monte Carlo approach to MDPs [10] recognizes that one does not need to play out every step, if some states are encountered repeatedly. A multi-armed bandit algorithm is used to choose between further exploration of such states, and simple exploitation of the previously-chosen actions.

Some of the most promising applications of MCTS are in computer programs to play the game of Go, a task that has been highly resistant to previous algorithms. MCTS-based Go programs are the first systems able to compete at the professional level on a reduced (9x9) board. Initial efforts at Monte Carlo Go played random moves on both sides in each run-out of the game tree, but current versions [5] include a dictionary of 30,000 locally-defined "stupid moves" that the program should avoid. Because these heuristic guidelines involve only a few cells, they can be checked rapidly in the random exploration of the tree.

The polyagent modeling construct can be viewed as a form of MCTS.

- Each ghost corresponds to a single run-out of the MDP using the simulator.
- The ghost logic embodies locally-defined movement heuristics. In a combat model, these include attraction to a mission objective, varying movement speed based on terrain and presence or absence of the adversary, and attraction or repulsion to pheromones representing friendly and adversarial forces.
- Because ghosts' movements are stochastic, weighted by the pheromone fields in their vicinity, each ghost samples a possibly different trajectory.

The conventional approach to an MDP begins by analyzing the problem statement to derive the transition and reward distributions, and from these derives a behavior policy. The MCTS (and polyagent) approach begins by defining the possible local behaviors of the entities in the problem and the influences on them, if only approximately. As these behaviors are repeatedly sampled, the MCTS approach effectively generates statistical distributions over state transitions. In other words, traditional MDP methods begin with distributions and generate an optimal description of behavior. MCTS begins with an approximate description of behavior, and generates distributions (and an approximation to the optimal policy).

4 Counting Possible Futures

How many different futures does this approach explore? We develop this value by successive refinement.

Consider a scenario in which, over σ shifts, each avatar sends $g*\sigma$ ghosts, where g is the number of ghosts issued per shift. In one recent application, $n = 5$ avatars each sent out $g = 2$ ghosts per shift over $\sigma = 100$ shifts into a book of 60 maps. Each ghost could in principle follow a distinct path through the book of pheromones. In practice, environmental constraints mean that many ghosts follow similar paths, and our probability distributions reflect the resulting distribution of trajectories.

A state of the world consists of the state of all avatars. Because we can capture multiple avatar states concurrently, we capture a number of states of the world equal to the product of the number of states visible for each avatar. A naive estimate of the number of possible futures is $(g*\sigma)^n \sim 3.2*10^{11}$, but this is an overestimate, for two reasons:

1. The number of ghosts that have visited a given page depends on the page. Pages further in the future see fewer ghosts.
2. A ghost interacts with later ghosts by way of the field that it increments, and this field evaporates over time. So we should not count all ghosts equally.

Assume that we are at shift σ and page τ < σ, so that the page in question has been visited. Shift 1 is now on page σ, and was on page τ (σ −τ) time steps ago, so the amount of the deposit g from shift 1 that remains is $g*E^{\sigma-\tau}$. The most recent deposit, made at σ, contributes g. So each avatar's "virtual presence" on the page is $g \sum_{i=1}^{\sigma-\tau} E^i = gE \frac{1-E^{\sigma-\tau}}{1-E}$. Fig. 4 shows the number of representatives for each entity at shift 100 as

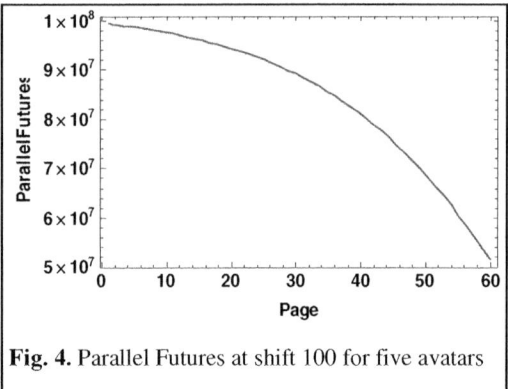

Fig. 4. Parallel Futures at shift 100 for five avatars

a function of page. For example, in the near future (pages 10 and lower), we are exploring nearly 40 alternative behaviors for each avatar. The concave nature of the curve is felicitous. It means that the drop-off in parallelism is gradual until we get to more distant futures, where the forecast horizon effect [17] (the increasingly random divergence of future trajectories under nonlinear iteration) makes forecasts less reliable anyway.

The number of states explored on each page is this value raised to the power of the number of entities. Averaging this value over the 60 pages yields an average number of parallel futures of 8.4 x 10^7. This is several orders of magnitude lower than the 3.2 x 10^{11} estimate based on 200 ghosts per avatar, but still far more than a single-trajectory simulation can explore.

There is an important trade-off in this computation. We could run all of an avatar's ghosts through the system in a few shifts, resulting in less pheromone loss to evaporation and thus a higher value for the number of parallel futures that we are exploring. However, fewer shifts might not allow the system to converge. We use 100 shifts because experience shows that the probability distributions will be converged by that point, but this value is very conservative. If in fact the distributions are converged earlier, we could produce more parallel futures by distributing the same total number of ghosts across fewer shifts. Just how much benefit could we realize?

Fig. 5 plots the number of parallel futures at page 20 against the total number of shifts for 200 ghosts, evenly divided across the shifts. As the number of shifts increases, the number of parallel futures increases rapidly (due to the larger number of ghosts reaching page 20), then drops faster than linearly (due to the evaporation effect). For instance, if the probability distributions converged sufficiently by shift 40, we could live with 40 shifts of 5 ghosts each and thus increase the number of parallel futures by more than an order of magnitude. In doing so, we would reduce the number of pages T by increasing the time interval between them, so this increase in parallel futures would have to be traded against the time resolution that we desire.

Not all of these futures are distinct. Environmental constraints will cause many of them to fall together, so the actual number of meaningful distinct branches in the futures will typically be many orders of magnitude less than the upper bounds that we have estimated. But a decision-maker can be assured that the branches considered result from a much more thorough review of possibilities than would be provided by the far fewer replications possible with a single-trajectory simulation.

This analysis highlights the importance of understanding the convergence of the probability distributions that polyagents produce. If we could reduce the number of shifts we run without compromising convergence, we would not only speed up computation, but also increase the number of parallel futures that we are exploring. Our ongoing research includes developing formalisms based on information geometry [1, 13] for monitoring the convergence of the fields that polyagents generate.

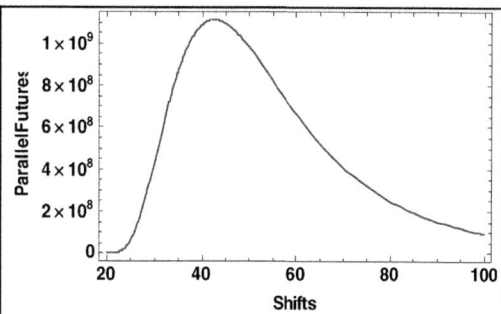

Fig. 5. Alternative Futures at page 20, as a function of the number of shifts across which 200 ghosts are distributed. Evaporation factor $E = 0.95$.

5 Analyzing Multiple Futures

Computational artifacts generated by polyagents can yield probability distributions that are not only intrinsically useful, but also a natural point of interfacing with other reasoning technologies. First, we introduce the sample data with which we illustrate our methods. Then we show how some distributions can be evaluated directly from pheromone fields, and how sampling methods can estimate other distributions that are not directly computable from the original fields.

5.1 Experimental Data

Consider a simulated wargame in which one force ("Red") is currently in the north-east of the playbox in a region γ, and the other ("Blue") is moving toward Red with the objective of getting Red's strength in γ below 25% of its initial strength. Red's objective is to attack and harass Blue. Fig. 6a shows the initial positions of the 16 companies in each force, and the region γ. Fig. 6b shows the ghosts generated by both forces, with all 60 pages superimposed. The dispersion of the ghosts suggests the breadth of alternative futures that they explore.

Fig. 7 shows the evolution of the Red pheromone field on pages 0, 30, and 60. As τ increases, the field becomes more diffuse, reflecting the increased uncertainty in unit locations as we forecast further into the future. The reduction in overall strength of the

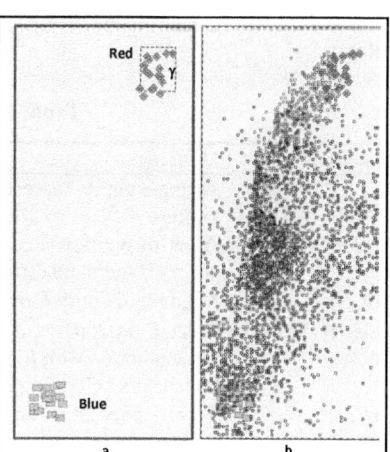

Fig. 6. Initial laydown of demonstration scenario (a) and ghosts on all pages (b)

field reflects Red attrition in encounters with Blue.

5.2 Evaluating Distributions

The fields generated directly by ghosts reflect the probability of finding an entity at a location. We can derive distributions of various conditions from these fields. Such derivative distributions could be used (for instance) by an external reasoner to forecast when a course of action is likely to terminate and in what state. We illustrate these methods with conditions that depend on the number of entities in a defined subregion of the AOI. Other conditions are discussed in more depth elsewhere [19], including those that depend on the number of forces in the entire AOI, those that depend on distances between forces and designated locations or other forces, and conditional distributions. Table 1 summarizes our notation.

Fig. 3 illustrates a page from the book of pheromones, with a gradient representing the pheromone field over the entire AOI, and a subregion of particular interest. A com-

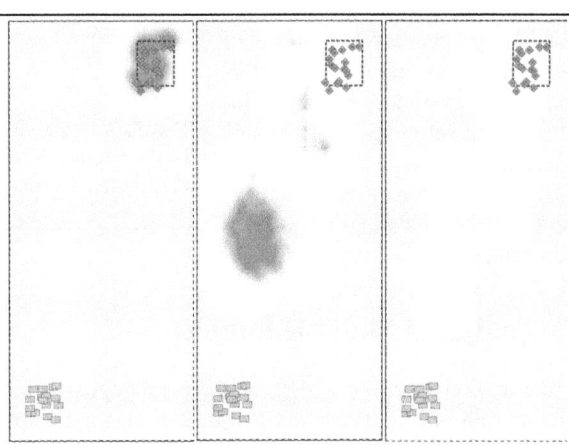

Fig. 7. Red pheromone field at $\tau = 0$ (left), 30 (center), and 60 (right)

mon class of condition depends on the strength of a given force within the region. For example, a Blue attack might terminate when the Red strength within a defended region γ falls below 25%. We define Red strength as the number of Red units, thus an integer.

Table 1. Notation for Examples

Notation	Meaning
E	A single entity, represented by a single avatar. Subscripts distinguish distinct entities.
R, B	A set of entities (Red or Blue), represented by multiple avatars (with subscripts if there are different entities belonging to the same force)
$S(E, \tau)$	Strength of entity E on page τ (= average strength of E's ghosts on that page)
$\Phi(E, \tau)$	Total E pheromone deposited by ghosts of entity E on page τ. We use the same notation with R or B to indicate the total amount of pheromone from all the avatars belonging to the designated group.
$\Gamma(E, \tau)$, $\Delta(E, \tau)$, $\Lambda(E, \tau), \ldots$	Total E pheromone in named region $\gamma, \delta, \lambda, \ldots$ Again, we overload the function to handle groups of entities.
(x_γ, y_γ)	Coordinates of named point γ in pheromome map
$\phi(E, x, y, \tau)$	E pheromone strength in cell (x, y) on page τ (with usual overloading for R and B)
$p(E, x, y, \tau)$	$\phi(E, x, y, \tau)/\Phi(E, \tau)$ = probability that E (R, B) is at (x, y, τ)

A naïve approach computes $\Gamma(R, \tau)/\Phi(R, \tau)$, which estimates the percentage of Red in the region, and reports if this ratio falls below 0.25. Fig. 8 shows this ratio for our example as a function of look-ahead. The proportion of pheromone in the region drops very low, then actually climbs later in the battle as Red is repulsed by Blue.

This approach is incomplete for two reasons.

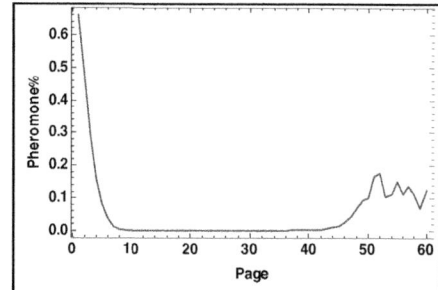

Fig. 8. % Red Pheromone in γ as Function of Page

1. It allows only a Boolean condition. For some purposes we would like to know a probability distribution over the proposition that Red is below 25% in the region.
2. The simple ratio estimates the percentage of Red's *current* strength in the region. Often we are more interested in the percentage of Red's strength at some previous time.

To address the first issue, note that the actual number of Red entities in the region follows a binomial distribution. Whether or not each Red entity is in the region is a Bernoulli trial whose probability of success is estimated by $\Gamma(R, \tau)/\Phi(R, \tau)$. This interpretation depends on the independence of the movements of the ghosts that generate the fields. At first glance, this assumption seems unjustified. In our combat example, the ghosts are certainly *not* moving indepen-

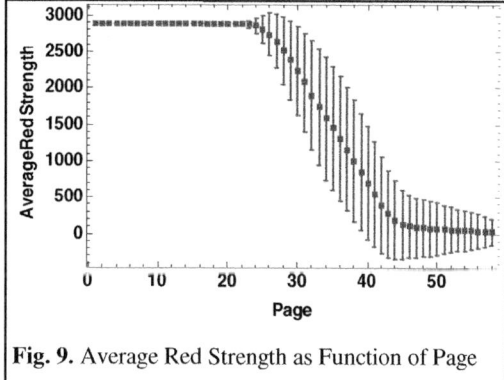

Fig. 9. Average Red Strength as Function of Page

dently of one another, but represent fighting units subject to the same combat forces and thus likely to move together. However, as discussed in Section 3.2, the probability field does in fact represent the probability of ghost location, conditioned on environmental factors. The ghosts' movements are independent, *conditional* on the environmental factors that the polyagent framework takes into account. We can thus use the binomial theorem to estimate the distribution of likely avatar locations.

On this basis, the probability that exactly $k \le n \equiv |R|$ Red entities are in γ is just

$$\binom{n}{k}\left(\frac{\Gamma(R,\tau)}{\Phi(R,\tau)}\right)^{k}\left(1 - \frac{\Gamma(R,\tau)}{\Phi(R,\tau)}\right)^{n-k} \tag{2}$$

To address the second condition, $S(R, 0)$ gives us the effective number of Red entities on page 0. So we can express k as a fraction of this original strength. Fig. 9

shows the average strength of the Red ghosts in our scenario as a function of page. The error bars are $\pm 1\sigma$.

The probability $p(C_1, \tau)$ that Red's strength in region γ at time τ is below 25% of its original strength is then derived by summing the probability from Equation 2, starting with the case where Red's strength is 0 (the lower bound in the summation). Naively, the upper bound is 25% of the original strength. Two qualifications are needed. First, since we have defined strength as an integer and are summing over successive strength values, we need to take the floor of this product. Second, if the current strength is already below 25%, we cannot sum past the current strength. The resulting sum is Equation 3.

$$p(C_1, \tau) = \sum_{i=0}^{Min(\lfloor .25*S(R,0)\rfloor -1, S(R,\tau))} \binom{n = S(R,\tau)}{i} \left(\frac{\Gamma(R,\tau)}{\Phi(R,\tau)}\right)^i \left(1 - \frac{\Gamma(R,\tau)}{\Phi(R,\tau)}\right)^{n-i} \tag{3}$$

In our example, this probability is vanishingly small on the first three pages, but approaches unity thereafter, due to the rapid movement of Red toward Blue (reflected in the precipitous drop of Red pheromone in γ shown in Fig. 8 and the subsequent high attrition of Red reflected in Fig. 9).

Sometimes we may want to detect a condition like C_2, for which the population in region γ exceeds 60% of the original strength. The computation is almost the same, except that now we sum from the lower limit (the larger of 60% of the original strength, or the actual strength at τ) up to the strength at τ. Again, we have to take the floor of 60% of the original strength plus 1 in order to insure an integer, and if the current strength is already above this level, we should start there instead, yielding Equation 4.

$$p(C_2, \tau) = \sum_{i=Max(\lfloor .6*S(A,0)\rfloor +1, S(A,\tau))}^{S(A,\tau)} \binom{n = S(A,\tau)}{i} \left(\frac{\Gamma(A,\tau)}{\Phi(A,\tau)}\right)^i \left(1 - \frac{\Gamma(A,\tau)}{\Phi(A,\tau)}\right)^{n-i} \tag{4}$$

5.3 Conditional Distributions

Let $\{C_i\}$ be propositions over state variables (e.g., $C_7 \equiv unitAStrength > 10$). The previous section showed how to derive probability density functions $p(C, \tau)$ for these over time. One common application of these time-varying distributions is for some other application to assess that at some point in the future being modeled by the polyagent system, a condition C_i is in fact satisfied. Further reasoning will then require the distributions of other state assertions *conditioned on* $p(C_i, \tau) = 1$, e.g, $p(C_j, \tau|C_i)$. This section discusses ways to do this.

If the propositions are independent, conditioning doesn't change anything. But how can we know that they are dependent? Omitting τ for clarity,

1. We have $p(a)$ and $p(C)$.
2. We want $p(a|C)$.
3. One way to get this would be to compute $p(a, C)$ and then compute $p(a|C) = p(a, C)/p(C)$.

So the real issue is how to get the joint probabilities for any pair of propositions. The Red and Blue pheromone fields from which we evaluate the margins are aggregated over all futures. How can we tease apart those futures in which both conditions are satisfied from those in which only one is satisfied?

There has been some theoretical work on deriving a joint distribution from margins [4, 12], but our attempts to exploit this work in the context of stigmergic systems have not yielded satisfactory results [19]. In practice, a supplementary sampling approach has proven much more effective.

Consider the joint probability $p(Red, Blue)$ of finding Red and Blue at the same location. As a thought experiment, imagine that each ghost deposits an interaction pheromone proportional to the number of ghosts of the other side in its cell. The resulting field is just what we want. But the process violates the stigmergic principle of handling all interchanges through the environment, and is likely to incur computational penalties, of two sorts. First, ghosts have to sense one another directly. Second, storage of the joint pheromone will be costly.

A more promising approach is to have each ghost deposit an echo pheromone proportional to the field it senses from its counterpart. For example, each Red ghost would deposit a Red-Echoing-Blue (REB) pheromone. The resulting field differs from the original Blue field because it is deposited only where Red actually visits. Thus the REB field is $p(B|R)$. If this is the conditional distribution we want, we're done. If we want the joint (say, to compute $p(R|B)$, we can multiply by $p(R)$, which we already have. The additional computation involved to do the echo deposit is fairly trivial, but we do have to store an additional time-varying pheromone field for each interaction pair, which will consume space.

Since joint distributions are in general of interest to other algorithms and not to our ghosts themselves, there is no need to store the time-varying field. Instead, we can log relevant information (e.g., unit ID, strength, location, shift number) from each ghost as it passes each page. In a typical application, we have on the order of 10^4 cells per page and on the order of 60 pages, so each pheromone flavor requires on the order of 10^6 scalars. Each avatar typically generates 200 ghosts in all over 100 shifts, and we can limit our attention to the last 40 or so ghosts per avatar, representing the converged state of the system. Thus we have to log 40 ghosts x 4 information items x 60 pages = 9600 scalars per avatar. Logs for 100 avatars consume only on the order of 10^6 scalars, from which we can generate many different combinations of conditions. We select from the logged ghosts those that satisfy conditions of interest to them, have them deposit pheromone on a single static map, and analyze it with the methods described above. For example, to explore the joint distribution of strength and location, we can sample ghosts in different bins of strengths and generate their spatial pheromone distribution.

6 Conclusion

Digital pheromones are an effective means of coordination among multiple agents in a wide array of domains. In many systems, they summarize the behaviors of many similar agents, and so it makes sense to interpret them as probability fields over that space of behavior. This interpretation offers three main benefits.

First, it permits us to relate the polyagent modeling construct to other stochastic search methods, specifically the application of Monte Carlo tree search to Markov decision processes. This interpretation allows us to leverage theoretical results from the MCTS and MDP literature in engineering polyagent applications.

Second, the field information is no longer just an internal coordination artifact among the agents, but becomes a meaningful product of the computation in its own right.

Third, fields interpreted as probability distributions are a useful way to communicate the resulting forecasts to a wide range of other applications that understand the world in terms of probabilities. By expressing our results as probability distributions, we enable the consumers of these forecasts to reason about the uncertainty inherent in statements about the future in a commonly understood mathematical language. Conversely, when an application requires probabilistic estimates, generating these estimates by conventional single-trajectory simulation can be prohibitively expensive, while this technique can generate them with a single run of a polyagent model.

There is no free lunch. Polyagent-based exploration of multiple futures achieves its great breadth at the expense of detail, as seen in the difficulty in obtaining some joint distributions. When ghosts react to one another through probability fields, rather than through direct interactions, some of the information that would be gained in a one-on-one interaction is lost. Nevertheless, this approach offers access to distributional information in dynamic, non-stationary environments that would otherwise be intractable to probabilistic reasoning.

Acknowledgments

This work would not be possible without experimental support provided by Bob Matthews, Jorge Goic, and Andrew Yinger, and has benefited from comments by John Sauter and Jacob Crossman. The observations of a careful reviewer helped clarify the mathematical presentation.

References

[1] Amari, S.-I., Nagaoka, H.: Methods of Information Geometry. American Mathematical Society (2007)
[2] Brueckner, S.: Return from the Ant: Synthetic Ecosystems for Manufacturing Control. Dr.rer.nat. Thesis at Humboldt University Berlin, Department of Computer Science (2000), http://dochost.rz.hu-berlin.de/dissertationen/brueckner-sven-2000-06-21/PDF/ Brueckner.pdf
[3] Brueckner, S., Belding, T., Bisson, R., Downs, E., Parunak, H.V.D.: Swarming Polyagents Executing Hierarchical Task Networks. In: Proceedings of Third IEEE International Conference on Self-Adaptive and Self-Organizing Systems (SASO 2009), San Francisco, CA, pp. 51–60. IEEE, Los Alamitos (2009), http://www.newvectors.net/staff/parunakv/SASO09rTAEMS.pdf
[4] Cheeseman, P., Stutz, J.: On The Relationship between Bayesian and Maximum Entropy Inference. In: Proceedings of 24th International Workshop on Bayesian Inference and Maximum Entropy Methods in Science and Engineering, AIP Conference Proceedings, pp. 445–461 (2004), http://ti.arc.nasa.gov/m/pub/archive/0807.pdf
[5] Coulom, R.: The Monte-Carlo Revolution in Go. In: The Japanese-French Frontiers of Science Symposium (JFFoS 2008), Roscoff, France (2009)

[6] Gmytrasiewicz, P.J., Durfee, E.H.: A Rigorous, Operational Formalization of Recursive Modeling. In: Proceedings of the First International Conference on Multi-Agent Systems (ICMAS 1995), San Francisco, CA, pp. 125–132 (1995), http://citeseerx.ist.psu.edu/viewdoc/summary?doi=10.1.1.56.1248

[7] Gilmer Jr., J.B., Frederick, J.S.: Alternative implementations of multitrajectory simulation. In: Proceedings of the 30th Conference on Winter Simulation, Washington, D.C., United States, pp. 865–872. IEEE Computer Society Press, Los Alamitos (1998)

[8] Gilmer Jr., J.B., Frederick, J.S.: Study of an ergodicity pitfall in multitrajectory simulation. In: Proceedings of Proceedings of the 33nd Conference on Winter simulation, Arlington, Virginia, pp. 797–804. IEEE Computer Society, Los Alamitos (2001)

[9] Kearns, M., Mansour, Y., Ng, A.: A Sparse Sampling Algorithm for Near-Optimal Planning in Large Markov Decision Processes. In: The Sixteenth International Joint Conference on Artificial Intelligence, pp. 1324–1331. Morgan Kaufmann, San Francisco (1999),http://www.cis.upenn.edu/~mkearns/papers/sparseplan.pdf

[10] Kocsis, L., Szepesvári, C.: Bandit based Monte-Carlo Planning. In: Fürnkranz, J., Scheffer, T., Spiliopoulou, M. (eds.) ECML 2006. LNCS (LNAI), vol. 4212, pp. 82–293. Springer, Heidelberg (2006), http://citeseerx.ist.psu.edu/viewdoc/download?doi=10.1.1.102.1296&rep=rep1&type=pdf

[11] Łatek, M., Axtell, R.L., Kaminski, B.: Bounded rationality via recursion. In: Proceedings of Eighth International Conference on Autonomous Agents and Multi-Agent Systems (AAMAS 2009), Budapest, Hungary, pp. 457–464. IFAAMAS (1846), http://delivery.acm.org/10.1145/1560000/1558076/p457-latek.pdf?key1=1558076&key2=1979263521&coll=&dl=&CFID=15151515&CFTOKEN=6184618

[12] Li, T., Zhu, S., Ogihara, M., Cheng, Y.: Estimating joint probabilities from marginal ones. In: Kambayashi, Y., Winiwarter, W., Arikawa, M. (eds.) DaWaK 2002. LNCS, vol. 2454, pp. 31–41. Springer, Heidelberg (2002)

[13] Murray, M.K., Rice, J.W.: Differential Geometry and Statistics. Chapman and Hall, Boca Raton (1993)

[14] Parunak, H.V.D., Brueckner, S.: Modeling Uncertain Domains with Polyagents. In: Proceedings of International Joint Conference on Autonomous Agents and Multi-Agent Systems (AAMAS 2006), Hakodate, Japan, pp. 111–113. ACM, New York (2006), http://www.newvectors.net/staff/parunakv/AAMAS06Polyagents.pdf

[15] Parunak, H.V.D., Brueckner, S.: Concurrent Modeling of Alternative Worlds with Polyagents. In: Antunes, L., Takadama, K. (eds.) MABS 2006. LNCS (LNAI), vol. 4442, pp. 128–141. Springer, Heidelberg (2007), http://www.newvectors.net/staff/parunakv/MABS06Polyagents.pdf

[16] Parunak, H.V.D.: Real-Time Agent Characterization and Prediction. In: Proceedings of International Joint Conference on Autonomous Agents and Multi-Agent Systems (AAMAS 2007), Industrial Track, Honolulu, Hawaii, pp. 1421–1428. ACM, New York (2007), http://www.newvectors.net/staff/parunakv/AAMAS07Fitting.pdf

[17] Parunak, H.V.D., Belding, T.C., Brueckner, S.: Prediction Horizons in Polyagent Models. In: Proceedings of Sixth International Joint Conference on Autonomous Agents and Multi-Agent Systems (AAMAS 2007), Honolulu, HI, pp. 930–932 (2007), http://www.newvectors.net/staff/parunakv/AAMAS07PH.pdf

[18] Parunak, H.V.D., Brueckner, S., Weyns, D., Holvoet, T., Valckenaers, P.: E Pluribus Unum: Polyagent and Delegate MAS Architectures. In: Antunes, L., Paolucci, M., Norling, E. (eds.) MABS 2007. LNCS (LNAI), vol. 5003, pp. 36–51. Springer, Heidelberg (2008), http://www.newvectors.net/staff/parunakv/MABS07EPU.pdf

[19] Parunak, H.V.D.: Interpreting Digital Pheromones as Probability Fields. In: Proceedings of the 2009 Winter Simulation Conference, Austin, TX, pp. 1059–1068 (2009), http://www.newvectors.net/staff/parunakv/WSC09Fields.pdf

[20] Parunak, H.V.D., Belding, T., Bisson, R., Brueckner, S., Downs, E., Hilscher, R., Decker, K.: Stigmergic Modeling of Hierarchical Task Networks. In: Di Tosto, G., Van Dyke Parunak, H. (eds.) MABS 2009. LNCS, vol. 5683, pp. 98–109. Springer, Heidelberg (2010), http://www.newvectors.net/staff/parunakv/MABS09rTAEMS.pdf

[21] Sauter, J.A., Matthews, R., Parunak, H.V.D., Brueckner, S.A.: Performance of Digital Pheromones for Swarming Vehicle Control. In: Proceedings of Fourth International Joint Conference on Autonomous Agents and Multi-Agent Systems, Utrecht, Netherlands, pp. 903–910. ACM, New York (2005), http://www.newvectors.net/staff/parunakv/AAMAS05SwarmingDemo.pdf

[22] Sauter, J.A., Matthews, R.S., Robinson, J.S., Moody, J., Riddle, S.P.: Swarming Unmanned Air and Ground Systems for Surveillance and Base Protection. In: Proceedings of AIAA Infotech@Aerospace 2009 Conference, Seattle, WA, AIAA (2009), http://www.newvectors.net/staff/parunakv/AIAA2009AirGround.pdf

[23] Shnerb, N.M., Louzoun, Y., Bettelheim, E., Solomon, S.: The importance of being discrete: Life always wins on the surface. Proc. Natl. Acad. Sci. USA 97(19), 10322–10324 (2000), http://www.pnas.org/cgi/reprint/97/19/10322

[24] Smith, L.A.: Disentangling Uncertainty and Error: On the Predictability of Nonlinear Systems. In: Mees, A. (ed.) Nonlinear Dynamics and Statistics. Birkhäuser, Boston (2001), http://www.maths.ox.ac.uk/~lenny/ni.ps.gz

[25] Valckenaers, P., Hadeli, K., Saint Germain, B., Verstraete, P., Van Brussel, H.: Emergent short-term forecasting through ant colony engineering in coordination and control systems. Advanced Engineering Informatics 20(3), 261–278 (2006)

[26] Wilson, W.G.: Resolving Discrepancies between Deterministic Population Models and Individual-Based Simulations. American Naturalist 151(2), 116–134 (1998)

Finding Forms of Flocking: Evolutionary Search in ABM Parameter-Spaces

Forrest Stonedahl and Uri Wilensky

Center for Connected Learning and Computer-Based Modeling
Northwestern University, Evanston, IL, USA
forrest@northwestern.edu, uri@northwestern.edu

Abstract. While agent-based models (ABMs) are becoming increasingly popular for simulating complex and emergent phenomena in many fields, understanding and analyzing ABMs poses considerable challenges. ABM behavior often depends on many model parameters, and the task of exploring a model's parameter space and discovering the impact of different parameter settings can be difficult and time-consuming. Exhaustively running the model with all combinations of parameter settings is generally infeasible, but judging behavior by varying one parameter at a time risks overlooking complex nonlinear interactions between parameters. Alternatively, we present a case study in computer-aided model exploration, demonstrating how evolutionary search algorithms can be used to probe for several qualitative behaviors (convergence, non-convergence, volatility, and the formation of vee shapes) in two different flocking models. We also introduce a new software tool (BehaviorSearch) for performing parameter search on ABMs created in the NetLogo modeling environment.

Keywords: parameter search, model exploration, genetic algorithms, flocking, agent-based modeling, ABM, multi-agent simulation.

1 Motivation

Agent-based modeling is a powerful simulation technique in which many agents interact according to simple rules resulting in the emergence of complex aggregate-level behavior. This technique is becoming increasingly popular in a wide range of scientific endeavors due to the power it has to simulate many different natural and artificial processes [1,3,22]. A crucial step in the modeling process is an analysis of how the system's behavior is affected by the various model parameters. However, the number of controlling parameters and range of parameter values in an agent-based model (ABM) is often large, the computation required to run a model is often significant, and agent-based models are typically stochastic in nature, meaning that multiple trials must be performed to assess the model's behavior. These factors combine to make a full brute-force exploration of the parameter space infeasible. Researchers respond to this difficulty in a variety of ways. One common approach is to run factorial-design experiments that either explore model behavior only in a small subspace or explore the full space but with very low resolution (which may skip over areas

T. Bosse, A. Geller, and C.M. Jonker (Eds.): MABS 2010, LNAI 6532, pp. 61–75, 2011.

of interest). A second common approach is to vary only a single parameter at a time, while holding the other parameters constant, and observe the effect of changing each parameter individually. However, because ABMs often constitute complex systems with non-linear interactions, these methods risk overlooking parameter settings that would yield interesting or unexpected behavior from the model.

As an alternative, we argue that many useful model exploration tasks may instead be productively formulated as *search problems* by designing appropriate objective functions, as we will demonstrate by example in the domain of simulated flocking behavior. In this paper, we introduce a new software tool (*BehaviorSearch*) that we have created for the purpose of searching/exploring ABM parameter spaces. Using *BehaviorSearch*, we offer a case study showing how search-based exploration can be used to gain insight into the behavior of two ABMs of flocking that have been implemented in the NetLogo modeling environment [21,18]. We also provide a comparison of the performance of three different search algorithms on several exploratory tasks for these two ABMs. In particular, we will show how genetic algorithms and hill-climbing can be used to discover parameter settings for these models that yield behaviors such as convergence, non-convergence, volatility, and specific flock shape formation. This approach can be useful for researchers to better understand the models they have created, the range of behavior their models are capable of producing, and which parameters have large impact on which behaviors. Flocking behaviors were chosen for this case study because flocking is a well-known example of a successful agent-based model, and can demonstrate a wide range of behaviors depending on the controlling parameters.

2   Related Work

Rather than using a full factorial experiment design for sampling points in the space, several more sophisticated sampling algorithms exist (e.g. Latin hypercube sampling, sphere-packing). These algorithms stem from the design of experiments (DoE) literature or more specifically the more recent design and analysis of computer experiments (DACE) literature (see [14] for a discussion of applying DACE methodology to ABMs). While appropriate experimental designs provide efficient sampling of the space in some situations, this is a separate direction from the search-oriented approach that we are pursuing here. In particular, we are interested in the use of genetic algorithms [7] (GAs) to search the ABM parameter spaces for behaviors of interest. Genetic algorithms have proven to be quite successful on a wide range of combinatorial search and optimization problems, and are thus a natural meta-heuristic search technique for this task. There is prior work on parameter-search and exploration in ABM, and considerably more on the problem of parameter-search in general.

Calvez and Hutzler have previously used a genetic algorithm (GA) to tune parameters of an ant foraging model [4], and discuss some of the relevant issues for applying GAs to ABM parameter search. However, in this case, the GA's performance was not compared to any other method, and the effectiveness of GAs for the ABM parameter search task has not been thoroughly investigated. Our present work contributes toward this goal. Specifically, we compare the performance of a genetic algorithm against a stochastic mutation-based hill-climber, as well as uniform random search, to serve as a baseline for comparison. We also explore a different domain (i.e. flocking models rather than ant foraging), and thus provide another perspective on the issue of automated model exploration.

Genetic algorithms have also been used to attempt to calibrate agent-based models with aggregate-level equation-based models as part of the SADDE methodology [15] for designing ABMs. Our research places an emphasis on exploration, as opposed to calibration or model design. The modeler may pose a question about the model's behavior which are potentially interesting, and the distribution of search results should answer that question, and may give additional insight into the interaction between parameters as well.

Other methods of exploration (besides genetic algorithms) have previously been considered. Most notably, Brueckner and Parunak proposed a meta-level multi-agent system to adaptively select points in the parameter-space to evaluate [2]. This swarm-based approach resembles particle swarm optimization [8] in that it uses a population of agents that combine global and local information to choose a direction to move in the search space, but it also considers whether to run additional simulations to improve the confidence of results at locations in the space. Brueckner and Parunak also mention in passing that genetic algorithms would be an appropriate choice for this type of search problem, but they did not follow this path, and only offer results from the novel multi-agent optimization algorithm they proposed. A comparison of genetic algorithms with this, and other swarm-based approaches, would be an interesting area for future work.

Genetic algorithms have also been employed in parameter-search problems which are not ABM, but closely related fields. For instance, genetic algorithms have been applied to search for rules in cellular automata (CA) that will produce a certain behavior (e.g. density classification) [11]. Cellular automata models could be considered a highly restricted case of agent-based models, and the cell state transition rules could perhaps be considered the *parameters* of such models, in which case this would constitute searching the parameter space. However, agent-based simulations more typically have numeric parameters, and whereas CA rules are naturally represented by binary switches, and the density-classification task is closer to a multi-agent system coordination problem, rather than an agent-based simulation.

Our present investigation is also inspired by Miller's work on active non-linear testing [9], which demonstrated the use of meta-heuristic optimization (genetic algorithms and hill climbers) for searching the parameter-space of the *World3* simulation, a well-known system dynamics model (SDM). Our work departs from Miller's in two respects: 1) model stochasticity (which is less frequently present in SDMs) is not addressed in those experiments, and 2) the characteristics of search spaces produced by agent-based models likely differ from those which are produced by aggregate equation-based models.

3   Methods

3.1   Flocking Models Overview

For our case study we explore the parameter-space of two agent-based models, searching for a variety of target behaviors. The two ABMs are the Flocking model [20] (denoted as *Flocking*) and the Flocking Vee Formations model [23] (denoted as *Flocking VF*). While the parameters of these two models are discussed briefly below, an in-depth discussion of these models is beyond the scope of this paper. Thus, we invite interested readers to examine the models themselves, which are both available in the NetLogo models library.

Flocking closely resembles the seminal ABM of swarming behavior in artificial birds (playfully dubbed "boids") that was introduced by Reynolds as a way to create life-like cinematic animation of flocking birds or other flying/swimming/swarming creatures [13]. The behavior of each "boid" is influenced by three basic rules, which provide impetus toward alignment, coherence, and separation. The relative influences of each are controlled by the parameters max-align-turn, max-cohere-turn, and max-separate-turn, respectively. Additionally there are parameters controlling the distance at which birds have knowledge of other birds (vision), and the minimum distance of separation which birds attempt to maintain (minimum-separation). For this first model, exploratory search tasks include the discovery of parameters that yield quick directional convergence (Section 4.1), non-convergence (Section 4.2), and volatility of the aggregate flock's heading over time (Section 4.3).

Flocking VF is based loosely on an extension of Reynolds' work that was proposed by Nathan and Barbosa [12], attempting to produce the vee-shaped patterns often observed in large migratory birds, such as Canada geese. *Flocking VF* has 8 controlling parameters, which account for fine-grained control over bird vision (vision-distance, vision-cone, obstruction-cone), takes into account benefits of "updraft" from nearby birds (updraft-distance, too-close), as well as flying speeds and acceleration (base-speed, speed-change-factor, and max-turn). The final exploratory search task is to seek parameters that best yield V-shaped flock formations, in both *Flocking* and *Flocking VF* (Section 4.4).

3.2   Search Algorithms

For each search task, we tested three different search algorithms: uniform random search (RS), a random-mutation hill climber (HC), and a genetic algorithm (GA). For all of the search methods, each ABM parameter's value was encoded as a sequence of binary digits (bit string) using a Gray code[1], and all the parameters' bit strings were concatenated to create a string that represents one point in the parameter-space. A bit string is evaluated by decoding it into the ABM parameter settings, and running the model with those parameters.

---

[1] A high-order binary encoding requires flipping 4 bits to change from 7 (0111_2) to 8 (1000_2). In a Gray code, consecutive numbers only require a single bit flip, thus creating a smoother mapping from numbers into binary search spaces.

The RS method simply generates one random bit string after another, and in the end chooses the one that best elicited the desired model behavior. RS is a naive search techniques, which we included as a baseline for comparison, to determine whether using more sophisticated meta-heuristics (such as the HC and GA) were indeed helpful.

Our HC is primarily a local search algorithm. It starts with a random bit string (s). A new string (s_{new}) is generated from s (each bit of s gets flipped with probability 0.05, which is the *mutation-rate*). If s_{new} is better than s (generates behavior that judged closer to the desired target behavior), then the HC chooses s_{new} as the new s, and the process repeats. If the HC becomes stuck (after 1000 unsuccessful move attempts), it will restart at a new random location in the search space, which makes this a quasi-local search method.

Our GA is a standard generational genetic algorithm [7], with a population size of 30, a crossover rate of 0.7, and a mutation rate of 0.05, using tournament selection with tournament size 3. The GA is a more sophisticated search mechanism than HC or RS, and there are several reasons to believe that it might perform better. First, the GA is population-based, which allows it to explore multiple regions of the space simultaneously (more of a global search technique). Second, genetic algorithms have previously been shown to perform well on a variety of nonlinear and multi-modal search/optimization problems. Third, genetic algorithms (like the biological processes of evolution that inspired them) often have a way of coming up with creative or unexpected solutions to a problem, which humans would not have considered. However, depending on the how the search space is structured, simpler approaches may be more effective. For example, it was shown that a HC performed better on a problem that was specifically designed with the expectation that GAs would work well on it [10]. One important consideration, is whether there are so-called *building blocks* in the solution-space, which the GA is able to discover and combine (via genetic crossover) to form better solutions. Phrased at the level of the agent-based model, this question becomes: are there certain combinations of several parameter settings, each of which partially produce desired target behavior, and when combined together produce that behavior even more strongly? If so, the GA may be able to take advantage of that structure in the search space to efficiently find solutions.

The objective function (or "fitness function" in the parlance of evolutionary computation) was always averaged across 5 model runs (replicates) with different random seeds, to reduce variability stemming from model stochasticity. While this variability is essentially "noise" from the search algorithm's perspective, it is simply a reflecting the fact that running the ABM results in a range of behavior depending on the initial placement of the birds. Our objective functions are attempting to characterize the presence or absence of a certain behavior *on average*, and short of running the simulation with every possible initial condition (which is impossible), there will always be some uncertainty about the objective function measure. Taking the average value from several replicate runs of the simulation, however, reduces this uncertainty and smooths the search landscape.

The objective functions were different for each task, and will be discussed individually in each of the investigations below (Sections 4.1-4.4). For efficiency, objective function values were cached after being computed[2]. The search algorithms were stopped after they had run the ABM 12000 times. Each search was repeated 30 times (except for the *volatility* exploration in Section 4.3, which was repeated 60 times for improved statistical confidence), to evaluate search performance and ensure that search findings were not anomalous.

3.3   BehaviorSearch

To perform these searches, we developed a new tool called *BehaviorSearch* [16], which was implemented in Java, and interfaces with the NetLogo modeling environment, using NetLogo's *Controlling API*. *BehaviorSearch* is an open-source cross-platform tool that offers several search algorithms and search-space representations/encodings, and can be used to explore the parameter space of any ABM written in the NetLogo language. The user specifies the model file, the desired parameters and ranges to explore, the search objective function, the search method to be used, and the search space encoding, and then *BehaviorSearch* runs the search and returns the best results discovered, and optionally the data collected from all of the simulations run along the way. *BehaviorSearch* supports model exploration through both a GUI (see Figure 1), and a command line interface. A beta-release of *BehaviorSearch* is freely available for download[3]. The software design purposefully resembles that of the widely-used *BehaviorSpace* [19] parameter-sweeping tool that is included with NetLogo. Our intent is to make advanced search techniques accessible to a wide range of modelers so that the methods and ideas discussed in this paper can be put into practice.

4   Explorations

4.1   Investigation 1: Convergence

The convergence of swarm-based systems is one potential property of interest, and has been formally studied for some theoretical cases [5]. Thus, the first behavior of interest for the *Flocking* model was the ability of birds starting at random locations and headings to converge to be moving in the same direction (i.e. directional, not positional, convergence). In order to make the search process effective, we must provide a quantitative measure to capture the rather qualitative notion of convergence. This quantitative measure (the objective function) will provide the search with information about how good one set of parameters is, relative to another, at achieving the goal. Specifically, we would like to find

---

[2] The goal of caching is to avoid repeating expensive computations. However, because the model is stochastic, re-evaluating points in the search space could lead to different results than the cached values, meaning that the search process is affected by caching. For further discussion of noise/uncertainty and fitness caching, see [17].

[3] Available at: http://www.behaviorsearch.org/

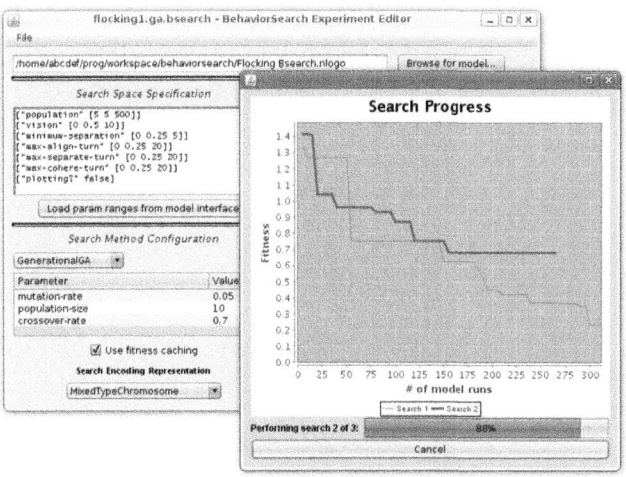

Fig. 1. Screenshot of the BehaviorSearch GUI, displaying search progress

parameters that yield very little variation between birds' headings. Thus, we will attempt to minimize the following objective function:

$$f_{nonconverged} = stdev(\{v_x(b) \mid b \in B\}) + stdev(\{v_y(b) \mid b \in B\}) \qquad (1)$$

where $v_x(b)$ and $v_y(b)$ are the horizontal and vertical components of the velocity of bird b, and B is the set of all birds. The standard deviation ($stdev$), which is the square root of the variance, serves as a useful measure of the variation for velocity, and we must apply it in both the x and y dimensions. A value of $f_{nonconverged} = 0$ would indicate complete alignment of all birds. We measure $f_{nonconverged}$ after 75 ticks (model time steps). While 75 ticks is effective here for finding parameter settings that cause the flock to quickly converge, if we were instead interested in the long-term behavior of the system, a longer time limit would be more appropriate.

The plot of search progress (Figure 2) shows that on average the HC may have found better model parameters early in the search, but in the end the GA's performance was superior (t-test, $p < 0.01$). Both GA and HC significantly outperformed random search. The best parameters found in each run (Figure 3) shows us that it is crucial for birds to have long-range vision, and that even a small urge to cohere is detrimental to convergence. The wide spread for max-separate-turn suggests that convergence is not very sensitive to this parameter (given the other parameter settings). Figure 3 also shows one possible converged state from running the model using the best parameters found by the GA.

4.2   Investigation 2: Non-convergence

Next, we probed for parameter settings that cause the birds not to globally align. For this task, we simply maximized the same objective function we

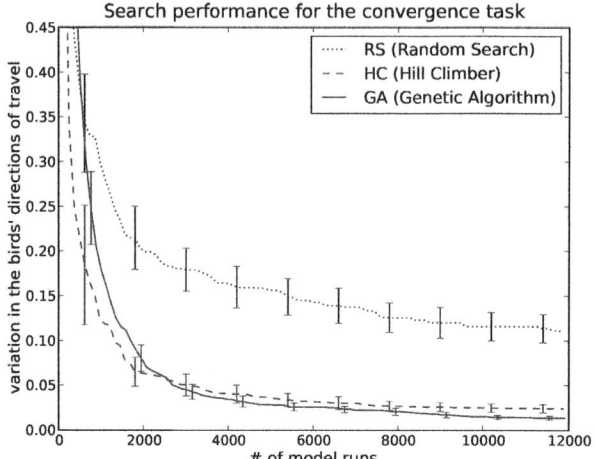

Fig. 2. Search performance for the convergence task, comparing how efficiently the GA (*genetic algorithm*), HC (*hill climber*), and RS (*random search*) can find parameters that cause the flock to quickly converge to the same heading. (Error bars show 95% confidence intervals on the mean).

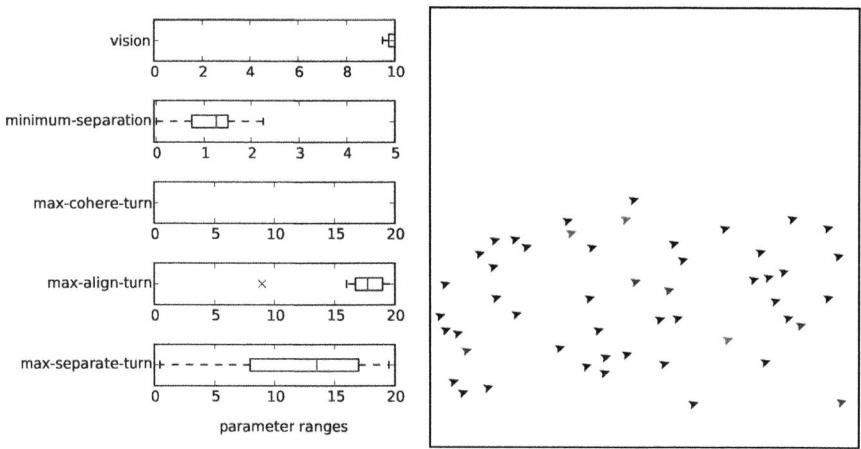

Fig. 3. *LEFT:* Distribution of model parameter settings found to cause quickest convergence in each of the 30 GA searches. All box-and-whisker plots presented in this paper show the median line within the lower-to-upper-quartile box, with whiskers encompassing the remainder of the data, apart from outliers which are marked with x's. *RIGHT:* Visualization of the flock (after 75 model steps) using the best parameters the GA discovered.

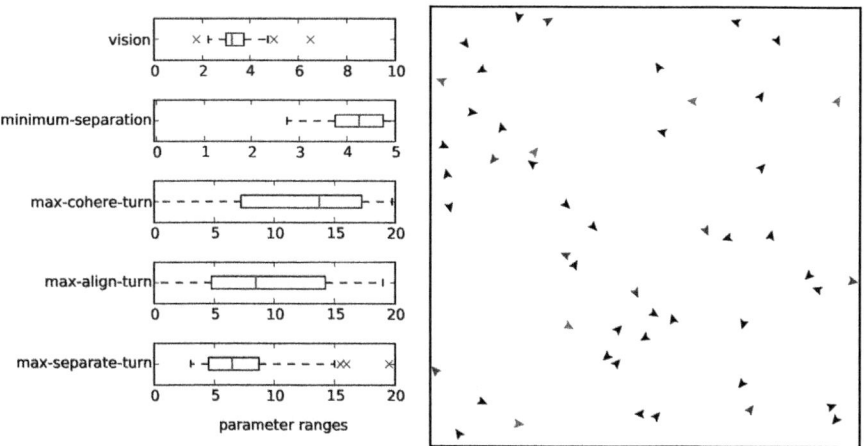

Fig. 4. *LEFT:* Distribution of model parameter settings found to cause non-convergence in each of the 30 GA searches. *RIGHT:* Visualization of a non-converged flock using the best parameters the GA discovered.

minimized in Section 4.1. This task turned out to be rather trivial, as all three search methods (GA, HC, and RS) very quickly found parameter settings that yielded little or no flock alignment. That such behavior is rather common in the parameter space is illustrated by Figure 4, which shows a wide distribution of best parameters. The results suggest that for non-convergence, it is helpful for birds to have a low-to-medium vision range, desire a large amount of separation from each other (minimum-separation), and act to achieve the separation (non-zero max-separate-turn). Digging deeper, the results tell us that it is the relationship between parameters that matters; if minimum-separation is larger than vision each bird will seek to avoid any other bird as soon as it sees it, as separation takes precedence over the align/cohere rules.

4.3   Investigation 3: Volatility

Our third experiment sought parameters for the *Flocking* model that would yield the most volatility (or changeability) in global flock heading, by attempting to maximize $f_{volatility}$, as defined in (4).

$$\overline{v_x}(t) = mean(\{v_x(b) \mid b \in B\} \text{ at tick } t \tag{2}$$

$$\overline{v_y}(t) = mean(\{v_y(b) \mid b \in B\} \text{ at tick } t \tag{3}$$

$$f_{volatility} = stdev(\overline{v_x}(t) \text{ for } t = 400..500) + stdev(\overline{v_y}(t) \text{ for } t = 400..500) \tag{4}$$

Again, on average the GA was slightly more successful than the HC in eliciting flock heading volatility, and both significantly outperformed random search (Figure 5). Only 5 out of the 60 GA searches' best parameter settings had a non-zero

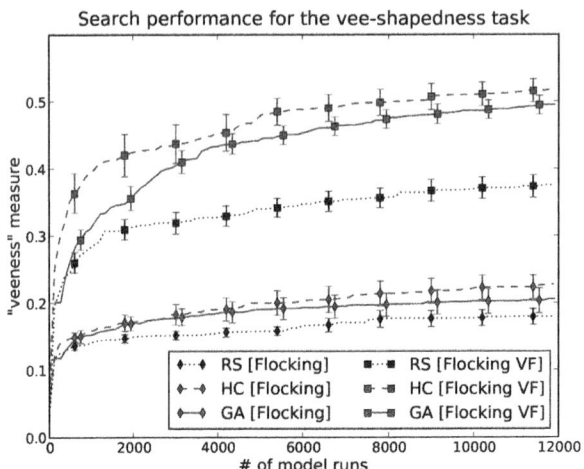

Fig. 5. Comparison of search algorithm performance for the flock heading volatility task. The final mean performance of the GA was better than the HC (t-test, $p < 0.05$), but not substantially so. (Error bars show 95% confidence intervals on the mean).

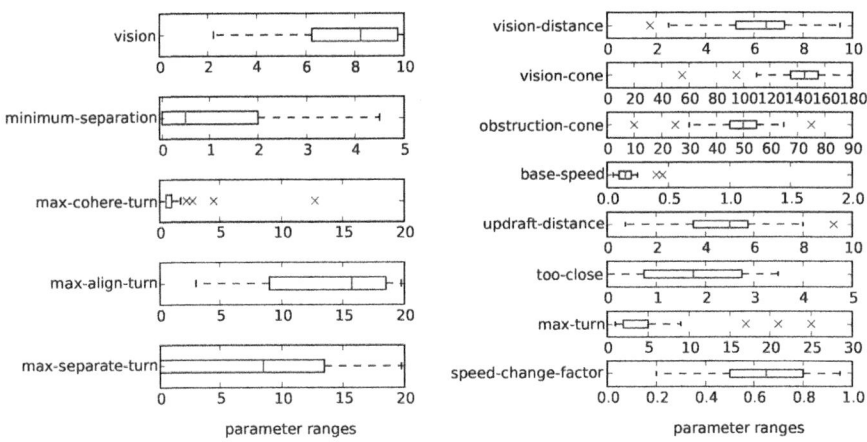

Fig. 6. *LEFT:* Distribution of model parameter settings (from each of the 30 GA searches) found to cause the most volatility in flock heading. *RIGHT:* Visualization of the flock after 500 model steps (also showing each bird's path over the last 100 steps), using the best parameters found by the GA.

value for minimum-separation, indicating that birds flying close together is a key factor for maximal volatility. Long-range vision, and large effects of max-align-turn and max-cohere-turn are also important (see Figure 6). The flight pattern of a flock exhibiting considerable volatility is shown in Figure 6. The single bird positioned at the left side in the rear is at least partially responsible for shift in flock heading, because of the strong coherence parameter.

Despite taking the average of 5 replications, noise due to model stochasticity was still significant. For example, the search reported finding settings yielding 0.99 volatility, but averaging 1000 runs at those settings showed true volatility of 0.41. This fact could bias the search toward parameters that occasionally yield very high volatility, over those that consistently yield moderately high volatility. Both goals are potentially interesting for model exploration; however, appropriate noise reduction methodology is a worthy subject for future research.

4.4   Investigation 4: Vee Formations

The final experiment was to search both the *Flocking* and *Flocking VF* models for a more complex behavior, which we shall refer to as *veeness*. *Veeness* measures the degree to which birds are flying in vee, or more generally, echelon formations. Our specific questions are: 1) Do any parameter settings cause *Flocking* to exhibit *veeness*? 2) How much better can *Flocking VF* do? and 3) What parameters are most important for the best vee/echelon creation?

To calculate *veeness*, we first cluster all the birds in the world into separate flocks, according to proximity (within 5 distance units of another bird in the flock) and directional similitude (less than 20 degrees angular difference in heading). A flock with less than 3 birds is assigned a flock veeness score of 0. Otherwise, it is calculated by choosing the optimal *point bird* and left/right echelon angles (which must be between 25 and 50 degrees, comprising a mid-range of echelon angles observed in nature [6]) for the flock. For a given point bird, the left and right echelon angles are calculated separately, by first dividing flock-mates into those to the right or left, relative to the point bird. The echelon angles are then chosen such that they minimize the mean-squared-error difference between the echelon angle and the angle between the point bird and all following birds on that side. Flock groupings with echelon angles and flock veeness scores can be seen in Figure 9. The flocking score for the flock is the reciprocal of the mean-squared-error value for the best "point" bird, rescaled so that a flock in perfect echelon/vee formation has a score of 1.0. Overall *veeness* is a weighted average (by flock size) of the veeness scores of individual flocks. *Veeness* was measured every 100 model ticks, between 1000 and 2000 ticks. Searches for both *Flocking* and *Flocking VF* used 30 birds and the same veeness metric.

Unlike in previous experiments, the HC search method performed slightly better than the GA (see Figure 7), but the difference was not statistically significant. For the Flocking model, RS was not far behind the GA and HC, but was considerably worse than the other methods for the Vee Flocking model.

The results show that *Flocking* can create formations that appear only mildly vee-like at best, but *Flocking VF* can (as expected) create much better vees (as

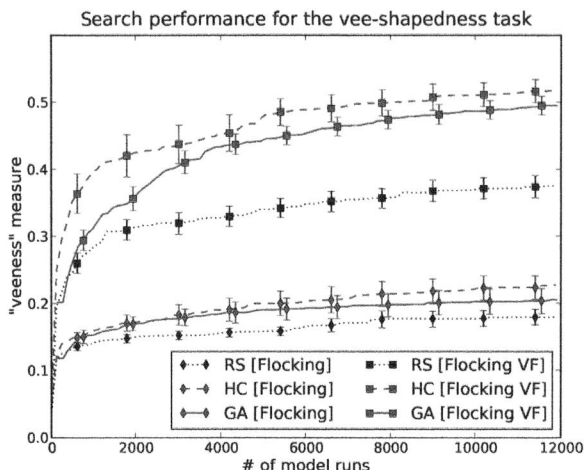

Fig. 7. Comparison of search performance for the vee-shapedness task on both the Flocking and Flocking Vee Formation models. (Error bars show 95% confidence intervals on the mean).

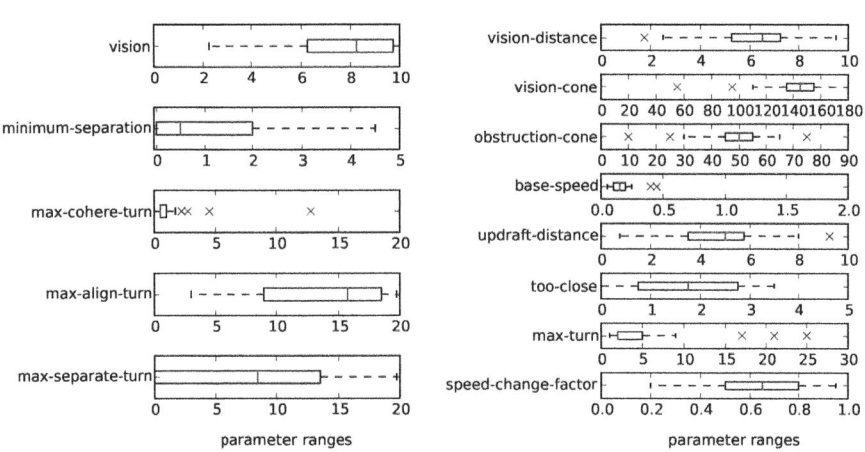

Fig. 8. Distribution of model parameter settings found to yield the best vees in the Flocking model (*left*), and the Flocking Vee Formation model (*right*), in each of the 30 HC searches

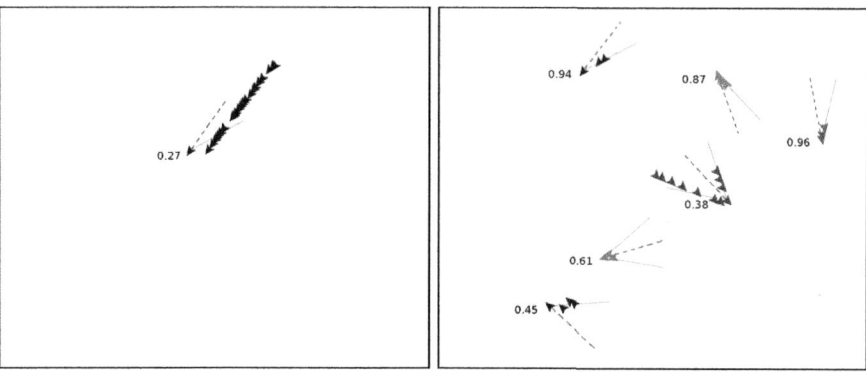

Fig. 9. Visualization of a run of the Flocking model (*left*), and the Flocking Vee Formation model (*right*), using the best "vee-forming" parameters found by the 30 HC searches. Birds are shaded by flock group, dashed lines show average flock heading relative to the "point" bird, and gray lines show best-fit angles for right and/or left echelons of the vee formation. The numeric "veeness" measure for each individual flock is also shown.

shown in Figure 9). For *Flocking VF* to produce the best vees (according to our chosen *veeness* metric), the vision-cone angle should be large, perhaps roughly 3 times larger than the obstruction-cone angle, the bird's base-speed and max-turn angle should generally be low, but the speed-change-factor should not be too small. We will not elaborate on specific implications of these findings for the *Flocking VF* model here, but broadly argue that findings such as these can lead modelers to a better understanding of their model by cognitively linking changes in model parameters with the qualitative behavior being investigated.

5 Conclusion and Future Work

Beyond the specific results concerning the behavior of two particular agent-based models (Flocking and Vee Flocking), there are several more general conclusions that may be drawn from this case study. First, evolutionary algorithms such as the GA and HC are indeed effective means of exploring the parameter space of ABMs. Their performance was vastly superior to RS, except in the cases where the task was too easy (e.g. nonconvergence) or too hard (veeness in *Flocking*) to make substantial progress. (The difficulty of the search task relates to how dense or sparse the desired target behavior is in the search space: parameter settings that cause the Flocking model to not converge are plentiful in the parameter space, whereas parameter settings that cause good vee formations are either extremely rare or nonexistent.) Second, by running multiple searches on a stochastic model and looking at the distribution of best-found parameter settings, rather than just the single best setting for the parameters, we can uncover trends (or at least postulate relationships) about the interactions between model parameters and behavior. One interpretation is that we are implicitly performing a type of sensitivity analysis on the *search process* for a particular *behavior*, but that the results of that analysis can tell us something about the model. Note that the trends we find are unlikely to be global (characterizing the whole parameter space), but apply only to a local view that is focused on regions of the parameter space where the target behavior is expressed mostly strongly.

These results also suggest several important areas for future work. First, it is unclear what circumstances favor the use of a genetic algorithm over a simpler hill climbing search mechanism. Second, the performance results presented here may be dependent on any number of *search algorithm parameters* (not to be confused with *model parameters*), such as the population size, mutation rate, crossover rate, elitism, or chromosomal representation. While we attempted to choose reasonable values for these search parameters, it is likely that by tuning these parameters, the algorithms' efficiency could be improved. Furthermore, poorly chosen search parameters could lead to worse performance than random search, and should thus be avoided. Also, in future work, we would like to investigate the use of other search algorithms (such as simulated annealing, and particle-swarm optimization). Finally, additional consideration should be given to the treatment of model stochasticity and noisy objective functions; while running fewer replicates of model runs takes less time for searching, large quantities of noise can inhibit search progress. In general, the prospects seem bright for using meta-heuristic search, such as genetic algorithms, to improve model exploration and analysis. It is our hope that these promising prospects will encourage ABM practitioners to flock toward, and eventually converge on, new methodologies for model parameter exploration that take advantage of these ideas.

Acknowledgments. We especially wish to thank William Rand for constructive feedback on this research, Luis Amaral for generously providing computational resources to carry out our experiments, and the National Science Foundation for supporting this work (grant IIS-0713619).

References

1. Bankes, S.: Agent-Based Modeling: A Revolution? PNAS 99(10), 7199–7200 (2002)
2. Brueckner, S.A., Parunak, H.V.D.: Resource-aware exploration of the emergent dynamics of simulated systems. In: AAMAS 2003: Proceedings of the Second International Joint Conference on Autonomous Agents and Multi-Agent Systems, pp. 781–788. ACM, New York (2003)
3. Bryson, J.J., Ando, Y., Lehmann, H.: Agent-based modelling as scientific method: a case study analysing primate social behaviour. Philosophical Transactions of the Royal Society B: Biological Sciences 362(1485), 1685–1698 (2007)
4. Calvez, B., Hutzler, G.: Automatic Tuning of Agent-Based Models Using Genetic Algorithms. In: Sichman, J.S., Antunes, L. (eds.) MABS 2005. LNCS (LNAI), vol. 3891, pp. 41–57. Springer, Heidelberg (2006)
5. Cucker, F., Smale, S.: Emergent behavior in flocks. IEEE Transactions on Automatic Control 52(5), 852–862 (2007)

6. Heppner, F., Convissar, J., Moonan Jr, D., Anderson, J.: Visual angle and formation flight in Canada Geese (Branta canadensis). The Auk, pp. 195–198 (1985)
7. Holland, J.: Adaptation in Natural and Artificial Systems. University of Michigan Press, Ann Arbor (1975)
8. Kennedy, J., Eberhart, R.: et al.: Particle swarm optimization. In: Proceedings of IEEE International Conference on Neural Networks, vol. 4, pp. 1942–1948. IEEE, Piscataway (1995)
9. Miller, J.H.: Active nonlinear tests (ANTs) of complex simulation models. Management Science 44(6), 820–830 (1998)
10. Mitchell, M., Holland, J., Forrest, S.: When will a genetic algorithm outperform hill climbing? In: Cowan, J.D., Tesauro, G., Alspector, J. (eds.) Advances in Neural Information Processing Systems, vol. 6, pp. 51–58. Morgan Kaufmann, San Mateo (1994)
11. Mitchell, M., Crutchfield, J.P., Das, R.: Evolving cellular automata with genetic algorithms: A review of recent work. In: Proceedings of the First International Conference on Evolutionary Computation and Its Applications, Russian Academy of Sciences, Moscow (1996)
12. Nathan, A., Barbosa, V.: V-like formations in flocks of artificial birds. Artificial Life 14(2), 179–188 (2008)
13. Reynolds, C.W.: Flocks, herds and schools: A distributed behavioral model. In: SIGGRAPH 1987: Proceedings of the 14th Annual Conference on Computer Graphics and Interactive Techniques, pp. 25–34. ACM, New York (1987)
14. Sanchez, S.M., Lucas, T.W.: Exploring the world of agent-based simulations: simple models, complex analyses. In: WSC 2002: Proceedings of the 34th Conference on Winter Simulation, pp. 116–126 (2002)
15. Sierra, C., Sabater, J., Augusti, J., Garcia, P.: SADDE: Social agents design driven by equations. In: Methodologies and Software Engineering for Agent Systems. Kluwer Academic Publishers, Dordrecht (2004)
16. Stonedahl, F., Wilensky, U.: BehaviorSearch [computer software]. Center for Connected Learning and Computer Based Modeling, Northwestern University, Evanston, IL (2010), http://www.behaviorsearch.org/
17. Stonedahl, F., Stonedahl, S.: Heuristics for sampling repetitions in noisy landscapes with fitness caching. In: GECCO 2010: Proceedings of the 12th Annual Conference on Genetic and Evolutionary Computation. ACM, New York (2010) ([in press])
18. Tisue, S., Wilensky, U.: NetLogo: Design and implementation of a multi-agent modeling environment. In: Proceedings of Agent 2004. pp. 7–9 (2004)
19. Wilensky, U., Shargel, B.: BehaviorSpace [computer software]. Center for Connected Learning and Computer Based Modeling, Northwestern University, Evanston, IL (2002), http://ccl.northwestern.edu/netlogo/behaviorspace
20. Wilensky, U.: NetLogo Flocking model. Center for Connected Learning and Computer-Based Modeling, Northwestern University, Evanston, IL (1998)
21. Wilensky, U.: NetLogo. Center for Connected Learning and Computer-based Modeling, Northwestern University, Evanston, IL (1999)
22. Wilensky, U., Rand, W.: An introduction to agent-based modeling: Modeling natural, social and engineered complex systems with NetLogo. MIT Press, Cambridge (in press)
23. Wilkerson-Jerde, M., Stonedahl, F., Wilensky, U.: NetLogo Flocking Vee Formations model. Center for Connected Learning and Computer-Based Modeling, Northwestern University, Evanston, IL (2010)

On the Profitability of Incompetence

Eugen Staab and Martin Caminada

University of Luxembourg,
Faculty of Science, Technology and Communication,
L–1359 Luxembourg
{eugen.staab,martin.caminada}@uni.lu

Abstract. The *exchange of information* is in many multi-agent systems the essential form of interaction. For this reason, it is crucial to keep agents from providing unreliable information. However, agents that provide information have to balance between being highly competent, in order to achieve a good reputation as information provider, and staying incompetent, in order to minimize the costs of information acquisition. In this paper, we use a multi-agent simulation to identify conditions under which it is profitable for agents either to make an investment to become competent, or to economize and stay incompetent. We focus on the case where the quality of the acquired information cannot objectively be assessed in any immediate way and where hence the information end users have to rely on secondary methods for assessing the quality of the information itself, as well as the trustworthiness of those who provide it.

Keywords: Social Epistemology, Dishonesty, Formal Argumentation, Reputation Systems, Incentive Compatibility.

1 Introduction

When purchasing information, one wants to be sure of the quality of the information in question. However, if one is not an expert oneself in the relevant domain, assessing the quality of information can be difficult. For the sellers of information (which we will simply refer to as "the consultants") this provides an incentive for dishonesty. After all, gaining real expertise costs significant efforts as well as time and money. If the consumer of information (which we will refer to as "the client") has difficulties assessing the quality of the provided information, then why not pretend to have a higher level of expertise than one actually has? As long as the chance that the client detects this dishonesty is low, and so the reputation will most probably not be damaged, a consultant can charge the same price for his advice, yet spend less resources on keeping up-to-date regarding the state of the art.

The issue of low quality information has been studied in [1,2]. What is new, however, is that we have now developed a model and a software simulator thereof that is able to compute the profit for the consultants of either a strategy of hard work or a strategy of taking it easy when it comes to staying up to date with the state of the art. In particular, we are able to provide some insight on which strategy yields the most profitable results under which circumstances.

T. Bosse, A. Geller, and C.M. Jonker (Eds.): MABS 2010, LNAI 6532, pp. 76–92, 2011.

2   Argumentation and Informedness

The aim of this section is to formalize the concept of informedness by means of formal argumentation. This establishes the background theory for the remaining practical part of the paper.

In standard epistemic logic (S5), informedness is basically a binary phenomenon. One either has knowledge about a proposition p or one does not. It is, however, also possible to provide a more subtle account of the extent to which one is informed about the validity of proposition p. Suppose Alex thinks that Hortis Bank is on the brink of bankruptcy because it has massively invested in mortgage backed securities. Also Bob thinks that Hortis is on the brink of bankruptcy because of the mortgage backed securities. Bob has also read an interview in which the finance minister promises that the state will support Hortis if needed. However, Bob also knows that the liabilities of Hortis are so big that not even the state will be able to provide significant help to avert bankruptcy. From the perspective of formal argumentation [3], Bob has three arguments at his disposal.

A: Hortis Bank is on the brink of bankruptcy, because of the mortgage backed securities.
B: The state will save Hortis, because the finance minister promised so.
C: Not even the state has the financial means to save Hortis.

Here, argument B attacks A, and argument C attacks B (see eq. (1)). In most approaches to formal argumentation, arguments A and C would be accepted and argument B would be rejected.

$$A \longleftarrow B \longleftarrow C \tag{1}$$

Assume that Alex has only argument A at his disposal. Then it seems reasonable to regard Bob as more informed with respect to proposition p ("Hortis Bank is on the brink of bankruptcy") since he has a better knowledge of the facts relevant for this proposition and is also in a better position to defend it in the face of criticism.

The most feasible way to determine whether someone is informed on some given issue is to evaluate whether he is up to date with the relevant arguments and is able to defend his position in the face of criticism. One can say that agent X is more informed than agent Y if it has at its disposal a larger set of relevant arguments.

We will now provide a more formal account of how the concept of informedness could be described using formal argumentation. An *argumentation framework* [3] is a pair (Ar, att) where Ar is a set of arguments and att is a binary relation on Ar. An argumentation framework can be represented as a directed graph. For instance, the argumentation framework $(\{A, B, C\}, \{(C, B), (B, A)\})$ is represented in eq. (1).

Arguments can be seen as defeasible derivations of a particular statement. These defeasible derivations can then be attacked by statements of other defeasible derivations, hence the attack relationship. Given an argumentation framework, an interesting question is what is the set (or sets) of arguments that can collectively be accepted. Although this question has traditionally been studied in terms of the various fixpoints of the characteristic function [3], it is equally well possible to use the approach of argument labelings [4,5]. The idea is that each argument gets exactly one label (accepted, rejected, or abstained), such that the result satisfies the following constraints.

1. If an argument is labeled accepted then all arguments that attack it must be labeled rejected.
2. If an argument is labeled rejected then there must be at least one argument that attacks it and is labeled accepted.
3. If an argument is labeled abstained then it must not be the case that all arguments that attack it are labeled rejected, and it must not be the case that there is an argument that attacks it and is labeled accepted.

A labeling is called complete iff it satisfies each of the above three constraints. As an example, the argumentation framework of eq. (1) has exactly one complete labeling, in which A and C are labeled accepted and B is labeled rejected. In general, an argumentation framework has one or more complete labelings. Furthermore, the arguments labeled accepted in a complete labeling form a complete extension in the sense of [3]. Other standard argumentation concepts, like preferred, grounded and stable extensions can also be expressed in terms of labelings [4,5]. Algorithms and proof procedures can be found in [6,7,8,9,10,11].

In essence, one can see a complete labeling as a reasonable position one can take in the presence of the imperfect and conflicting information expressed in the argumentation framework [12,13]. An interesting question is whether an argument *can* be accepted (that is, whether the argument is labeled accepted in at least one complete labeling) and whether an argument *has to be* accepted (that is, whether the argument is labeled accepted in each complete labeling). These two questions can be answered using formal discussion games [6,7,8,11]. For instance, in the argumentation framework of eq. (1), a possible discussion would go as follows.

Proponent: Argument A has to be accepted.
Opponent: But perhaps A's attacker B does not have to be rejected.
Proponent: B has to be rejected because B's attacker C has to be accepted.

The precise rules which such discussions have to follow are described in [6,7,8,9,11]. We say that argument A can be *defended* iff the proponent has a winning strategy for A. We say that argument A can be *denied* iff the opponent has a winning strategy against A.

If informedness is defined as justified belief, and justified is being interpreted as defensible in a rational discussion, then formal discussion games can serve as a way to examine whether an agent is informed with respect to proposition p, even in cases where one cannot directly determine the truth or falsity of p in the objective world. An agent is informed on p iff it has an argument for p that it is able to defend in the face of criticism.

The thus described approach also allows for the distinction of various grades of informedness. That is, an agent X can be perceived to be at least as informed as agent Y w.r.t. argument A iff either X and Y originally disagreed on the status of A but combining their information the position of X is confirmed, or X and Y originally agreed on the status of A and in every case where Y is able to maintain its position in the presence of criticism from agent Z, X is also able to maintain its position in the presence of the same criticism.

When $AF_1 = (Ar_1, att_1)$ and $AF_2 = (Ar_2, att_2)$ are argumentation frameworks, we write $AF_1 \sqcup AF_2$ as a shorthand for $(Ar_1 \cup Ar_2, att_1 \cup att_2)$. Formally, agent X is at least as informed with respect to argument A as agent Y iff:

1. A can be defended using AF_X (that is, if X assumes the role of the proponent of A then it has a winning strategy using the argumentation framework of X), A can be denied using AF_Y (that is, if Y assumes the role of the opponent than it has a winning strategy using the argumentation framework of Y), but A can be defended using $AF_X \sqcup AF_Y$, or
2. A can be denied using AF_X, A can be defended using AF_Y, but A can be denied $AF_X \sqcup AF_Y$, or
3. A can be defended using AF_X and can be defended using AF_Y, and for each AF_Z such that A can be defended using $AF_Y \sqcup AF_Z$ it holds that A can also be defended using $AF_X \sqcup AF_Z$, or
4. A can be denied using AF_X and can be denied using AF_Y, and for each AF_Z such that A can be denied using $AF_Y \sqcup AF_Z$ it holds that A can be denied using $AF_X \sqcup AF_Z$.

In the example mentioned earlier (eq. (1)) Alex has access only to argument A, and Bob has access to arguments A, B and C. Suppose a third person (Charles) has access only to arguments A and B. Then we say that Bob is more informed than Alex w.r.t. argument A because Bob can maintain his position on A (accepted) while facing criticism from Charles, where Alex cannot. A more controversial consequence is that Charles is also more informed than Alex w.r.t. argument A, even though from the global perspective, Charles has the "wrong" position on argument A (rejected instead of accepted). This is compensated by the fact that Bob, in his turn, is more informed than Charles w.r.t. argument A. As an analogy, it would be fair to consider Newton as more informed than his predecessors, even though his work has later been attacked by more advanced theories.

It can be interesting to compare the thus defined notion of argumentation-based informedness with the notion of knowledge as modeled by traditional (S5) modal logic. Knowledge, from a conceptual point of view, is often defined as "justified true belief". When using S5 and S4 based modalities, the notion of knowledge is usually simplified as "true belief", whereas in our argumentation approach, we take the other way and define informedness as "justified belief". The difference between the modal logic approach and the argumentation approach is an important one, since it has consequences for the domains where these approaches are applicable. As an example, consider an expert on climate change who predicts a global temperature increase of 2° C by the year 2050. Whether or not this claim is true or not cannot immediately be assessed in any objective way. However, what can be assessed is whether the backing of this claim can stand a critical assessment using the information that is currently available. That is, is the expert able to defend his position against possible counterarguments? Similar observations can be made not only with respect to climate change, but also with respect to issues like the world's energy resources, or the viability of the long-term investment strategy of a pension fund. The reputation of the experts who work in these fields cannot be purely determined in terms of feedback from the objective world, since in many occasions this feedback will only reveal itself at the end of one's professional life. In many cases one cannot determine whether a statement is *true*; one can only determine whether it is *well-informed*.

3   Model

We consider a client/consultant-scenario, that is, a scenario where consultants advise their clients on a certain issue. We model the knowledge on which the consultants advise their clients by a chain of arguments:

$$A_1 \longleftarrow A_2 \longleftarrow \ldots \longleftarrow A_{N_{\mathrm{arg}}} \tag{2}$$

Here, any argument A_i (for $1 < i \leq N_{\mathrm{arg}}$) defeats its predecessor argument A_{i-1}. As a consequence, if N_{arg} is even, then all arguments A_i with even indices are accepted, and all arguments with odd indices are rejected. For odd N_{arg}, it is the other way around[1].

At the beginning of a simulation, only argument A_1 is known to the consultants and only this argument is known in the whole society, i.e., it represents the "state of the art". To model the discovery/emergence of new information (e.g., through research), we make a certain number of new arguments available to the consultants in each round. This represents the evolution of the state of the art. The number of new arguments per round will be fixed for a simulation and is denoted by ΔN_{arg}. The simulation is finished when all N_{arg} arguments have been made available. During simulation, the structure of the chain of arguments looks as follows ($k \leq i$ must hold):

$$\overbrace{A_1 \leftarrow \cdots \leftarrow A_k}^{\substack{\text{"state of the art"}}} \leftarrow \cdots \leftarrow A_i \leftarrow \overbrace{A_{i+1} \leftarrow \cdots \leftarrow A_{i+\Delta N_{\mathrm{arg}}}}^{\substack{\text{added to the "state of the art"}\\\text{in the next round}}} \leftarrow \cdots \leftarrow A_{N_{\mathrm{arg}}} \tag{3}$$

$$\underbrace{}_{\substack{\text{known to a certain}\\\text{consultant}}}$$

In each round, consultants can decide how many new arguments they want to procure. We assume that the consultants extend their already known chain of arguments with new arguments always in a seamless manner, i.e., without gaps. This assumption was made in order to be in line with argument games (such as described in [6,7,8]) where each uttered argument is a reaction to a previously uttered argument, thus satisfying the property of *relevance* [14].

---

[1] Although it would have been possible, and to some extent even more natural, to use a tree-shaped argumentation framework instead of just a linear one, we do not expect our current simplification to significantly affect the outcome of the simulator.

3.1   Expenses, Turnover and Profit

For the sake of simplicity, we model the cost of an argument by some constant c_{arg}. This means that to get for instance the knowledge about argument A_{10}, a consultant has an overall expense of $10 \cdot c_{\mathrm{arg}}$ (recall that arguments can only be procured in a row). We write n_{arg} to denote the total number of arguments acquired by a specific consultant (where $n_{\mathrm{arg}} \leq N_{\mathrm{arg}}$). Then, the expenses E of a consultant can be computed as:

$$E = n_{\mathrm{arg}} \cdot c_{\mathrm{arg}} \qquad (4)$$

The turnover of a consultant is defined as the sum of the money that the consultant has been paid. Of course, the consultant is paid only for those consultations where he actually is better informed than the client; we call these "successful consultations". Let S be the multiset that contains all amounts that have been paid to a certain consultant. This consultant's turnover T is defined as:

$$T = \sum_{p \in S} p \qquad (5)$$

The profit P of a consultant is defined as the difference between his turnover and his expenses:

$$P = T - E \qquad (6)$$

3.2   Consultancy Strategies

Consultants generally want to provide as little information as necessary, because this way they can give more consultations. At the same time, consultants want to give advice that makes them appear knowledgeable – in order to increase their reputation. Therefore, in our model, a consultant advises a client always with the argument that has the lowest index above the client's knowledge and that is compliant with the consultant's latest known argument, i.e., that has the same parity. In other words, provided that a consultant knows enough arguments, he provides a client with *two* arguments, if the latest argument known to the client is of the same parity as the latest argument known to the consultant, and with *one* argument otherwise. These arguments become known to the client.

We consider two strategies for how consultants can increase their knowledge:

Well-informed strategy *(WELL):* A consultant procures arguments as soon as these become available, so as to be always up-to-date with the aim to achieve a good reputation.

Ill-informed *(ILL):* A consultant procures arguments only as to appear knowledgeable to the clients. More precisely, only upon encountering a client who is as informed as the consultant (before or after the consultation), or even better informed, the consultant procures a number of new arguments, which we set to 2. Although this strategy could be made much more sophisticated, we show that under certain conditions it outperforms the *WELL*-strategy already in this form.

Consultants that follow the *WELL*-strategy are always as competent as possible, whereas consultants that follow the *ILL*-strategy become increasingly incompetent with increasing ΔN_{arg}. The *ILL*-strategy allows consultants to offer their advice at a lower price, because they have to invest less in new information. However, this comes at the cost of risking a decrease in reputation, because clients do not want to be advised by a consultant who is not better informed than they are.

3.3   Selection of Consultants

In our model, clients rate consultants according to two criteria: the *price* demanded by the consultants, and their *reputation*.

Price: Clients prefer relatively cheap consultants. The price is agreed upon by client and consultant before an interaction takes place.

Reputation: A client wants to get advice from consultants with a good reputation. In this context, reputation reflects the characteristics of the consultant that cannot be agreed upon beforehand, because they can generally not be checked after an interaction. For instance, in our scenario, clients are generally unable to check provided information for correctness.

We denote a consultant i's current reputation by r_i and represent his price for the upcoming round in form of "cheapness", denoted by c_i. The details on how the reputation and cheapness are computed in our model are given later. For now, it suffices to know that both values are in the interval $(0, 1]$. A high cheapness and a high reputation make a consultant attractive. A parameter $\alpha \in [0, 1]$ defines which of the two criteria the clients think is more important. The "attractiveness" a_i of consultant i is defined as (and is recomputed each round):

$$a_i = \alpha \cdot c_i + (1 - \alpha) \cdot r_i \tag{7}$$

A high α favors cheaper consultants, while a low α favors more reputable consultants. In each round, each client selects a new consultant. Attractiveness values are first centered around a mean of 0.5 (to weaken the impact of extreme outliers), and then normalized to $[0, 1]$, giving a_i'. Finally, a client selects consultant i with the following probability[2]:

$$P_i = \frac{a_i'}{\sum_j a_j'} \tag{8}$$

If a client meets a consultant who is not better informed than he is, the client repeats the selection procedure.

---

[2] In the implementation, we reserve for each consultant i a disjoint interval with length P_i, and generate for each client a uniform random number that selects his consultant: by the interval it falls on (note that a consultant can be selected by several clients).

Price Computation. Let δ be the *profit margin* of a consultant, with $\delta \in [0, \infty)$, where $\delta = 0.5$ represents for instance a profit margin of 50%. Using a certain profit margin δ, a consultant i computes his current price p_i as follows:

$$p_i = (1 + \delta)\frac{E}{|S|} \tag{9}$$

Here, $\frac{E}{|S|}$ is a heuristic to provide cost recovery, where E models the expenses (see eq. (4)), and $|S|$ is the number of successful consultations so far (see eq. (5)). Still, no client would choose a consultant that is more expensive than the acquisition of the information itself. Hence, we limit the price to the cost of *one* argument (see also Sect. 3.2). We map each price to the interval $(0, 1]$ and transform it into cheapness c_i as follows:

$$c_i = \frac{\min_j(p_j)}{p_i} \tag{10}$$

In this way, the cheapest consultant has maximal cheapness 1, and the ratios between the prices are preserved, as can easily be shown:

$$\forall i, j : \frac{c_i}{c_j} = \frac{\min_k(p_k)}{p_i} \cdot \frac{p_j}{\min_k(p_k)} = \frac{p_j}{p_i} \tag{11}$$

Reputation Computation. In our model, clients use a *reputation system* [15] to share their experiences with consultants. This allows clients to better estimate the trustworthiness of the consultants and thus to better select their future consultants. We assume "perfect" conditions for the reputation system, because this will make it harder for the consultants with the *ILL*-strategy to hold their ground. These perfect conditions consist of:

- *honest reporting* of the clients, i.e., clients do not bias their experience,
- all clients have the same idea of how to fuse the experiences with consultants, and so a *global reputation score* can be computed, and
- *total information sharing*, i.e., every client shares *all* his experiences with every other client.

To minimize the impact of specifics of the reputation system on our results, we try to keep it as simple as possible. We propose a system that measures the reputation of a consultant based on the number of bad and good experiences with that consultant. Because clients cannot verify the arguments, they have a bad experience with a consultant only if the consultant is not better informed than they are. Such an interaction is evidence for a consultant following the *ILL*-strategy; in rare cases, this interaction can also be misleading evidence, namely in the case where the consultant is actually following the *WELL*-strategy and the client's knowledge is state of the art. How often the evidence is misleading depends on how fast new information becomes available (ΔN_{arg}); for $\Delta N_{\text{arg}} \geq 3$ for instance, the consultants that follow the *WELL*-strategy are always ahead of the clients, and so a bad experience implies an encounter with a consultant following the *ILL*-strategy. The clients share their experience and maintain for each consultant i a global counter $\mathcal{G}_i$ of good experiences, and a global counter $\mathcal{B}_i$ of bad experiences. Then a reputation score is computed as follows (we follow the trust value computation from [16]):

$$r'_i = \frac{\mathcal{G}_i + 1}{\mathcal{G}_i + \mathcal{B}_i + 2} \tag{12}$$

It follows that at the point where no experience with a consultant has been made yet ($\mathcal{G}_i = \mathcal{B}_i = 0$), his reputation is 0.5. To make reputation comparable to cheapness, we map it to $(0, 1]$ as follows:

$$r_i = \frac{r'_i}{\max_j(r'_j)} \tag{13}$$

As for cheapness, the most reputable consultant has reputation 1, and ratios between reputation scores are preserved (proof analogously to eq. (11)).

4   Simulations

We have implemented a simulator for our model. The aim of this simulator is to reveal the impact of the different model parameters on the profit of the two consultancy strategies. In other words, we want to identify the parameter settings for which the *ILL*-strategy is more profitable than the *WELL*-strategy.

4.1   Experiments

Each experiment was repeated 2^{10} times. Mean profits and corresponding standard deviations were computed, separately for the two consultancy strategies. To account for the fact that consultancy makes only sense when a consultant can advise several clients, we chose a much higher number of clients (2^{10}) than consultants (2^7). The sets of clients and consultants are fixed. At the outset, all consultants procure 2 initial arguments[3]. We varied the following parameters:

- the number of arguments becoming available each round ($\Delta N_{\mathrm{arg}} \in \{2, 4, 6, 8\}$),
- the fraction of consultants that use the *ILL*-strategy ($f_{ILL} \in \{0.1, 0.5, 0.9\}$), where the remaining consultants use the *WELL*-strategy,
- the profit margin ($\delta \in \{0.1, 0.5\}$), and
- the factor α that regulates the importance of the consultants' price and reputation for the clients ($\alpha \in [0, 1]$).

---

[3] We also run the experiments with all consultants procuring 4 initial arguments. As a result, the profit of the *ILL*-consultants increased in all cases. Because of the limited space, these results are not shown here.

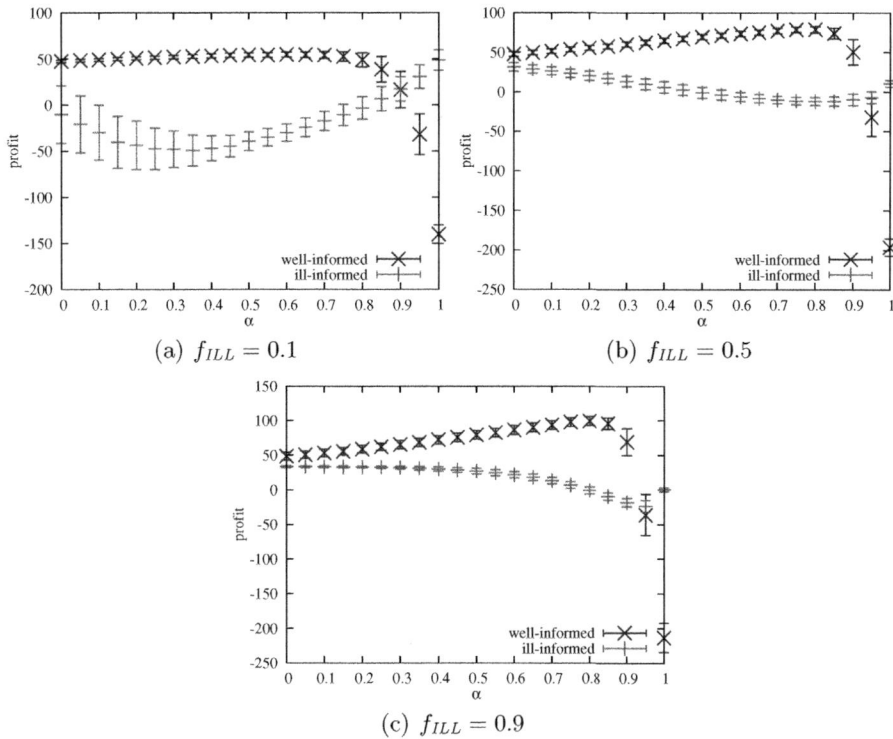

Fig. 1. Impact of fraction of *ILL*-consultants ($\Delta N_{\mathrm{arg}} = 2$ and $\delta = 0.1$)

4.2   Results

In the following, we analyze the results of selected experiments[4]. In all figures, the x-axis gives α, which defines how clients chose their consultants, i.e., for $\alpha = 0$, clients select consultants solely based on their reputation, and attach more importance to the price for increasing α; for $\alpha = 1$, clients only look at the price of the consultants (see also Sect. 3.3). The y-axis gives the profit of the consultants for both consultancy strategies.

Impact of Fraction of *ILL*-Consultants. At the outset, we look at the impact of f_{ILL} on the consultants' profit. To this end, we first fix the parameters $\Delta N_{\mathrm{arg}} = 2$ and $\delta = 0.1$. The results that are shown in Fig. 1 reveal that for small α, the profit of the two types of consultants converge for increasing f_{ILL}, whereas for large α (with a center roughly around 0.8) they develop in different directions. The profit of *ILL*-consultants is in certain areas very low — and even

---

[4] Another set of results was presented in [17]. However, the current model is more reasonable in fundamental points like price and reputation computation, and thus the results of the old model are not considered here.

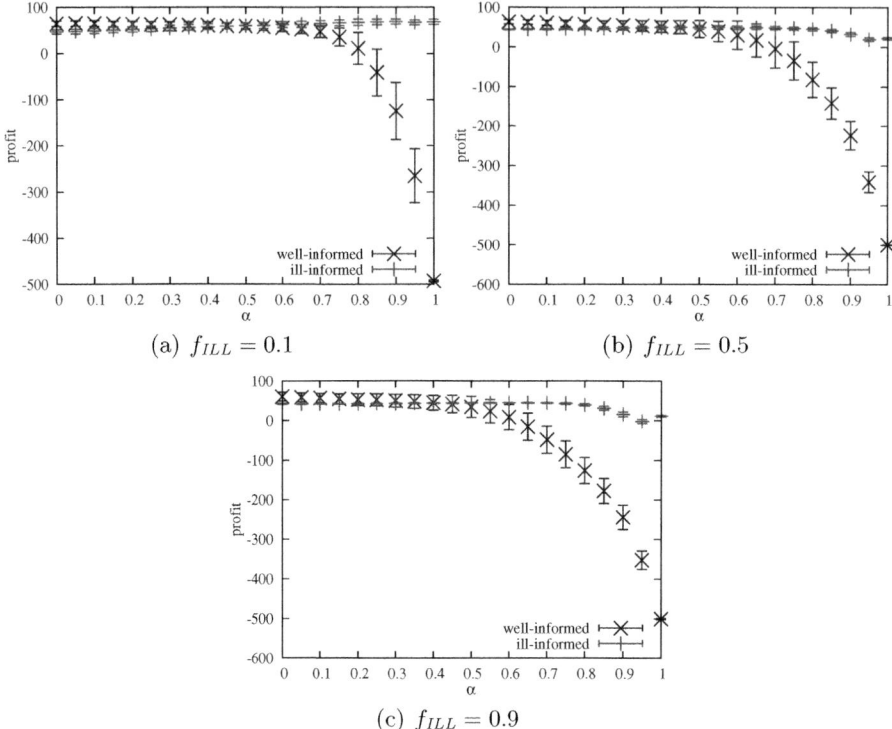

(a) $f_{ILL} = 0.1$ (b) $f_{ILL} = 0.5$

(c) $f_{ILL} = 0.9$

Fig. 2. Impact of fraction of ILL-consultants ($\Delta N_{\mathrm{arg}} = 4$ and $\delta = 0.1$)

negative. By looking at the data, we found that the reason for this is their bad reputation (due to a high rate of unsuccessful consultations, for which they are not paid), and their price which is not considerably better in this scenario. For increasing f_{ILL}, these "negative areas" seem to shift to the right: we found in the data that the average attractiveness of ILL-consultants is increasing for low α, while for the $WELL$-consultants it is increasing for higher α (up to a certain point of α). This an effect of a complex interplay of price, reputation and selection, and we currently have no exact explanation for this. For very high α, one can see a drop in the profit of $WELL$-consultants, because the price is becoming decisive for selection here.

As can be seen from Fig. 2, where ΔN_{arg} is higher, an increase in f_{ILL} causes the drop of the profit of $WELL$-consultants for high α to become more intense. The reason is that now it becomes harder for $WELL$-consultants to offer competitive prices, and so, since they get more competitors for increasing f_{ILL}, it becomes harder for them to make profit, especially when clients care much about the price. For the same reason the profit of ILL-consultants is (slightly) decreasing for high α and increasing f_{ILL}: a higher number of ILL-consultants has to share the profit. Still, their profit increases relatively to the profit of the $WELL$-consultants.

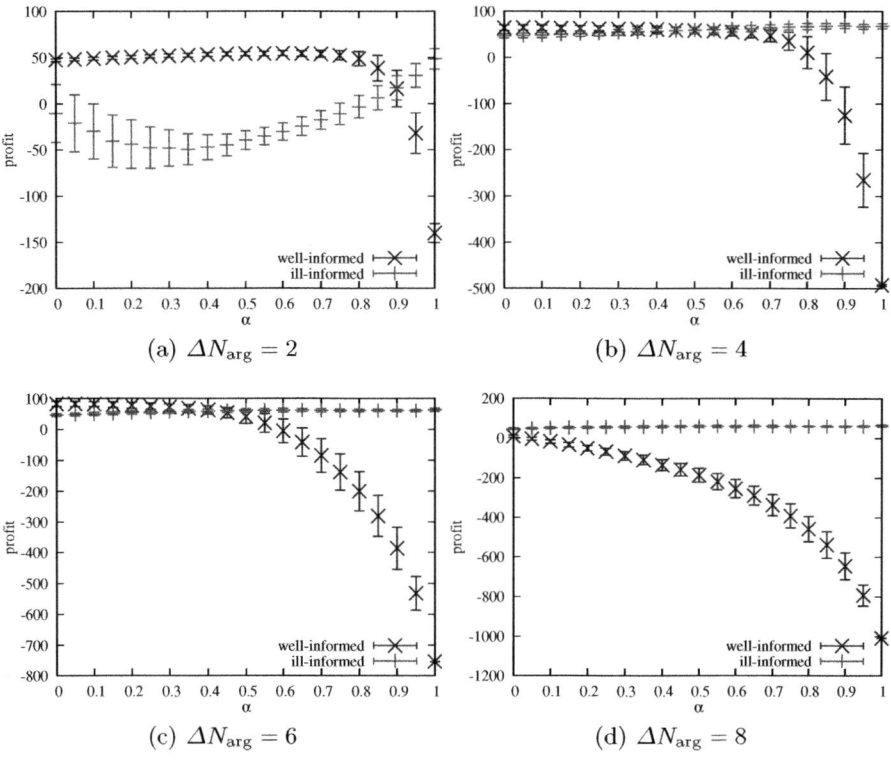

Fig. 3. Impact of ΔN_{arg} ($\delta = 0.1$, $f_{ILL} = 0.1$)

Note that in Figure 1(c) for $\alpha = 0.95$, both strategies make negative profit. This is due to the limitation of the price to the price of one argument (see Sect. 3.3), which is in this case not sufficient to provide cost recovery.

Impact of ΔN_{arg}. We now look at the impact of a higher speed of arguments becoming available (ΔN_{arg}). Figure 3 shows results for varying ΔN_{arg} and fixed δ and f_{ILL}. It can be observed that the profit of the *ILL*-strategy increases in comparison to the *WELL*-strategy for increasing ΔN_{arg}. The reason for this is that for a higher ΔN_{arg}, the *WELL*-consultants have to invest more in the arguments to keep up with the state of the art, and thus are more expensive. Being selected less often, they have to ask for higher prices to compensate their loss (they are continually procuring arguments). For $\Delta N_{\mathrm{arg}} = 8$, that even goes so far as to make it in general unprofitable to follow the *WELL*-strategy, independent of the clients' preferences α. At the same time, the *ILL*-consultants have more successful consultations, and thus are paid more. This is because for increasing ΔN_{arg}, *ILL*-consultants are chosen more regularly by the clients, and so are better informed about the informedness of the clients.

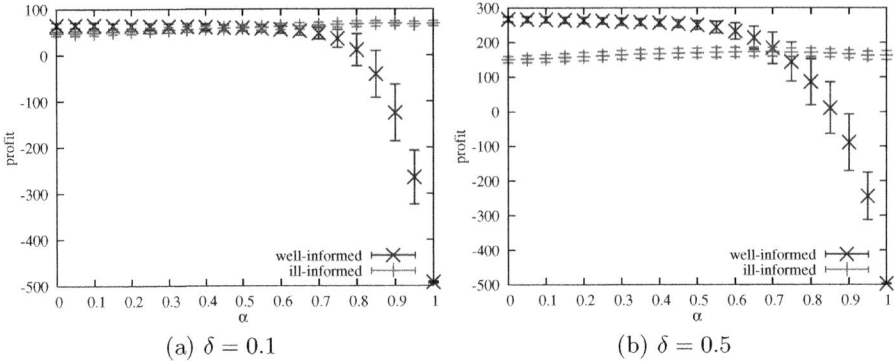

Fig. 4. Impact of profit margin ($\Delta N_{\mathrm{arg}} = 4$, $f_{ILL} = 0.1$)

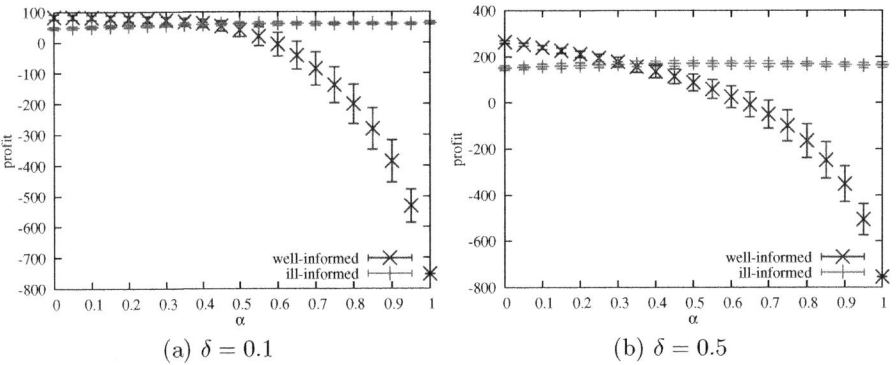

Fig. 5. Impact of profit margin ($\Delta N_{\mathrm{arg}} = 4$, $f_{ILL} = 0.5$)

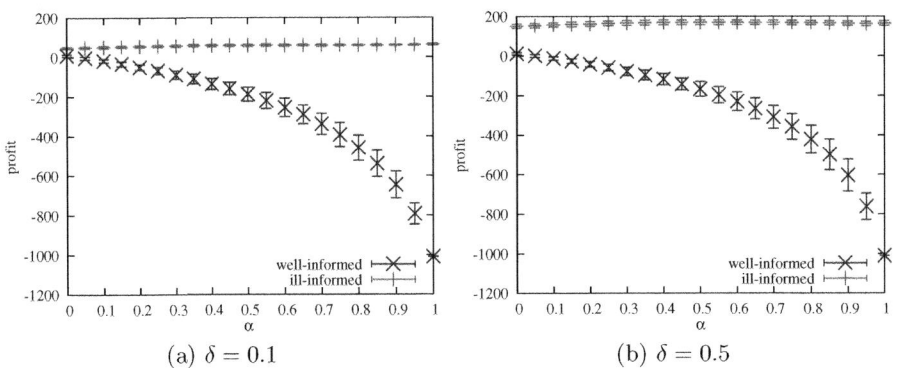

Fig. 6. Impact of profit margin ($\Delta N_{\mathrm{arg}} = 8$, $f_{ILL} = 0.1$)

Impact of Profit Margin. Up to now, we have looked at a profit margin of $\delta = 0.1$. Figures 4, 5 and 6 show what happens when δ is increased; the left figures show $\delta = 0.1$, the right figures show $\delta = 0.5$. In general, it can be seen that a higher profit margin increases the maximal profit (e.g., look at the scale of the y-axis). Apart from that, in Figures 4 and 5, the profit of the *WELL*-strategy is increased for low α, but not affected much for high α. The point where the increase ceases to take place, seems to be where the two profit curves intersect. This holds also for Fig. 6 where the two profit curves move away from each other (there is no intersection). It is also confirmed by the other results not shown in this paper. This leads us to the conjecture that the profit margin amplifies the difference between the profit of the two types of consultants.

5   Conclusions and Perspectives

In this paper, we have compared the profit that consultants yield when following two different strategies: staying as competent as possible, and staying preferably incompetent. In our model, we found that there are scenarios where it is more profitable to stay incompetent. In particular, this is increasingly the case when:

- the speed with which the state of the art changes (ΔN_{arg}) is high,
- clients prefer cheap to reputable consultants (there are exceptions when both ΔN_{arg} is small and f_{ILL} is high), or
- the fraction of incompetent consultants is high (and ΔN_{arg} is not too low).

The impact of the profit margin seems to be more complex. However, it appears to act as an amplifier in that it increases the difference between the profit of the two consultancy strategies.

Our finding that considerations of reputation are sometimes not sufficient to counterbalance incentives for providing low quality information has also been observed in the field of economics, where the role of credit rating agencies has received significant criticism, before as well as after the recent credit crisis. Mathis et al. claim that considerations of reputation might not be sufficient to dissuade rating agencies from giving a too positive rating to certain structured products [18]. Other criticism regarding the low added value of rating agencies has been provided by [19,20,21]. Despite the highly questionable performance of the credit rating agencies, as witnessed in the recent credit crisis, it is striking to see that the ratings industry has continued to operate, while still being relied on both by regulators and by the public [22]. Although some important differences between the domain of credit ratings and the domain studied in our software simulator do exist (for instance the low number of rating agencies compared to the relatively high number of consultants in our simulator) it is striking to see that our findings on the profitability of incompetence do not fundamentally deviate from what has been observed in economics.

The reputation system implemented in the current paper is relatively simple and straightforward. An alternative would be to implement a more advanced approach, like [23,24], which essentially uses a trust-net for weighting the other agents' opinions. Where in [23,24] reporting to the reputation system is assumed to be honest, ReGret [25,26] goes one step further and considers the possibility of dishonest reporting. In our current work, however, the problem studied is not so much dishonest reporting (we assume all client agents to be honest) but fundamental limitations regarding the extent to which a client is able to evaluate the quality of the advise it has purchased. That is, we show that even when all reporting to the reputation system is honest, it can still be the case that the *ILL*-consultants achieve the best economic performance. Nevertheless, the reputation system could be made more clever. For instance, clients could look retrospectively at what their consultants advised them on: is this *older advice* conflicting with what a client *currently believes*? Depending on how much the client believes the real world has changed in between, he can retroactively reduce the reputation of the respective consultants – which would not be justified though if his current believes are incorrect.

There are many ways of how to extend our current model, and to make it more realistic. First of all, the price computation could be extended with ideas from the field of economics: instead of caring just about cost recovery, consultants could proactively reduce their price in order to attract more clients; this would involve models for market analysis. Also, the possibility of bankruptcy could be considered. Furthermore, in our model, clients select their consultants autonomously, but all have the same preference regarding price and reputation. This can be extended by defining a probability density function (PDF) over the clients' preferences, and choosing the preference of a client from this distribution. Domain specific knowledge should be used to define a meaningful PDF. Analogously, the number of arguments getting available each round to the consultant (ΔN_{arg}) could be described by a PDF. Also, this work did not address the issue of dynamics, e.g., clients that adapt their preferences over time. Finally, more complex argumentation frameworks could be explored, possibly involving trees instead of the relatively simple linear structure treated in the current paper.

Acknowledgments

We would like to thank Yining Wu (Interdisciplinary Lab for Intelligent and Adaptive Systems) and Tibor Neugebauer (Luxembourg School of Finance) for their useful comments.

References

1. Frankfurt, H.G.: On Bullshit. Princeton University Press, Princeton (2005)
2. Caminada, M.: Truth, lies and bullshit; distinguishing classes of dishonesty. In: Social Simulation Workshop at the International Joint Conference on Artificial Intelligence, SSIJCAI (2009)
3. Dung, P.: On the acceptability of arguments and its fundamental role in nonmonotonic reasoning, logic programming and n-person games. Artificial Intelligence 77, 321–357 (1995)

4. Caminada, M.: On the issue of reinstatement in argumentation. In: Fisher, M., van der Hoek, W., Konev, B., Lisitsa, A. (eds.) JELIA 2006. LNCS (LNAI), vol. 4160, pp. 111–123. Springer, Heidelberg (2006)
5. Caminada, M., Gabbay, D.: A logical account of formal argumentation. Studia Logica 93(2-3), 109–145 (2009); Special issue: new ideas in argumentation theory
6. Prakken, H., Sartor, G.: Argument-based extended logic programming with defeasible priorities. Journal of Applied Non-Classical Logics 7, 25–75 (1997)
7. Vreeswijk, G., Prakken, H.: Credulous and sceptical argument games for preferred semantics. In: Brewka, G., Moniz Pereira, L., Ojeda-Aciego, M., de Guzmán, I.P. (eds.) JELIA 2000. LNCS (LNAI), vol. 1919, pp. 239–253. Springer, Heidelberg (2000)
8. Caminada, M.: For the sake of the Argument. Explorations into argument-based reasoning. Doctoral dissertation Free University Amsterdam (2004)
9. Modgil, S., Caminada, M.: Proof theories and algorithms for abstract argumentation frameworks. In: Rahwan, I., Simari, G. (eds.) Argumentation in Artificial Intelligence, pp. 105–129. Springer, Heidelberg (2009)
10. Caminada, M.: An algorithm for computing semi-stable semantics. In: Mellouli, K. (ed.) ECSQARU 2007. LNCS (LNAI), vol. 4724, pp. 222–234. Springer, Heidelberg (2007)
11. Caminada, M., Wu, Y.: An argument game of stable semantics. Logic Journal of IGPL 17(1), 77–90 (2009)
12. Caminada, M., Pigozzi, G.: On judgment aggregation in abstract argumentation. Journal of Autonomous Agents and Multi-Agent Systems (2009)
13. Rahwan, I., Tohmé, F.: Collective argument evaluation as judgement aggregation. In: Proceedings of the 9th International Conference on Autonomous Agents and Multiagent Systems, AAMAS 2010 (2010)
14. Caminada, M.: Semi-stable semantics. In: Dunne, P., Bench-Capon, T. (eds.) Computational Models of Argument; Proceedings of COMMA 2006, pp. 121–130. IOS Press, Amsterdam (2006)
15. Resnick, P., Kuwabara, K., Zeckhauser, R., Friedman, E.: Reputation systems. Commun. ACM 43(12), 45–48 (2000)
16. Staab, E., Fusenig, V., Engel, T.: Towards trust-based acquisition of unverifiable information. In: Klusch, M., Pěchouček, M., Polleres, A. (eds.) CIA 2008. LNCS (LNAI), vol. 5180, pp. 41–54. Springer, Heidelberg (2008)
17. Staab, E., Caminada, M.: Assessing the impact of informedness on a consultant's profit. Technical report, University of Luxembourg (2009), http://arxiv.org/abs/0909.0901
18. Mathis, J., McAndrews, J., Rochet, J.: Rating the raters: are reputation concerns powerful enough to discipline rating agencies? Journal of Monetary Economics 56, 657–674 (2009)
19. Ferru, G., Liu, L.G., Stiglitz, J.E.: The procyclic role of rating agencies: evidence from the east asian crisis. Economic Notes 28(3), 335–355 (1999)
20. Sinclair, T.: The new masters of capital; American bond rating agencies and the politics of creditworthyness. Cornell University Press (2005)
21. Sy, A.: Rating the rating agencies: anticipating currency crises or debt crises? Journal of Banking & Finance 28, 2845–2867 (2004)
22. Spatt, C.: Discussions of 'ratings shopping and asset complexity: A theory of rating inflation'. Journal of Monetary Economics 56, 696–699 (2009)
23. Schillo, M., Funk, P., Rovatsos, M.: Using trust for detecting deceitful agents in artificial societies. Applied Artificial Intelligence 14(8), 825–848 (2000)

24. Yu, B., Singh, M.P.: A social mechanism of reputation management in electronic communities. In: Klusch, M., Kerschberg, L. (eds.) CIA 2000. LNCS (LNAI), vol. 1860, pp. 355–393. Springer, Heidelberg (2000)
25. Sabater, J., Sierra, C.: Regret: reputation in gregarious societies. In: Agents, pp. 194–195 (2001)
26. Sabater, J., Sierra, C.: Reputation and social network analysis in multi-agent systems. In: AAMAS 2002: Proceedings of the First International Joint Conference on Autonomous Agents and Multiagent Systems, pp. 475–482. ACM, New York (2002)

Mechanisms for the Self-organization of Peer Groups in Agent Societies

Sharmila Savarimuthu, Maryam Purvis, Martin Purvis,
and Bastin Tony Roy Savarimuthu

Department of Information Science, University of Otago,
Dunedin, New Zealand
{sharmilas,tehrany,mpurvis,tonyr}infoscience.otago.ac.nz

Abstract. New mechanisms for group self-organization in agent societies are investigated and examined in the context of sharing digital goods. Specifically we illustrate how cooperative sharers and uncooperative free riders can be placed in different groups of an electronic society in a decentralized manner. We have simulated a decentralized, open P2P system which self-organizes itself to avoid cooperative sharers being exploited by uncooperative free riders. Inspired by human society, we use social mechanisms such as tags, gossip and ostracism. This approach encourages sharers to move to better groups and restricts free riders without necessitating centralized control, which makes the system appropriate for current open P2P systems.

Keywords: Multi-agent Based Simulation, Cooperation, Sharing behavior and Artificial Societies.

1 Introduction

One of the common problems in a P2P network is that of free riders. In our context, free riders are those agents or nodes that do not contribute to the collective goals of the network society, but make use of the resources of the network [9]. These free riders decrease the overall performance of the society by contributing to the degradation of the common good [4] without contributing to the community. In a way, they can be considered as parasites.

Many existing approaches to social regulations in ecommerce employ a centralized mechanism to control free riders, whereby the system eliminates antisocial behaviour by employing a monitoring or governor agent [6, 9]. But these centralized mechanisms are computationally expensive for a system and can represent a bottleneck. Centralized control systems need a central manager to monitor and carry out punishment or to provide an incentive mechanism, which is not suitable for decentralized systems, due to the explosion of state spaces. In an open system it is inappropriate to rely on a centralized monitoring authority that monitors all possible state spaces that an agent can be in. Scalable modern P2P systems are entirely decentralized and open; hence to deal with this dynamic nature of digital societies, there is a need for a decentralized solution for dealing with the free-riding problem.

T. Bosse, A. Geller, and C.M. Jonker (Eds.): MABS 2010, LNAI 6532, pp. 93–107, 2011.
© Springer-Verlag Berlin Heidelberg 2011

In this work we propose a decentralized solution that makes use of social mechanisms such as tagging, gossip and ostracism. The inspiration to use social mechanisms for our work comes from the human societies, which have evolved over millennia to work effectively in groups. For human beings group mechanisms provide social machinery that supports cooperation and collaboration. In this work, inspired by human society, we propose a new mechanism for agents to self-organize themselves into different groups, based on their behavior and in a decentralized manner.

2 Background and Related Work

Previous research has shown that tags can improve cooperation among participants and can induce "altruistic" behavior [3, 7]. For example, some researchers have shown that tag-based mechanisms have been successful in the evolution of cooperation using the Iterated Prisoner's Dilemma/ Prisoner's Dilemma (IPD/PD) games [3, 8].

By playing the "donation game", agents employing tagging achieved altruism in the model described by Riolo, Cohen and Axelrod [7]. In their model, tag and tolerance values are used to form groups, and an agent donates to another when the difference between its tag values is within the agent's tolerance level. Also an agent in their system could be a member of more than one group. In that case, that agent may donate to or receive from the group members of all those groups. This mechanism has been shown to achieve altruism among peers by making use of tags.

The knowledge sharing game is about sharing knowledge (information/skill) within a society that is composed of sharers and non-sharers. In the context of the knowledge sharing game [10-12], it is shown that tagging can help to increase sharing behaviour. The work presented in [10] describes the effect of tag-based mechanisms for sustaining knowledge through sharing behavior, and it describes the conditions under which sharing behavior spreads through the society and how knowledge is shared and sustained in the society.

In the work of Purvis, Savarimuthu, Oliveira and Purvis [6], the cooperative self-organization of peers in different groups was achieved in playing the PD game, by making use of tags and monitoring agents, where the population had a mixture of cooperators and non-cooperators. By employing a monitoring agent for each group, the system evolved into groups partitioned according to the performances of their group members. Each monitoring agent employed a voting mechanism within the group to determine which agents were the most and least cooperative members of the group. Then the most cooperative member was allowed to move to a new group, and the least cooperative member was expelled from the group. Those peers who left or were expelled from their groups obtained membership in a new group only if the local monitor agent of the other (new) group accepted them. Since the local monitor agents picked players for their group based on performance, the high performing player had a good chance to get entry into the best group, and the reverse conditions applied for the worst performing player. As a result, the players entered into groups based on their performances. But this approach was still semi-centralized, because it required a local monitoring agent for each group. In addition it was a closed system model, so it did not fully support open, distributed P2P systems.

In Hales's work [3], the PD game was played in a P2P network among nodes. This work extends his previous work on tags, to networks, where a 'neighbor list of nodes' is considered to be a tag and 'movement of node in a network' is modeled as a mutation. His results showed that tags work well for P2P systems in achieving cooperation, scalability and robustness.

In our present work, instead of the PD game, we have adopted the more practical scenario of sharing digital goods in electronic societies. We investigate how we can achieve the separation or self-organization of groups based on their behavior in a decentralized manner and in an open society. Such a system would help to protect cooperators from being exploited by the non-cooperators. It would also restrict the non-cooperators from taking advantage of cooperators and restrict their entree to better groups where the access to resources are better and hence the quality of service/performance is higher. By doing so, the performance of the whole system can be improved, because resources can be distributed in greater proportion to the better performing groups. Otherwise it will be difficult to shield the cooperators from the defectors who rarely or never share their resources. For easy understanding, we differentiate our system from the system of Purvis, Savarimuthu, Oliveira and Purvis [6], see Table 1.

Table 1. Differences between the earlier system and our present system

Earlier system	Present system
Semi-centralised	Decentralised
Used monitoring agents	No monitoring, distributed
Used voting mechanism	Used gossip mechanism
Closed system	Open system

3   Experimental Model

Our experimental model presents a social situation in which the agents have the option to share or not share. Sharing costs the donor who shares. But the receiver receives the benefit (b) without incurring any cost (c). The sharer who shares the file loses -1 as a cost. The receiver who receives the file gets 2 as a benefit. Non-sharing is the selfish option which benefits the individual but is not good for the society. Sharing leads to the betterment of the society as opposite to the non-sharing which deteriorates the common good. Everyone will be better off if everyone shares. Since the donating agent spends some effort (e.g. bandwidth) in the process of donating, it incurs some cost in our model. That sharing agent could have decided to be selfish and thereby avoid incurring that cost. Thus free riding becomes a threat to the society, causing damage to the common good. This is the issue of the "Tragedy of the Commons" [4]. Some of the model properties and mechanisms used in our experiments are described below:

3.1 Tag Groups

The tags we use are simply markings that are "visible" to other agents and are employed for grouping purposes. Some natural biological tagging examples are birds flocking together, animals forming herds, and ants forming a colony. They interact within their tagged group – they act together, and those small interactions among them can lead to the emergence of collective behavior. Thus the tagging mechanism that we use is inspired by nature, and it has been widely used to model the behaviour of artificial agent societies. A simple way to think of these tags is to assume that they represent group identifiers for sets of agents: agents having the same tags belong to the same group. Tagging is thus a straightforward and lightweight approach for facilitating cooperation [3].

3.2 Gossip Mechanism

Gossip has long been an effective mechanism for passing information in human society [2, 14]. Similarly in agent societies, agents use gossip to learn about other agents [5]. This mechanism maintains partial (i.e. not complete) information about agents in the society in a distributed and scalable fashion within the system. This gossip mechanism can be considered as 'distributed referral', and it is described more fully in the experimental setup.

3.3 Social Ostracism

Agents will refuse to interact (share resources) with another agent if that other agent is identified as the "worst", i.e. the least cooperative agent in the group. If other agents are not interacting with the worst agent, the worst agent will eventually choose to leave the group on its own, since it no longer has opportunities to increase its wealth. This is a kind of 'ostracism' [1, 15].

3.4 Agent Attributes

In experiments described in this paper, the agents have fixed, randomly assigned attribute values which represent how they behave. One agent attribute concerns cooperation: agents have a randomly assigned cooperation value between 0 and 10 that represents how much they cooperate (share), with 0 representing maximally uncooperative and 10 representing maximally cooperative. This value is known as the cooperativeness of the agent. Agents with low cooperativeness, hardly or never share. These agents are known as free riders. Agents also have a tolerance value between 1 and 10, which characterizes how much non-cooperation the agent can tolerate before it decides to leave the group. A value of 1 identifies the least tolerant, and 10 identifies the most tolerant.

4 Experimental Setup

In our experimental arrangement agents are engaged in the sharing of digital goods in a P2P environment of a simulated artificial agent society. In the initial setup 100 agents are put into five random groups. The group is called a "tag group" which can be imagined to be represented by a tag (badge). Agents within a group have the same tag. They interact within their group, and they can also move to other groups under certain conditions. In such cases they join the other, jumped-to group, and the tag changes accordingly. Each agent has a gossip blackboard to store the gossip messages from other agents of its group. Each agent also has a memory of any previous groups to which it has belonged. Each agent is initialized with a random cooperative value and a random tolerance value. The experiment was executed for 5000 iterations. The procedure of the experiment is explained in detail below.

4.1 Gossiping

In every iteration, a certain random percentage of the players (agents) may ask for files from other players of their group. A player can gossip about the outcome of an interaction with another agent in its group (report whether the other agent was cooperative or not). In this gossip mechanism we assume that there is no lying. Since this happens within the group, the agent has no motivation to lie. In this fashion, every transaction is reported (gossiped about) to one of the other agents in the group. Thus the overall system has some partial information about the cooperativeness of each agent, maintained in a distributed way. The first 500 iterations (out of 5000) are played in this manner to build up a distributed gossip repository among the players. For further illustration, the operation of how peers publish gossip is outlined schematically in Algorithm 1. In the scheme illustrated in Algorithm 1, there are three players A, B and C, belonging to the same group. A is the taking-player, B is the giving-player, and C is the gossip holder.

Algorithm 1. To publish gossip

```
begin
    A requests for file to B ;
    if B shares then
    |   A gossips good about B to C;
    else
    |   A gossips bad about B to C ;
    end
end
```

Each peer has a limited amount of memory space for storing new gossip information. After reaching the storage limit, the memory register rolls over, based on a First-In-First-Out (FIFO) algorithm.

After 500 iterations, the agents begin using the received gossip information to decide whether or not to play with a taking-player. When a player requests a file, the giving player can check with five other random agents (asking them what they know from the gossip information they have received) whether this asking agent is the worst cooperator of their group. The worst player is the one who has been uncooperative most of the times in its group (according to the available gossip information). If the taking-player is the worst player, the giving player refuses to interact with the taking-player. Otherwise this giving player interacts (sharing a file or not based on its own cooperativeness). The operation of how peers use gossip is outlined in Algorithm 2, where B and D are the players in the group. Assume here that B is the taking-player, D is the giving-player, and D collects the gossip information from any 5 other agents and checks whether B is the worst player (from the available gossip information) .

Algorithm 2. To use gossip within group

```
begin
    D requests 5 other players for gossip about B;
    D receives gossip;
    if B is the worst player then
    |   D refuses to play with B;
    else
    |   D plays with B;
    end
end
```

When only a few agents (less than 5) have gossip about a taking-player, then only the available information is taken into consideration. Sometimes it can be the case that none of the players has gossip about the taking-player. In such a case the taking-player is considered not to be the worst player, a privilege similar to what happens when a new player joins a group.

4.2 Leaving a Group

A player can leave a group if its tolerance level is surpassed or when its wealth has not increased recently. We call this agent a "hopping peer". If its tolerance limit is reached, that means this agent is in a group where others do not cooperate at the rate that meets this agent's minimum level of expectation. Thus after a number of such non-sharing events from the group members (breaching the agent's tolerance limit) the agent will decide to leave that group and move to another group.

In addition, making use of gossip information, the agents will stop playing with the worst player in their group. Every time they play, the giving-players check with other agents about the taking-players and check whether that player is considered to be the most uncooperative. If an agent is regularly rejected from play, then, of course, that agent's score will not increase. If, over a given period of play opportunities (here, 15 iterations), an agent's wealth has not increased, then it will choose to leave that group and move to another group. Since the other players in its current group are not playing with it, it will be better off moving to another group, irrespective of that group's co-operativeness/performance. Thus the worst player leaves the group on its own accord, without any control applied on it.

4.3 Joining a Group

The hopping peer then collects information about other groups from their group members. Then it decides to which group to request admission. Every agent has a memory record of its most recent groups (in our experiments the memory limit was set to 4). For example, assume agent E has been in 3 other groups before, as shown below in Table 2.

The first row of the Table 2 explains that, E has left group 1 at the 560th iteration, and the cooperation value of that group was 4.5 at that time. E left group 3 at the 700th iteration and group 2 at 1200th iteration. Since the composition of groups invariable change over time, the cooperativeness of any group will change as time progresses. So it is likely that the most recent information will be the most accurate and useful for an agent.   Since all agents have a memory of their previous groups, the hopping peer can collect this information from all its group members and calculates the latest information about other groups. In particular, the agents get to see which agent has moved into this group recently from other groups. Taking into consideration the most recent information available, the agent decides where to move based on this information.   For example assuming the current iteration is 1400, the latest information collected from the group members is given in Table 3.

Table 2. Previous group history   **Table 3.** Latest available information

Group No	Iteration No	Cooperativeness
1	560	4.5
3	700	6.0
2	1200	6.4

Group No	Iteration No	Cooperativeness
5	1330	8.1
3	1170	7.5
2	1200	6.4
1	1199	3.8

Assume here that agent L intends leaving group 4, and Group 4's cooperativeness is 6.6 at that moment. From the latest information agent L knows about other groups and their cooperation value. For agent L, groups 5 and 3 are better, since the cooperation value in those groups appear to be higher than L's current group. Groups 2 and 1 are lower-ranked groups. So agent L chooses to move to the groups in the order of their ranking.

If L is intolerant of its current group (which means it is not happy about the cooperativeness of its current group), it will try to enter into the best group that it can find. This is the case of an agent being "too good" for its current group and wanting to move to a more cooperative group. But if the better groups on its list don't allow entry into their groups, then the intolerant agent L may determine that there is no group available that is better than its current group, and it will remain in its current group. In this case its tolerance limit is reset to 0.

On the other hand, an agent may not be good enough for its current group – it is being shunned by the other members for being the worst member of its group. Because of play rejections, its wealth will not advance, and it will want to leave and find some other group in which it can find players to play with. If the better groups do not allow entry, the agent will go to lower and lower groups, since it is better off moving to any new group rather than staying in the current group where it is known as the worst player.

How a player gets entry to another group is explained in the following section.

4.4 Calculating the Entry Value

The hopping peer asks any randomly chosen agent in the group to which it seeks entry for permission to enter. We call this permission-granting agent in the group to which entry is sought, the "checking peer". The checking peer will accept agents whose cooperativeness values are greater than or equal to a value calculated by a formula (given below). This hopping peer will gain permission to enter the group whenever its cooperativeness is greater or equal to the group's entry value calculated by the following formula:

$$EV = AC - (C1 / (SL - S)^{C2}) + C3^{(S-SU)}$$

The group Entry Value (EV) is calculated considering the given group's Average Cooperativeness (AC) and its group Size (S). AC is the average cooperativeness of the group calculated through the gossip mechanism, and S is the size of the group. C1, C2, C3 are constants whose values in our experiments are 25, 2, 10, respectively. These constants were adjusted to make the EV expression appropriate for two "boundary values", the upper size limit of a group (SU) and the lower size limit of a group (SL). It is inappropriate or inefficient for groups of players or traders to become too big or too small. In our experiments, SU was set to be 25, and SL was set to be 10. That means if the size of the group is 10 or below the entry qualification value is set at a low value, making entry into the group very easy to obtain. If the size is 25 or above the entry qualification value is set to a high value and that would make it difficult for any but the most cooperative agents to join. Any values of the EV expression that fall below 0 are set to 0, and entry values above 10 are set to 10. Thus a group's entry value is always between 0 and 10.

A simple example illustrates the use of this formula. Consider that a group's calculated cooperativeness (AC) is 6. When the group Size (S) is 14 the group Entry Value (EV) is 4.43. When the group Size (S) is 25 the Group Entry Value (EV) is 6.88. This can be identified in Figure 1 by examining the line Avg6 for size 14 and for size 25.

In our system, the checking peer needs to get an estimate of the cooperativeness of the hopping peer (the agent seeking entry). So the checking peer asks 5 randomly chosen players from the hopping peer's group about the hopping peer's cooperation. It is thus inquiring into gossip information from the hopping peer's group.

Consider a case where E and F are in different groups. E is the checking peer, and F is the hopping peer that wants to enter E's group. F asks E for entry, and E asks 5 other randomly chosen players in F's group for gossip information about F's cooperativeness. If F's estimated cooperativeness calculated through this gossip information is greater than or equal to the entry value (EV) of its group, the checking peer allows entry for the hopping player; otherwise it denies. In that case the hopping peer will try to enter into other groups. This process is outlined in Algorithm 3. The hopping peer will ultimately get into a group where its cooperativeness is eligible to enter. If no such group is available, the hopping peer stays in its current group.

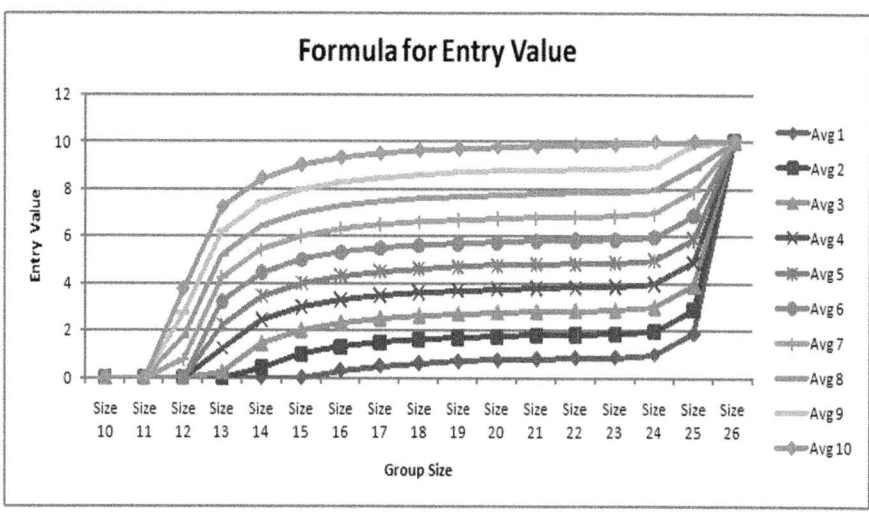

Fig. 1. Entry value calculated by the formula

Algorithm 3. To use gossip between groups

```
begin
    E requests 5 other players for gossip about F;
    E receives gossip about Fs estimated cooperativeness;
    E calculates entry value;
    if Fs estimated cooperativeness ≥ entry value then
    |   F gets entry;
    else
    |   F does not get entry;
    end
end
```

The entire process is repeated for many iterations, and gradually, some groups will emerge as elite groups with many cooperators, and other groups will have less cooperative players. As a consequence, these mechanisms achieve a separation of groups based on performance. The overall process is outlined in Algorithm 4. A demo video can be seen in this link [13].

4.5 Results and Comparison

To consider the overall performance of our mechanisms, we first explain the results from the earlier system [6] for comparative purposes. In that earlier result, all the 5

Algorithm 4. Pseudocode for the overall process

```
begin
    initialization;
    bootstrap agents in groups;
    foreach iteration do
        select random number of agents;
        if iteration is less than 500 then
            foreach selected agent do
                play with another agent in the group;
                collect payoff;
                gossip;                                    // Algorithm 1
            end
        else
            foreach selected agent do
                play with another agent based on gossip;   // Algorithm 2
                collect payoff;
                gossip;                                    // Algorithm 1
                if selected agent's tolerance level is met then
                    selected agent leaves the group;
                    joins another group under certain condition;  // Algorithm 3
                end
                if selected agent's wealth has not increased then
                    selected agent leaves the group;
                    joins another group under certain condition;  // Algorithm 3
                end
            end
        end
    end
end
```

groups started with a similar number of cooperators in each group. Later the groups were separated into 2 groups having most of the cooperators, 2 groups having most of the non-cooperators and the middle group having a mixed population of both. But thatearlier work employed localized group monitors and was therefore less scalable and distributed.

We present our results here using the decentralized approach in Figure 2. Initially all the five groups were randomly seeded and started with roughly similar average cooperativeness values among their members. They ended up showing a separation among the groups with respect to their cooperativeness values. Group4, with mostly the best cooperators, Groups 2 and 3, with mostly non-cooperators, Groups 1 and 5, with moderate ones. This partitioning was achieved using social mechanisms without central control.

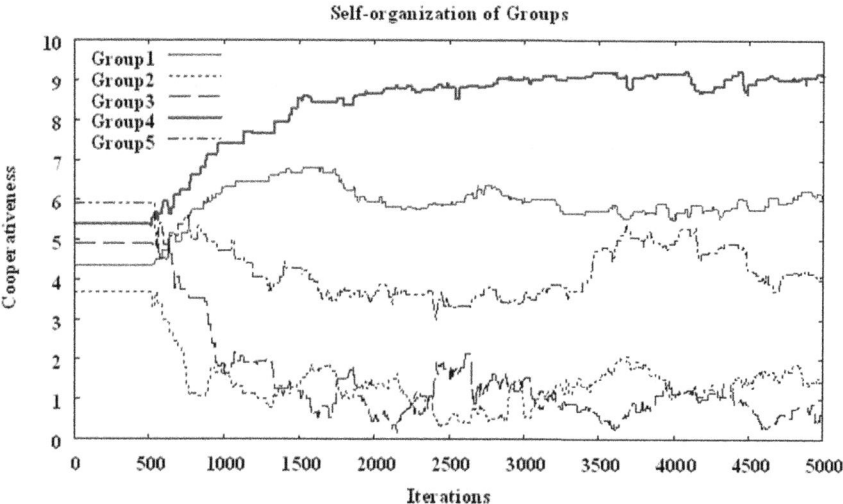

Fig. 2. Self-organization of groups based on cooperativeness in closed society

A paired-samples t-test was conducted to compare the separation of groups based on cooperativeness (standard deviation)) at the start and end of the runs. The paired t-test was performed with null hypothesis for 30 sample runs. The standard deviation of groups' cooperativeness at the start and end of the run were measured. There was a significant difference in the values at start (M=0.71, SD=0.25) and at end (M=3.27, SD=0.31) conditions. The average difference between the mean values (M=2.55, SD=0.07, N=30) was significantly greater than zero, t=33.77, two-tail p=(7.78*10^{-25}), providing evidence that our mechanism is effective in producing the separation of groups based on cooperativeness with a 95% confidence interval.

We also experimented by varying the number of agents that are contacted to collect gossip. The number of agents from which gossip was provided varied between 2, 5 and 15. From the 30 sample runs collected, the mean of the standard deviations of groups, for gossip size 2, 5 and 15 are 2.80, 3.22 and 3.23 respectively. We noticed significant difference when we compared 2 with 5. Collecting gossip from 5 agents has resulted in better separation than from 2 agents. But when we compared 5 with 15 there is not much difference in the separation. Collecting gossip from 15 agents (or less, if there are less than 15 agents in that particular group) has slightly improved the separation, but the difference was very small.

4.6 Adding Openness

Our aim has been to develop a self-organizing open and dynamic system, where new agents may come into the society and also agents may leave the society at any time. New unknown peers are allowed to join the society by gaining entry into the lowest ranked group. They can build their way up to higher groups, based on how well they perform in the eyes of their peers. A truly open and dynamic system will allow the formation of new groups and dismantling of existing groups according to the population size. Our aim was to achieve that in a decentralized manner without explicit control at the top level. Forming groups using tags is helpful, since it is scalable and robust. For higher numbers of peers, more tag groups can be formed, and that process will scale well for any number of peers. Now, in the new arrangement, agents are set to have lifespans, which determines how long the agents remain in the society and when they leave (i.e. "die"). At any time a new agent could join the society and an existing agent could leave when its lifespan is over. Thus we added openness to the society (agents can arrive and leave).

In our approach, a group splits into two if the size of group reaches certain limit (40). Based on the local gossip information in the splitting group, the top cooperators (first half) form one group and the rest (second half) form the other group. If the size of the group decreases and goes below certain limit (5) then the group dismantles. The remaining agents in the group go to the lowest group.

4.7 Results and Discussion

The self-organization of groups in the open society is shown in figure 3. The results from a sample run for 5000 iterations are presented in figure 3. Out of 5 initial groups, Group 4 dismantled. Group 3, which is the most cooperative group, split into two most cooperative groups, group 6 and 7. Group 5 also split into two groups 8 and 9, of which Group 9 is the lowest group. Note that the new groups formed by splitting have some difference in their cooperativeness since the most cooperative ones from the splitting group team up to form one group, and the rest form the other group. This is an ongoing process, because further groups will be formed and dismantled based on the arrival and leaving rates of the agents.

To test the scalability, we ran the experiment for 10000 iterations, by having the initial population set to be 100 in 5 initial groups and also having hundreds of agents enter the scene randomly over subsequent periods. Agents also leave the society when their life span is over. This experiment has scaled well by forming 23 groups over 10000 iterations, in which 11 of them have dismantled or split and the others are operational groups by the end of the iterations. It shows the system can scale well for any number of agents just by forming or dismantling groups dynamically. In open societies like these, agents cannot have a global view of all the groups. They have a limited view which means they know about the groups where the agents and its group members have been before.

It can also be observed from the results that the system mechanisms lead to the filtering out of the worst peers, and these mechanisms restrict those uncooperative peers from gaining access to the good, more cooperative, groups. This also helps to

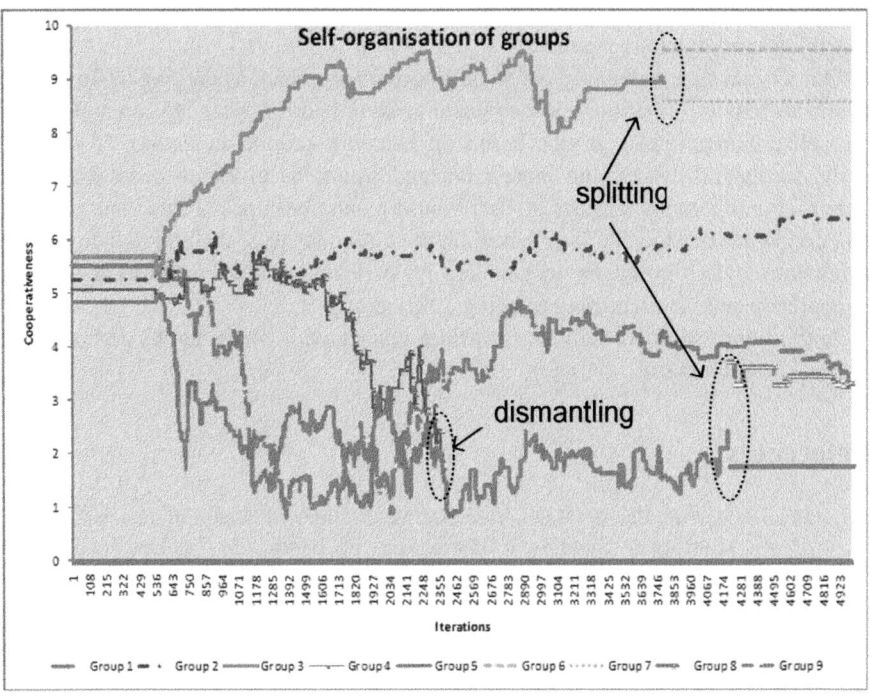

Fig. 3. Self-organization of groups based on cooperativeness in open society

improve the betterment of the society by protecting cooperators from not being exploited by free riders. The best players (most cooperative) get to access or/enter into any group. Thus the system has distributed operative mechanisms that lead to the following social principle for the individual agents: "the better you are the better your chances are".

Using the gossip mechanism, agents share their interaction experience with some other agents. Unlike most reputation mechanisms, where agents keep track of all the reputation information of other agents, our system distributes a subset of this information among the individuals in the group. This mechanism operates and converges to satisfactory results in the context of a partial-view of truth about the world states, which is a realistic and scalable feature of open agent societies. If any peer leaves a group, only a limited amount of information is lost, which ensures the robustness of the system. Peers might leave the society (because of bad behavior) and try to re-enter again. But our system filters out peers in separate groups, based on their behavior. It does not matter how many times an uncooperative agent would enter, it will inevitably end up in the worst group.

5   Conclusion and Future Work

The system presented in this paper is suitable for sharing digital goods in open P2P systems where the aim is to improve societal performance by avoiding free riding. It has produced self-organization, or the so called self-balancing of P2P systems, in a distributed and dynamic manner.

Our system takes advantage of social mechanisms, such as tagging to form groups, gossip to pass information, and ostracism to shun bad behavior. As a result, it shows the self-organization of groups based on behavior (cooperativeness). In our future work, we intend to examine more advanced situations in which peers dynamically alter their cooperation strategies. That would mean that a peer could start with a certain cooperative value, but later based on the circumstances, it could decide to change it accordingly. (It could try to enhance its performance by becoming a "bad guy" temporarily and then returning to being a "good guy").

In the future work we will also consider misbehavior of agents, by adding lying in the gossip mechanism.

References

1. de Pinninck, A.P., Bas, S.C., Schorlemmer, M.: Distributed Norm Enforcement: Ostracism in Open Multi-Agent Systems. In: Casanovas, P., Sartor, G., Casellas, N., Rubino, R. (eds.) Computable Models of the Law. LNCS (LNAI), vol. 4884, pp. 275–290. Springer, Heidelberg (2008)
2. Eugster, P., Felber, P., Le Fessant, F.: The "art" of programming gossip-based systems. ACM SIGOPS Operating Systems Review-Special topic: Gossip-Based Networking 41(5), 37–42 (2007)
3. Hales, D.: Self-Organising, Open and Cooperative P2P Societies - From Tags to Networks. In: Brueckner, S.A., Di Marzo Serugendo, G., Karageorgos, A., Nagpal, R. (eds.) ESOA 2005. LNCS (LNAI), vol. 3464, pp. 123–137. Springer, Heidelberg (2005)
4. Hardin, G.: The Tragedy of the Commons. Science 162, 1243–1248 (1968)
5. Jelasity, M., Montresor, A., Babaoglu, O.: Detection and removal of malicious peers in gossip-based protocols. In: FuDiCo II: S.O.S., Bertinoro, Italy (2004)
6. Purvis, M.K., Savarimuthu, S., De Oliveira, M., Purvis, M.A.: Mechanisms for Cooperative Behaviour in Agent Institution. In: Nishida, T., Klusch, M., Sycara, K., Yokoo, M., Liu, J., Wah, B., Cheung, W. (eds.) Proceedings of IEEE/WIC/ACM International Conference on Intelligent Agent Technology (IAT 2006), pp. 121–124. IEEE Press, Los Alamitos (2006) ISBN 0-7695-2748-5
7. Riolo, R.L., Cohen, M.D., Axelrod, R.: Cooperation without Reciprocity. Nature 414, 441–443 (2001)
8. Riolo, R.L.: The Effects of Tag-Mediated Selection of Partners in Evolving Populations Playing the Iterated Prisoner's Dilemma. Santa Fe Institute (1997)
9. Saroiu, S., Gummadi, P., Gribbe, S.: A measurement study of peer-to-peer file-sharing systems, Technical report UW-CSE-01-06002, University of Washington (2002)
10. Savarimuthu, S., Purvis, M.A., Purvis, M.K.: Altruistic Sharing using Tags. In: Proceedings of the 6th International Workshop on Agents and Peer-to-Peer Computing, Estoril, Portugal (2008)
11. Savarimuthu, S., Purvis, M.A., Purvis, M.K.: Emergence of Sharing Behavior in a Multi-agent Society using Tags. In: Proceedings of IEEE/WIC/ACM International Conference on Intelligent Agent Technology, Sydney, Australia, pp. 527–530 (2008)

12. Savarimuthu, S., Purvis, M., Purvis, M.: Tag-based model for knowledge sharing in agent society. In: Proceedings of the 8th International Conference on Autonomous Agents and Multiagent Systems, Budapest, Hungary, May 10-15, vol. 2 (2009); International Conference on Autonomous Agents. International Foundation for Autonomous Agents and Multiagent Systems, Richland, SC, pp. 1299–1300 (2009)
13. Self-organising groups (closed society), Video link on youtube,
    http://www.youtube.com/watch?v=a_3MOfeUy2Y
14. Rebecca, S.B.: Some Psychological Mechanisms Operative in Gossip. Social Forces 34(3), 262–267 (1956), http://www.jstor.org/stable/2574050
15. Thomsen, R.: The Origins of Ostracism, A Synthesis (Gyldendal: Copenhagen, 1972) (1972)

Multigame Dynamics: Structures and Strategies

David L. Sallach, Michael J. North, and Eric Tatara

Computation Institute, University of Chicago,
5735 South Ellis Avenue, Chicago, Illinois 60637, USA
{sallach,north}@uchicago.edu

Abstract. The dominant strategy among game theorists is to pose a problem narrowly, formalize that structure, and then pursue analytical solutions. This strategy has achieved a number of stylized insights, but has not produced nuanced game-theoretic solutions to larger and more complex issues such as extended international historical conflicts, or the detailed assessment of variegated policy alternatives. In order to model more complex historical and policy-oriented processes, it has been proposed that a broader computational approach to game theory that has the potential to capture richer forms of social dynamics be used, namely the 'multigame.' In the multigame approach there are multiple games each of which is open, prototypical, implicit, reciprocal, positional, variegated and historical. When later implemented, the multigame approach will offer the potential to rigorously model complex international historical conflicts and variegated policy alternatives that, heretofore, typically required qualitative analysis.

Keywords: Game theory, multigame, requirements, structures, strategies, roles.

1 Introduction

The dominant strategy among game theorists is to pose a problem narrowly, formalize that structure, and then pursue analytical solutions. This strategy has achieved a number of stylized insights, but has not produced nuanced game-theoretic solutions to larger and more complex issues such as extended international historical conflicts, or the detailed assessment of variegated policy alternatives. Nevertheless, game theory has supported a breadth of focus, from international strategies to economic interactions, that illustrates the potential of mathematical methods in the social sciences.

In order to model more complex historical and policy-oriented processes, a broader computational approach to game theory has been proposed which has the potential to capture richer forms of social dynamics, specifically, the 'multigame' model [1], [2]. This is not to say that narrower analytical solutions would or should not be pursued but, rather, that there is likely to be an extensive amount of contextual and situational definition before an adequately specified game could be formalized. However, such contextual and situational definition is necessary in its own right, and is an essential part of the game characterization for any particular problem.

T. Bosse, A. Geller, and C.M. Jonker (Eds.): MABS 2010, LNAI 6532, pp. 108–120, 2011.

2 Multigame Requirements

To achieve this larger role, multigames need to manifest a set of qualitative and interrelated characteristics. These requirements redefine both the nature of the game formalism, and the types of representation to which it may be applied.

2.1 Characteristics

Multigame models need to be: 1) multiple, 2) open, 3) prototypical, 4) implicit, 5) reciprocal, 6) positional, 7) variegated, and 8) historical. Each of these characteristics will be briefly described, including their contributions to the multigame framework.

Multiple Games. The defining characteristic of the broader multigame approach to game theory is that actors are permitted to play multiple games simultaneously. Communications and actions are often simultaneous moves in multiple concurrent games. This multiplicity means that the actor must take interactions among relevant games and players into account. Such considerations may include competing use of resources, and/or divergent objectives, expectations and actor answerabilities [3].

Actors may enter into a joint game which each actor, nonetheless, defines differently. An effective move in the most salient game may result in relative advantages or disadvantages in adjacent games and relationships. Accordingly, in the multigame environment, prioritization, tradeoffs and balance are necessary to shape player strategies that are both coherent and effective. The complexity of the resulting process suggests that, in many cases, the rationality of endogenous actors will be bounded rather than complete or perfect.

Agents engaged in game-based interaction cannot be seen as completely autonomous. Often they perform roles that are expressions of larger social and institutional structures. Associated with these roles are a variety of norms and expectations that are, themselves, created, maintained and evolved by a continuing flow of social interaction. Roles become defined within, and relative to, a wide range of structures, thereby providing a vital linkage between micro and macro social processes.

Open. Multigames are open-ended, in the sense that additional players can join games, current players can abandoned them, and new games can be initiated by current or prospective players. Moreover, the focus of a game can change as it evolves. Each of these characteristics makes formalization of the process more challenging, but also makes the representation more fluid and more consistent with the complexity of empirical games.

Prototypical. Turning to the nature of the games that actors play, the multigame paradigm defines three prototypical games: beneficent, instrumental[1] and coercive. Together, they define a broad range of available types of social games.

---

[1] This game type is sometimes called 'economic', but the characterization is overly narrow. There are other forms of instrumental trade-offs and negotiations, particularly in the political and military domains, that are also examples of instrumental (or interchangic) games.

Beneficent games involve a kind of mutual support that is seen in families and tribes, among neighbors, and within communities. They are organized around altruistic and voluntary actions. Types of support in beneficent games may vary, but accounting is not strict. The game tends to be mutually reinforcing over time, and a common dynamic is a virtuous spiral [4].

Instrumental games are familiar in political and economic forms. Prototypically, they involve arms-length transactions, with strict accounting, among actors with coupled dependencies. They involve complementary benefit and relative advantage and, like beneficent games, they are often self-reinforcing [5].

Coercive games involve the exchange, or threat, of force or violence. They are inherently adversarial, and prone to escalation. Reciprocity is frequently anticipatory, and actors tend to exaggerate comparative accounting toward their own priorities, resulting in a vicious spiral [6].

Multigames are prototypical in the sense that there is a conceptual core that defines the game type, while empirical games vary in their proximity to that core [7], [8]. For modeling purposes, these differences can be identified and dimensionalized. This form accommodates itself to the representation of an extensive variety of empirical games, including the emergence of calibrated strategies.

Each game prototype produces a resource for the successful actor that can accumulate over time. Beneficent games produce appreciation, respect and, ultimately, status. Instrumental games produce wealth or advantageous position. Coercive games produce power. In this regard, these outcomes correspond to the dimensions of social stratification first identified by Weber [9]: class, status and power, respectively. This mapping provides a clue as to how multigame patterns translate into persistent social structures [10], [11].

Implicit. Since game theory is designed for analytical and modeling purposes, rarely will endogenous social actors define their activities in game-theoretic terms. This is most clearly demonstrated by the historical reality of intensive social interaction long before the development of game theory. Accordingly, in a multigame paradigm, it will be unusual for agents to recognize games in fully articulated form. On the contrary, prospective games will usually present themselves in partial and implicit form (cf., [12]). Games thus take on fuller definition as they emerge, and their coevolution is a vital part of the multigame process. Actor responses to partially identified games is an essential aspect of multigame dynamics.

Reciprocal. For each game type, there is a reciprocal exchange type in which two actors engage in complementary interactions of the same type. Examples include friends exchanging small gifts, businesses exchanging material benefits, and military enemies exchanging armed forays. Because they are mutually reinforcing, they tend to persist [13].

It is also possible to have exchanges across game types. Examples include providing compensation for coercive resources or acts, using force to abduct children to rear, or providing home services in return for payment. Cross-game exchanges are also reciprocal, but may be subject to strains that arise from the admixture of motives. As such, they may be less stable and may exhibit a tendency to degenerate into complementary exchanges.

Both types of reciprocity are summarized in Table 1. Notice that the diagonal in Table 1 focuses on reciprocal exchanges of the same type, while non-diagonal cells represent exchanges across game types. To the extent that reciprocal game types are more stable than coupled games based solely on complementarity, there may be a tendency for off-diagonal games to collapse toward the diagonal.

Table 1. Reciprocal Multigames

	Beneficent	**Instrumental**	**Coercive**
Beneficent	Reciprocity of nurturance & support	Nurturant means of acquiring economic services	Nurturant means of acquiring coercive resources
Instrumental	Instrumental means of acquiring nurturant resources	Reciprocity of goods & services	Instrumental means of acquiring coercive resources
Coercive	Coercive means of acquiring nurturant resources	Coercive means of acquiring instrumental resources	Reciprocity of force & threat

Positional. Standard game theory usually defines payoffs on a single stylized dimension and then, where feasible, deduces optimal and/or probable outcomes. These focal payoffs arise from the narrow, formalized focus of the model. As described in the discussion of earlier characteristics, the multigame model is significantly more open and fluid. Technically, a multigame is not completed until all adversarial participants have withdrawn from the game (and no new replacements have joined or will join the game). As a result, outcomes are broader and less amenable to formalization. This requires the articulation of an alternate formalism.

One such alternate formalism is *positional* in nature [14]. Representing the possible positions within the game, their comparative advantages and disadvantages, and the constraints and affordances at each position, allows the state of the game to be assessed at each step. From each position, however assessed, new moves are possible.

For example, if an insurgent movement captures a capitol, the previous ruler(s) have the option of moving to a secure area and resuming the conflict. If a previous leader is captured or killed, the movement can select a replacement. If the disparity in resources is too great, partisans can go underground and operate covertly until open conflict becomes more feasible.

In positional multigames, as O'Brien [15] famously wrote, there are no final victories (but also no final defeats). Thus, if a *multigame* is typified [cf., 16], it will not have a distinguished final state. Rather, it will define the criteria relative to which the game is defined as completed, and defines a function to test the current state relative to those criteria. Consistent with this approach, there may be multiple sets of criteria that, when met, indicate the conclusion of the multigame in question, either in general, or for a specific actor.

As long as the game is active, positions of participants improve or deteriorate, but they remain a location from which relevant games can be furthered. Depending upon the forms of the relevant games, the relative strengths and weaknesses of the game(s) have the potential to be formally expressed. This approach makes the assessment process comparable to the one used by endogenous participants.

Variegated. There are discrete transitions in a multigame: an actor may live or die; a message may be received or lost; or an actor may have received a college degree or not. However, many aspects of the game are continuous in nature. Even in the examples previously described, the actor might also be wounded or otherwise disabled; parts of the message may have been received, or the entire message may arrive late; the student might be just six hours short of a degree, or have received a degree that is irrelevant to the situation at hand.

It is the mix of discrete and continuous choice and outcomes that contributes to the unique characteristics of the multigame. However, these mixtures introduce complexities beyond those found in a strictly discrete or strictly continuous game. Accordingly, multigames must be variegated, i.e., a mix, as appropriate, of binary, nominal, ordinal and quantitative types of data [17], [18]. This kind of data combination will require that operators associated with one or more data types will frequently need to be more sophisticated than those in common use today.

Historical. The characteristics of the multigame allow it to provide a much closer representation of historical settings and processes than does conventional game theory. Accordingly, the overall result is more relevant to historical interpretations and policy-oriented decisions.

While the described set of characteristics is applicable to the multigame paradigm, they do not automatically define distinct mechanisms. On the contrary, they operate together as a whole. While the net effect is likely to require richer, more complex mechanisms, the characteristics themselves are analytical in nature. They indicate diverse aspects of multigame models, but not *how* these aspects will be achieved.

2.2 Toward a Multidimensional Formalism

Games that address the characteristics described in the previous section are more expressive than conventional games. However, these advantages do not come without cost. Either the deductive efficacy of the game will be lost, or an analyzable formalism will need to be reconstructed. In fact, either alternative is possible. It is to these issues that the discussion now turns.

The Price of Expressiveness. Games cannot address the characteristics described in the previous section and still be investigated using tautly woven inferences. This capability is sacrificed to the complexities that allow the needed expressiveness.

Conventional game theory relies on certain simplifying assumptions. Preference functions to be applied, for example, must meet three requirements: 1) all alternatives are represented (completeness), 2) choices are consistently ordered (transitivity), and 3) omitted alternatives do not influence the ordering (independence) [19]. Multiple, open, historical processes do not observe these requirements and, therefore, appropriate modeling formalisms cannot avail themselves of these simplifications. Multigame modeling, in particular, does not rely upon these assumptions.

Integrated Multigame Space. The most straightforward way to represent multigame characteristics is to define an inclusive game space that captures and integrates the needed features. The space would include game types, game components, roles of those likely to play the game, a representative sample of the dimensions by which the game is constituted, as well as the value region within those dimensions that can be considered a prototype game of a specific kind.

3   Complex Multigames

To this point, multigames have been addressed as if the games in which a social actor participates are independent. However, multigames are often embedded, one within another. Some games dominate, and shape secondary, contributory games. Broad game structures can thereby be deeply intertwined. Roles, strategies and institutions can be defined in terms of, and dependent upon, many interlocking multigames. As a result, multigames may interlock across multiple scales.

In many important cases, multiple games are part of a coherent structure for each actor. To the extent that this is true, the emergent integral game is a skein of priorities, constraints, affordances and tradeoffs. In a war, for example, a state has coercive relations with adversaries, mutually supportive relations with allies (although with the potential of strains and tensions regarding the nature and extent of support), and a service/support relation with suppliers and trade partners. Each other party has a set of relations that are equally interwoven. The full assembly of multifaceted relations form a rich ecology, providing the backdrop against which all moves are played.

When the actors are large social institutions, populated by hundreds of actors, each with their own roles and strategies, issues of representation and analytical strategies must be addressed. Fine-grain representation will depend upon available data, but it will also be influenced by the level of analysis that is required.

In general, one of the key benefits of the multigame framework is the ability to represent games at various scales. To take advantage of this benefit, it is recommended that at least three levels be included in the model. An example would be a study of strategic interaction in which social institutions (such as the economy, religion and the state) provide focus, and the higher and lower levels (social systems and social movements, respectively) provide coarser and finer-grain contexts. This type of tripartite scaling can be applied at varying levels and, in each such case, the cross-tier focus allows for richer and more expressive dynamics.

In tracking emerging events, it may be necessary to identify, characterize, and follow finer-grain actors and actions. In visualization, this requirement can be envisioned as spikes downward from the focal levels, event spikes that may serve as inflection points that shape the direction of subsequent development.

4   Strategies and Roles

4.1   Strategies

The prototype games identified in Section 2 can be pursued using different types of strategies. Johnston [20] introduces an ideal type with three types of strategy, each manifesting varying assertiveness. Table 2a shows the forms these strategies would take when applied to the different prototype games.

Table 2a. Reciprocal Multigames by Strategy

	Compliant (soft)	**Defensive** (firm)	**Aggressive** (hard)
Beneficent	Unrestrained support, give freely without expectation of return	Attend to timing and adequacy of response, be prepared to diminish the level of reciprocity	Withdraw cooperation, shun
Instrumental	Relax competition, share opportunities, be tolerant of slow or incomplete responses	Compete, expect value-for-value, negotiate binding contracts	Demand hard bargains, seek to drive rival from the field
Coercive	Show respect for adversary, allow truces, permit conflict to subside	Return blow-for-blow, assess threats and prepare for possible attacks	Destroy enemy, amplify threats, attack without provocation, invent reasons to confront

Table 2a illustrates that a game of a particular type can be played using different strategies, ranging from compliant to aggressive[2]. This diversity of strategies is applicable to different game types, although what each strategic level means will differ, depending on the game type. Taking strategy into account means that an actor will have expectations, not only of what game types are being played but, also, what strategy is being used.

In the long run, it may be expected that reciprocities of game and strategy will be more stable and, thus, more common, than various types of asymmetries. However, since some of these patterns will be persistently path dependent, or context sensitive, reciprocal symmetries may be slow to emerge.

4.2 Roles and Relationships

Actor orientation will also be influenced by the roles that other players are perceived to play. Indeed, roles such as 'friend', 'enemy' and 'competitor' are commonly used by actors in determining the type of orientation that is appropriate. This pattern is described in Table 2b, the contents of which are similar to 2a.

As shown in Table 2b, affiliative relationships are characterized by compliant or soft strategies that tend to move overall the interchange towards the beneficent form. Thus we see attempts to relax the strict accounting arise in instrumental games, and de-escalation of tensions in coercive games.

Similarly, rival relationships shown in Table 2b tend to move off-diagonal games into on-diagonal economic forms characterized by defensive or firm actions. In this case we see the introduction of accounting into beneficent games and the limiting of positive amplification in feedback loops. We also see rivals attempting to calibrate their reprisals to match, but not exceed, the perceived intensity of previous attacks as well as defensive preparations, but not preemptive attacks.

---

[2] For clarity of discussion, strategies are divided into three types. However, the values ranging from extremely compliant to extremely aggressive are best understood as a continuum, and are implemented that way in strategic models.

Table 2b. Multigames by Role

	Affiliate (ally)	**Rival** (competitor)	**Adversary** (enemy)
Beneficent	Unrestrained support, give freely without expectation of return	Attend to timing and adequacy of response, be prepared to diminish the level of reciprocity	Withdraw cooperation, shun
Instrumental	Relax competition, share opportunities, be tolerant of slow or incomplete responses	Compete, expect value-for-value, negotiate binding contracts	Demand hard bargains, seek to drive rival from the field
Coercive	Show respect for adversary, allow truces, permit conflict to subside	Return blow-for-blow, assess threats and prepare for possible attacks	Destroy enemy, amplify threats, attack without provocation, invent reasons to confront

The adversarial relationships in Table 2b are shown to be aggressive or hard. They tend to create or intensify negative feedback loops. Beneficent games are undermined by failures to reciprocate, thus increasing the likelihood of inciting grievances in the other players. Instrumental games are also destabilized by reductions in reciprocity than are likely to threaten other players and cause them to stop seeing interchanges as economically valuable.

Parallel Effects. The reader will, of course, note that the descriptive cells in Table 2a and 2b are identical. This pattern suggests another potential source of efficiency in this representation. The fact that two sources, actor strategy and attributed role, can have similar effects, suggests that each may be defined along the same underlying dimension, and should be represented as such.

If the two effects pull in the same direction, the two sources may be expected to jointly deepen the overall effect. Alternatively, to the extent that their effects act in opposite directions, the strength of each will be attenuated. Such a pattern suggests a valuable insight into how multigames aggregate, one that is likely to be analytically useful.

If (and to the extent that) actors' role expectations are inconsistent with the players' actions, the actor in question may find it necessary to use a different label to shift them in semantic space. This type of relabeling is extensively considered in ACT theory [21]. The latter is definitely relevant to multigame dynamics, but is beyond the scope of the present discussion.

4.3   Illustrations of Multigame Interaction

Generic Example. A sample application of these ideas could consider two allied nations with dramatically different resource bases and a powerful common enemy. The allied nations may initially have an instrumental relationship characterized by economic trading with strict accounting. Simultaneously one of the allied nations may have a hard coercive relationship with the common enemy in the form of an active war. The other ally may have a reciprocal instrumental relationship with the common enemy that is slowly deteriorating due to increasing frequency of coercive interactions. As the war proceeds and the allied states weaken, they may shift to a moderately beneficent relationship characterized by soft interactions such as Lend-Lease style arrangements. If the struggle against the enemy turns around and the allies are victorious, the allies may normalize their relationship and return to an instrumental game of mutual economic trade. They may also form a new instrumental game with the now defeated adversary. This fluid flow between games shows the openness of the multigame approach.

Throughout the example, there is continual interplay between multiple simultaneous games. For example, before deciding to offer Lend-Lease arrangements the initially non-combative ally must consider not only the status of the instrumental game with their ally but also the implications of such an action for their separate but interrelated instrumental game with the powerful common enemy.

In this example, we can also see the importance of prototype reasoning. As described above, the Lend-Lease arrangement can be understood as a weakly beneficent act. However, it can also be understood, and publicly portrayed, as a weakly economic (instrumental) act and thus not a formal inducement for the enemy to declare war on the initially non-combative ally. The arrangement may, nonetheless, ultimately become part of a formal declaration of war. Of course, the Lend-Lease arrangement is both beneficent and instrumental, simultaneously. The resulting Lend-Lease game is thus well represented by a prototype concept that lies somewhere between the beneficent and instrumental game prototypes.

We also see the importance of implicitness in multigames in the way the players can further their interests by taking strategic advantage of the ambiguity in the definition of the game itself. Also, the variegated nature of multigames with discrete categories (e.g., formally declared enemy versus treaty ally) and continuous categories (e.g., a Lend-Lease arrangement that is at once both beneficent and instrumental) intermingling at the levels of both strategic thinking (e.g., sharing productive capacity) and discourse (e.g., public speeches on the imperative of abandoning accounting and lending a neighbor a garden hose when they have an unexpected house fire).

The example game is positional because the overall multigame never really ends, and no ultimate winner can be declared. All that occurs is continual fluid flow between games, with some games ending, new games beginning, and old games being revisited. In the example, we see a flow between several coercive games (e.g., two-party war and then three-party war) and interchanging games (e.g., two-party economic trade that later becomes three-party trade). However, none of this fluidity and open-endedness obviates the outcome and impact of specific games. Winning a major war really is different than losing!

Historical Example. The case of the Lend-Lease policies and practices during World War II allows more in-depth consideration of how multigames may manifest themselves on a global stage. Figure 1 shows several alternate routes by which lend-lease supplies might be conveyed. Route selection would be based on distance, cost and availability of transportation modes, the risks of interception and seizure during a specific time frame, etc.

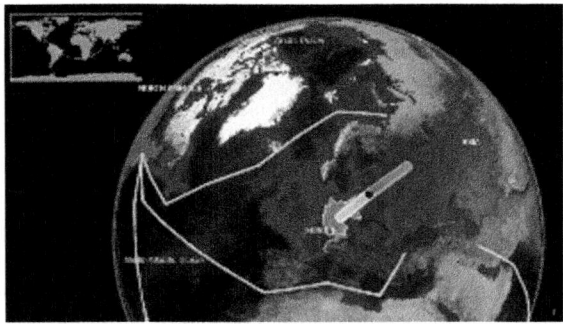

Fig. 1. Alternate Lend-Lease Routes

However, in any actual case, it will also be necessary to assess how committed or enthusiastic the donor nation is, and this will be relative to alternate uses of resources. Donor assessments may hinge on historic and/or cultural ties between the nations (or their lack), their alignment by regime type or policy, the potential for military coordination including the amount of trust that such cooperation is likely, and other related considerations [24, 25]. Specific model configurations and parameters may, of course, vary.

Table 3. Affect among Nations, 1941-1944

Duration	Unit of Analysis	Affect Toward
194105, 194105	nation	US, USSR, Germany
		{nil,nil},{-0.6,-0.75},{-0.75,-0.85}
		{-0.75,-0.75},{nil,nil},{0.75,-0.75}
		{-0.75,-0.75},{0.75,-0.9},{nil,nil}
194106, 194110	nation	US, USSR, Germany
		{nil,nil},{-0.3,-0.6},{-0.75,-0.85}
		{0.3,-0.5},{nil,nil},{-0.9,-0.9}
		{-0.75,-0.8},{-0.75,-0.9},{nil,nil}
194111, 194405	nation	US, USSR, Germany
		{nil,nil},{0.3,0.0},{-0.75,-0.85}
		{0.4,-0.4},{nil,nil},{-0.9,-0.9}
		{-0.75,-0.85},{-0.75,-0.9},{nil,nil}

If we consider lend-lease support to an outcome of game interaction, Table 3 shows how shifts in the ecology of active games can result in shifts in strategies. Assuming a monthly timestep, the first column indicates the duration of a specific pattern of play[3]. The second column indicates the scale of the actors. Multigames are designed to support the interaction of actors at multiple levels. An actor might be a faction, movement, nation, or alliance, among others, with actors at different scales having the capability of influencing each other.

---

[3] If the two numbers are identical, a point is indicated rather than duration.

The third column of Table 3 shows the particular actors included in the model, and their public solidarity versus private affect toward each other[4]. When private affect sharply contradicts public solidarity, it is a source of strategic instability. The data is designed to illustrate this, using a specific historical case.

Prior to the German invasion of Russia, both states display high solidarity toward the other but, at the same time, harbor deep antagonism. After the invasion, the solidarity and affect of both nations is more closely aligned. This indicates that the apparent beneficent games of early 1941 were instrumental at best, and part of the larger coercive game in which each was engaged.

Meanwhile, the solidarity and affect of the US toward the other two nations changes from being essentially equivalent to be significantly more positive toward the USSR (which is now an ally). However, there remains a discrepancy, insofar as the US shows a modest solidarity toward the USSR, while retaining tacit caution[5].

This historical example is suggestive rather than definitive. However, it does suggest how multigame dynamics can be coupled with history as a means of creating more richly textured models.

5   Conclusion

Multigame models have been developed in order to address social complexities. The particular objective of multigame modeling is to bring some of the strengths of game theory to more complex social domains such as historical interpretation and policy-oriented decisions. More specifically, they are designed to model historical discourse and policy-oriented decisions from both an exogenous and endogenous perspective. The present paper has addressed the characteristics a multigame requires, their implications for multigame formalisms and structures, and how strategic orientations and player roles translate into particular game types.

Multigame models are rooted in social theory. While this makes them somewhat abstract, it also provides the correlative virtue that they can be applied to a wide range of scenarios and situations. In particular, while narrower or more rigid modeling strategies will tend to make artificial assumptions, or otherwise distort the complex patterns found in historical cases, multigame dynamics can represent idiosyncrasies within a strategically compelling framework.

While multigames will necessarily be integrated with other social modeling techniques, most obviously social agent modeling and simulation (SAMS) [22, 23], the broader contribution will be to help advance social modeling as an enterprise. The ultimate benefit of multigame analysis will be in the ability to identify higher level interaction patterns among strategic actors.

This work extends and deepens the multigame concept, illustrating how it might be applied, and the analytical advantages of doing so. The authors hope this discussion clarifies that the multigame approach offers the potential to rigorously model complex

---

[4] The present model does not include self-solidarity or self-affect, although future models may.

[5] The public and private orientations of these nations might be assessed differently by different historians and subject matter experts. This summary is not intended to be definitive but, rather, illustrative about how multigame simulation may represent motives, intent and affect.

international historical conflicts and variegated policy alternatives that, heretofore, typically required qualitative analysis. The next steps in this research program, aspects of which are currently under way, are to design and develop a computational implementation of the multigame approach, and then to apply it to specific historical scenarios and policy issues.

Acknowledgments. Argonne National Laboratory, a US Department of Energy Office of Science laboratory, is operated by The University of Chicago under contract W-31-109-Eng-38. The authors gratefully acknowledge support for this project from the Office of Naval Research, Award No. N00014-09-1-0766.

References

1. Sallach, D.L.: Complex multigames: Toward an ecology of information artifacts. In: Sallach, D.L., Macal, C.M., North, M.J. (eds.) Proceedings of the Agent 2006 Conference on Social Agents: Results and Prospects, pp. 185–190. Argonne National Laboratory, Chicago (2006)
2. Sallach, D.L.: Interpretive agents and discourse-oriented games. In: Fourth Joint Japan-North America Mathematical Sociology Conference, Redondo Beach, CA (2008)
3. Kenny, R.W.: The good, the bad and the social: On living as an answerable agent. Sociological Theory 25, 268–291 (2007)
4. Carse, J.P.: Finite and Infinite Games. Ballantine, New York (1986)
5. Osborne, M.J., Rubinstein, A.: Bargaining and Markets. Academic Press, San Diego (1990)
6. Rummel, R.J.: Understanding Conflict and War: The Conflict Helix. John Wiley & Sons, New York (1976)
7. Rosch, E.: Principles of categorization. In: Rosch, E., Lloyd, B.B. (eds.) Cognition and Categorization, pp. 27–48. Lawrence Erlbaum, Hillsdale (1978)
8. Rosch, E.: Prototype classification and logical classification. In: Scholnick, E.K. (ed.) New Trends in Conceptual Representation: Challenges to Piaget's Theory?, pp. 73–86 Lawrence Erlbaum, Hillsdale (1983)
9. Weber, M.: Economy and Society: An Outline of Interpretive Sociology. Translated by G. Roth and C. Wittich. University of California Press, Berkeley (1978)
10. Bendix, R., Lipset, S.M. (eds.): Class, Status and Power: Social Stratification in Comparative Perspective. Free Press, New York (1966)
11. Kemper, T.D., Collins, R.: Dimensions of microinteraction. American Journal of Sociology 96, 32–68 (1990)
12. Sallach, D.L.: Games social agents play: A complex form. In: Joint Conference on Mathematical Sociology in Japan and America, Honolulu (2000)
13. Moody, M.: Serial reciprocity: A preliminary statement. Sociological Theory 26, 130–151 (2008)
14. Hajek, O.: Pursuit Games: An Introduction to the Theory and Applications of Differential Games of Pursuit and Evasion. Dover Publications, Mineola (1975)
15. O'Brien, L.F.: No Final Victories: A Life In Politics From John F. Kennedy to Watergate. Doubleday & Company, New York (1974)
16. Craig Cleaveland, J.: An Introduction to Data Types, pp. 144–152. Addison-Wesley, Reading
17. Sallach, D.L.: Comparing objects composed by abstract relationships. In: Proceedings of the ACM Hawaii International Conference on the System Sciences, Kailua Kona, HI, vol. III, pp. 89–93 (1989)

18. Sallach, D.L.: Logic for situated action. In: Takahashi, S., Sallach, D., Rouchier, J. (eds.) Advancing Social Simulation: The First World Congress, pp. 13–21. Springer, Tokyo (2007)

19. Gintis, H.: Game Theory Evolving: A Problem Centered Introduction to Modeling Strategic Interaction, pp. 18–31. Princeton University Press, Princeton (2009)

20. Johnston, A.I.: Cultural Realism: Strategic Culture and Grand Strategy in Chinese History, pp. 109–117. Princeton University Press, Princeton (1995)

21. Heise, D.R.: Expressive Order: Confirming Sentiments in Social Actions. Springer, New York (2006)

22. Sallach, D.L.: Social theory and agent architectures: Prospective issues in rapid-discovery social science. Social Science Computer Review 21, 179–195 (2003)

23. North, M.J., Macal, C.M.: Managing Business Complexity: Discovering Strategic Solutions with Agent-Based Modeling and Simulation. Oxford University Press, New York (2007)

24. Herring Jr., G.C.: Lend-lease to Russia and the origins of the Cold War. Journal of American History 56, 93–114 (1944-1945)

25. Munting, R.: Lend-lease and the Soviet war effort. Journal of Contemporary History 19, 495–510 (1984)

26. Sallach, D.L.: Modeling emotional dynamics: Currency versus field. Rationality and Society 20, 343–365 (2008)

Microstructure Dynamics and Agent-Based Financial Markets

Shu-Heng Chen[1], Michael Kampouridis[2], and Edward Tsang[2]

[1] AI-ECON Research Center, Department of Economics,
National Chengchi University, Taiwan
chen.shuheng@gmail.com
[2] School of Computer Science and Electronic Engineering, University of Essex, UK
mkampo@essex.ac.uk, edward@essex.ac.uk

Abstract. One of the essential features of the agent-based financial models is to show how price dynamics is affected by the evolving microstructure. Empirical work on this microstructure dynamics is, however, built upon highly simplified and unrealistic behavioral models of financial agents. Using genetic programming as a rule-inference engine and self-organizing maps as a clustering machine, we are able to reconstruct the possible underlying microstructure dynamics corresponding to the underlying asset. In light of the agent-based financial models, we further examine the microstructure both in terms of its short-term dynamics and long-term distribution. The time series of the TAIEX is employed as an illustration of the implementation of the idea.

1 Introduction and Main Ideas

It comes as no surprise to economists that there is no single strategy which can persistenly dominate all other strategies in the market. The idea of the best strategy is simply inconsistent with the intuitive notion of the efficient market hypothesis. While this feature is well expected among economists, the result shown by [7], generally known as the *overreaction hypothesis*, is still very appealing. They have found that successive portfolios formed by the previous five years' 50 most extreme winners considerably underperform the market average, while portfolios of the previous five years' 50 worst losers perform better than the market average[1].

Recently, a similar phenomenon has been rigorously analyzed and replicated in the agent-based finance literature, in particular, in the *H*-type model. In this literature, markets at any point in time are composed of different clusters (types) of agents. Agents who follow similar rules are considered to be in the same cluster. Each cluster is defined by the associated behavioral rules. The market microstructure is characterized by the *fractions* (distribution) of individuals over different clusters. Different distributions (microstructure) over the clusters may

---

[1] The overreaction hypothesis has been extensively examined in the finance literature. For a survey, see [10].

T. Bosse, A. Geller, and C.M. Jonker (Eds.): MABS 2010, LNAI 6532, pp. 121–135, 2011.
© Springer-Verlag Berlin Heidelberg 2011

have different impacts on the aggregates, and both the microstructure and the aggregates are evolving with feedbacks to each other.

Complex dynamic analysis of these models indicates two interesting properties. First, in the short run, it is *likely* that the market fractions are constantly changing. In particular, for each cluster, the market fraction can swing from very low to very high, i.e., switching between the majority and the minority. Second, in the long run, no single strategy can dominate the other, i.e., the market fraction converges to $1/H$ for each cluster. These two properties provide us with a basis to study the complex dynamics of microstructure, which we refer to together as the *market fraction hypothesis*, or as an abbreviation, the MFH. In fact, a number of empirical studies have already attempted to estimate the parameters associated with the MFH [5].

This paper, however, differs from the H-type models in two regards. First, we do not assume any prefixed behavioral rule (functional form) for any cluster (type) of agents; second, we do not assume that agents of the same type are homogeneous, while they can be *similar*. We consider that this departure will lead us to a more general and *realistic implication* of the MFH. Consider the three-type model as an example. In the fundamentalist-chartist-contrarian model, traders of the same type at any point in time behave in *exactly the same way*, and their functional forms of behavioral rules, in this case, their forecasts of the price in the next period, $\{E_{f,t}(p_{t+1})\}$, $\{E_{c,t}(p_{t+1})\}$ and $\{E_{co,t}(p_{t+1})\}$, are all known. Equations (1) to (3) are typical examples.

$$E_{f,t}[p_{t+1}] = p_t + \alpha_f(p_t^f - p_t), \quad 0 \leq \alpha_f \leq 1, \tag{1}$$

$$E_{c,t}(p_{t+1}) = p_t + \alpha_c(p_t - p_{t-1}), \quad 0 \leq \alpha_c. \tag{2}$$

$$E_{co,t}(p_{t+1}) = p_t + \alpha_{co}(p_t - p_{t-1}), \quad \alpha_{co} \leq 0. \tag{3}$$

Nevertheless, in the real world, the behavioral rules of each trader are expected to be heterogeneous, and even if they can be clustered into types, the representative behavior of each type is normally unknown[2].

1.1   Genetic Programming as a Rule-Inference Engine

In this paper, we assume that traders' behavior, including price expectations and trading strategies, is either not observable or not available. Instead, their behavioral rules have to be *estimated* by the observable market price. Using macro data to estimate micro behavior is not new as many H-type empirical agent-based models have already performed such estimations [5]. However, as mentioned above, such estimations are based on very strict assumptions upon which a formal econometric model can be built. Since we no longer keep these assumptions, an alternative must be developed, and in this paper we recommend *genetic programming* (GP).

---

[2] While the ideas of fundamentalists and chartists are the results of field work, abstracting the general observed behavior into a very specific mathematical model is a big leap.

The use of GP as an alternative is motivated by considering the market as an evolutionary and selective process[3]. In this process, traders with different behavioral rules participate to the markets. Those behavioral rules which help traders gain lucrative profits will attract more traders to *imitate*, and rules which result in losses will attract fewer traders[4]. This evolutionary argument in fact is, intuitively, the same as the evolution process considered by the H-type agent-based financial models. For example, their use of the Gibbs-Boltzman distribution is a formalization of this process. Genetic programming is another formalization which, unlike the former, does not rest upon any pre-specified class of behavioral rules. Instead, in GP, a population of behavioral rules is randomly initiated, and the survival-of-the-fittest principle drives the entire population to become fitter and fitter in relation to the environment. In other words, given the non-trivial financial incentive from trading, traders are aggressively searching for the most profitable trading rules. Therefore, the rules that are outperformed will be replaced, and only those very competitive rules will be sustained in this highly competitive search process[5].

Hence, even though we are not informed of the behavioral rules followed by traders at any specific time horizon, GP can help us infer what these rules are *approximately* by simulating the evolution of the microstructure of the market. Without imposing tight restrictions on the inferred behavioral rules, GP enables us to go beyond the simple but also unrealistic behavioral rules used in the H-type agent-based financial models. Traders can then be clustered based on more realistic, and possibly more complex behavioral rules[6].

1.2 Self-organizing Maps as a Clustering Machine

Once a population of rules is inferred from GP, it is desirable to cluster them based on a chosen similarity criterion so as to provide a concise representation of the microstructure. The similarity criterion which we choose is based on the *observed trading behavior*. Based on this criterion, two rules are similar if they are *observationally equivalent* or *similar*, or, alternatively put, they are similar if they generate the same or similar market timing behavior.

Given the criterion above, the behavior of each trading rule can be represented by its series of market timing decisions over the entire trading horizon,

---

[3] See [18] for his eloquent presentation of the *adaptive market hypothesis*.

[4] One may wonder how traders can imitate each others' rules by having a sample of behavior but not the rules underlying it. This question has been addressed in [4], where they proposed a mechanism called *business school* to show how the seemingly unobservable rules can be imitated.

[5] It does not necessarily mean that the types of traders surviving must be smart and sophisticated. They can be dumb, naive, randomly behaved or zero-intelligent. Obviously, the notion of rationality or bounded rationality applying here is *ecological* [21,11].

[6] [9] provides the first illustration of using genetic programming to infer the behavioral rules of human agents in the context of ultimatum game experiments. Similarly, [12] uses genetic algorithms to infer behavioral rules of agents from market data.

for example, 6 months. Therefore, if we denote the decision "enter the market" by "1" and "leave the market" by "0", then the behavior of each rule is a binary string or a binary vector. The length of these strings or the dimensionality of the vectors is then determined by the length of the trading horizon. For example, if the trading horizon is 125 days long, then the dimension of the market timing vector is 125. Once each trading rule is concretized into its market timing vector, we can then easily cluster these rules by applying Kohonen's *self-organizing maps* (SOMs) [15] to the associated clusters.

The main advantage of SOMs over other clustering techniques such as K-means is that the former can present the result in a *visualizable* manner so that we can not only identify these types of traders but also locate their 2-dimensional position on a map, i.e., a distribution of traders over a map. Furthermore, if we suppose that we do not have dramatic crustal plate movement so that the map is fixed over time, then the distribution of traders over the map can, in effect, be comparable over time. This provides us with a rather convenient grasp of the dynamics of the microstructure directly as if we were watching the population density on a map over time.

However, the assumption of crustal stability does not hold in general; therefore, *maps over time are not directly comparable.* To make them comparable, some adjustments are needed. The idea of adjustment is also very intuitive. If the dominant strategy remains unchanged from period A to period B, then when we apply the dominant trading strategy derived from period A to another period B, the strategies should behave in a way that is similar to the dominant strategy derived from period B, if it is not exactly the same. This motivates us to *emigrate* all trading strategies from one map (the home map) to the other (the host map) in such a way that each emigrant shall find its new cluster on the host map based on the same similarity metric. In this manner, we can reconstruct a time-invariant version of the map, and comparison can be made upon this reconstruction.

The rest of the paper is organized as follows. Section 2 provides a brief description of the version of genetic programming used in this paper. Section 3 demonstrates the self-organizing map constructed based on the description in Section 1.2. A time series of these maps is constructed accordingly and the maps are then analyzed both in their short-term dynamic behavior (Section 3.1) and long-term distribution behavior (Section 3.2). The analysis is further consolidated with the results from multiple runs (Section 3.3). Section 4 examines the short-term dynamics and long-term distribution behavior of a rather small self-organizing map. In Section 5, we present our concluding remarks.

2   Genetic Programming

In this paper, we use the financial GP system introduced by Edward Tsang at University of Essex, known as Eddie. Eddie, standing for Evolutionary Dynamic Data Investment Evaluator, applies genetic programming to evolve a population of artificial financial advisors or, alternatively, a population of market-timing

<Tree> ::= If-then-else <Condition> <Tree> <Tree> | Decision
<Condition> ::= <Condition> "And" <Condition> |
                <Condition> "Or" <Condition> |
                "Not" <Condition> |
                VarConstructor <RelationOperation> Threshold
<Variable> ::= MA_12 | MA_50 | TBR_12 | TBR_50 | FLR_12 |
             FLR_50 | Vol_12 | Vol_50 | Mom_12 | Mom_50 |
             MomMA_12 | MomMA_50
<RelationOperation> ::= ">" | "<" | "="
Decision is an integer, Positive or Negative implemented
Threshold is a real number

Fig. 1. The Backus Normal Form of EDDIE

strategies, which guide investors on when to buy, to hold, or to sell. These artificial financial agents (market timing strategies) are formulated as decision trees in Eddie, which, when combined with the use of GP, are referred to as *Genetic Decision Trees* (GDTs).

Each of these market-timing strategies (GDTs) is syntactically (grammatically) produced by the Backus Normal Form (BNF) [3]. Figure 1 presents the Backus Normal Form (BNF) of the GP. As we can see, the root of the tree is an If-Then-Else statement. Then the first branch is a boolean (testing whether a technical indicator is greater than/less than/equal to a value). The 'Then' and 'Else' branches can be a new Genetic Decision Tree (GDT), or a decision, to buy or not-to-buy (denoted by 1 and 0).

What is also shown in Figure 1 is a list of major terminals (technical indicators) used for growing our GDTs. These terminals are moving average (MA), trade break-out rule (TBR), filter (FLR), volatility (Vol), momentum (Mom), momentum moving average (MomMA). The GDTs generated from these terminals under the BNF are very similar to those generated in [1,6,19]. Also see Figure 2 below.

The fitness function used to evolve GP is mainly built upon the confusion matrix [20], which is presented in Table 1. Each point in time, each GDT makes a recommendation to buy (positive prediction) or not to buy (negative prediction). We call a decision (prediction) to buy *true positive* if it leads to a positive profit, and *false positive* if it leads to a negative profit. Similarly, a decision not to buy is called *true negative* if it helps to avoid a negative profit and is called *false negative* if it causes investor to miss a profitable opportunity.

Table 1. Confusion Matrix

	Actual Positive	Actual Negative
Positive Prediction	True Positive (TP)	False Positive (FP)
Negative Prediction	False Negative (FN)	True Negative (TN)

With this matrix, we can develop the following three metrics:

Rate of Correctness
$$RC = \frac{TP + TN}{TP + TN + FP + FN} \quad (4)$$

Rate of Missing Chances
$$RMC = \frac{FN}{FN + TP} \quad (5)$$

Rate of Failure
$$RF = \frac{FP}{FP + TP} \quad (6)$$

Li [17] combined the above metrics and defined the following fitness function:

$$ff = w_1 * RC - w_2 * RMC - w_3 * RF \quad (7)$$

where w_1, w_2 and w_3 are the weights for RC, RMC and RF respectively. These weights are given in order to reflect the preferences of investors. For instance, a conservative investor would want to avoid failure; thus a higher weight for RF should be used. However, tuning these parameters does not seem to affect the performance of the GP [17]. For our experiments we chose to include strategies that mainly focus on correctness and reduced failure. Thus these weights have been set to 1, 1/6 and 1/2 respectively.

Table 2 presents other GP parameters for our experiments. The GP parameters for our experiments are the ones used by Koza [16]. Only the tournament size has been changed (lowered), and the reason for that was because we were observing premature convergence. Other than that, the results seem to be insensitive to these parameters.

Table 2. Tableau of GP Control Parameters

GP Parameters

Max Initial Depth	6
Max Depth	17
Generations	50
Population size	500
Tournament size	2
Reproduction probability	0.1
Crossover probability	0.9
Mutation probability	0.01
$\{w_1, w_2, w_3\}$	$\{1, 1/6, 1/2\}$

Given the fitness function above and a set of historical data, GP is then applied to evolve these market-timing strategies in a standard way. After evolving a number of generations, what stands (survives) at the end (the last generation)

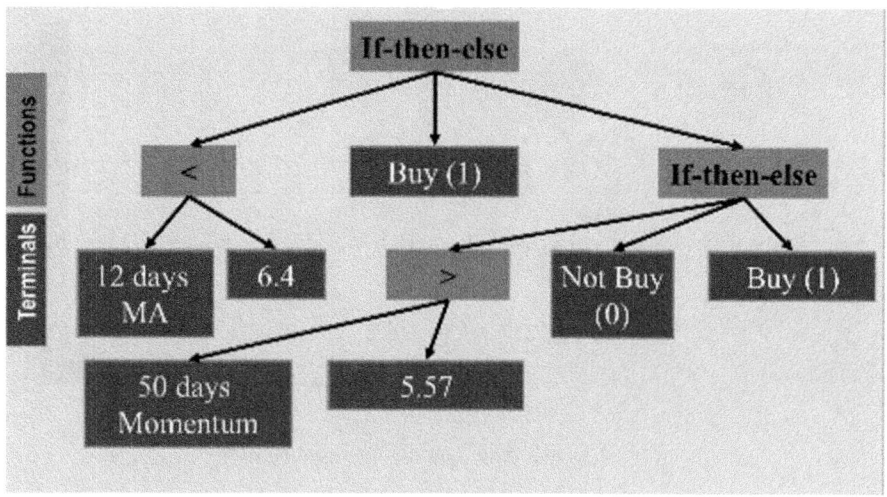

Fig. 2. An Example of Genetic Decision Trees

is, presumably, a population of financial agents whose market-timing strategies are financially rather successful. An example of one best fitted GDT is given in Figure 2.

3   An Illustration from the Taiwan Stock Market

Figure 3 gives a concrete illustration of the idea presented above (Sections 1.1 and 1.2). Here, 500 artificial traders are grouped into *nine* clusters. The parameter value '500' refers to the *population size* used in genetic programming, i.e., the rule-inference stage, whereas the parameter value '9' is due to a 3×3 two-dimensional SOM employed in the rule clustering stage. In a sense, this could be perceived as a snapshot of a nine-type agent-based financial market dynamics. Traders of the same type indicate that their market timing behavior is very similar. The market fraction or the size of each cluster can be seen from the number of traders belonging to that cluster. Not surprisingly, they are not evenly distributed. Figure 3 shows that the largest cluster has a market share of 37.6% (188/500), whereas the smallest cluster has a market share of only 0.4% (2/500).

Once we can have a snapshot of the market fraction, we can go further over a series of snapshots so as to have a picture of the dynamics of the market fraction or the dynamics of the market microstructure. However, as we mentioned before, the SOMs constructed from different periods are not directly comparable; therefore, to make them all comparable, we have to first choose a base period and fix the map, i.e., to take the centroid of each cluster as given. In this particular example, we choose the second half of the year 2007 as the base. Once the centroids are given, all points (vectors) in other maps shall *immigrate* into this

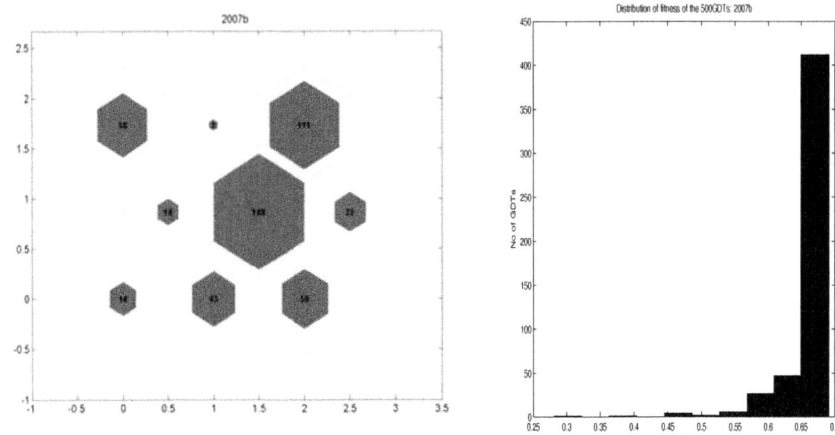

Fig. 3. 3×3 Self-Organizing Feature Map

The left panel shows the SOM constructed based on the 500 financial decision trees generated by GP using the daily data of the TAIEX from July 2007 to December 2007. The right panel gives the associated histogram of the fitness of these 500 GDTs.

fixed map, and they are re-clustered based on their similarity to these fixed centroids. Figure 4 shows the reconstruction of these maps in this manner.

This figure has the *market fraction maps* from the year 2006 to the year 2007, crossing 4 different periods[7]. These maps were constructed by using the second half of 2007 as the base period. This figure gives a clear picture of what we mean by *market fraction dynamics*. First of all, we notice that the distribution over the clusters is uneven over time. In each period of time, some clusters obviously dominate others, but that dominance changes over time. This can be seen from the constant renewing of the major blocks. This eye-browsing inspection motivates us to formulate two hypotheses which we already experienced from the dynamics of H-type agent-based financial models.

3.1   Short-Term Dynamics

The first hypothesis regards the *short-run dynamics of market fraction*. Each type of trader can be a dominant group (majority) for some of the time, but the duration of its dominance can only be temporal. The quick turnover of the dominant cluster or its short duration is consistent with the impression of the *swinging dynamics* as we saw in the 2-type agent-based financial models, e.g., [14]. However, in addition to eye-browsing the swing, it is desirable to have an objective measure of *how persistent a dominant cluster can be*. To do so, we need an operational meaning of dominance. Even though there is no unique way of doing this, we find the following threshold to be quite general and useful.

---

[7] We, of course, have a total of 34 maps from the year 1991 to the year 2007, and it is impossible to show them all.

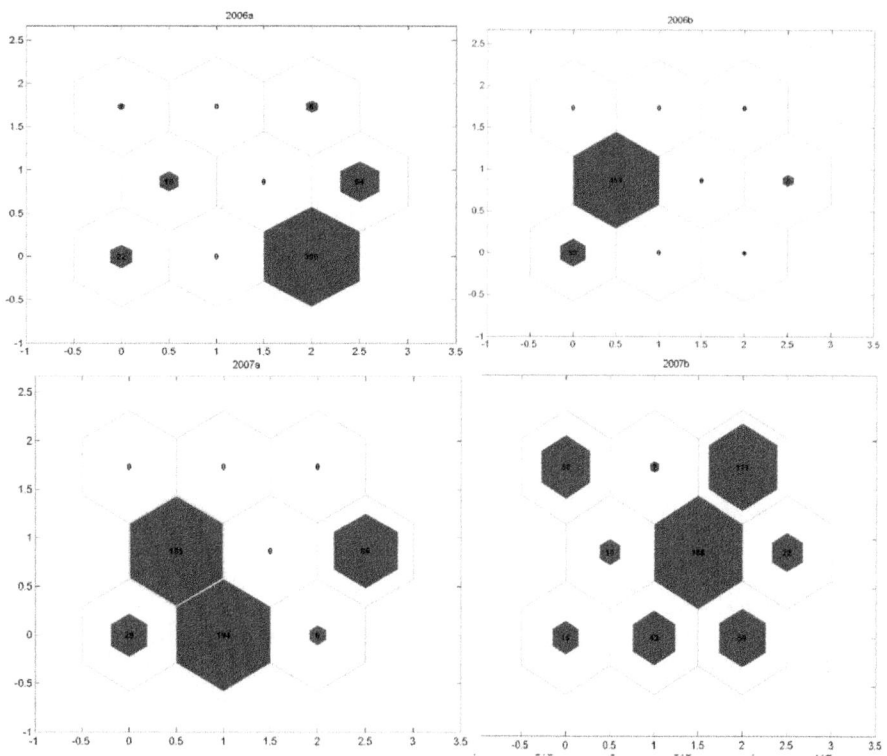

Fig. 4. Market Fraction Dynamics: Map Dynamics

The four SOMs above are constructed using the daily data of the TAIEX from 2006 to 2007. From the top-left panel to the bottom-right panel, they correspond to the first half and seconf half of year 2006 (2006a, b) and the first half and second half of the year 2007 (2007a, b). Except for the last one, 2007b, the other three are reconstructed by using 2007b as the base (see Section 1.2).

$$\bar{q} = \frac{1+p}{H+p}, \tag{8}$$

where H is the number of clusters, and p, a non-negative integer, is a control parameter for the *degree of dominance*. Hence, a cluster is dominant if its market fraction exceeds this threshold. By varying the parameter p, one can therefore have an operational meaning that is consistent with our intuition regarding dominance. For example, if $H = 2$ (a two-type model) and $p = 2$, a cluster can be dominant only if its market fraction is greater than a $\bar{q}$ of 75%, a standard much higher than just breaking the tie (one half). Of course, the higher the p, the higher the threshold.

Figure 5 presents the *dominance-duration statistics* of each type of trader. Basically, we keep track of the persistent time of each dominance. Once after a type of trader become dominant, we count how many periods in a row that it

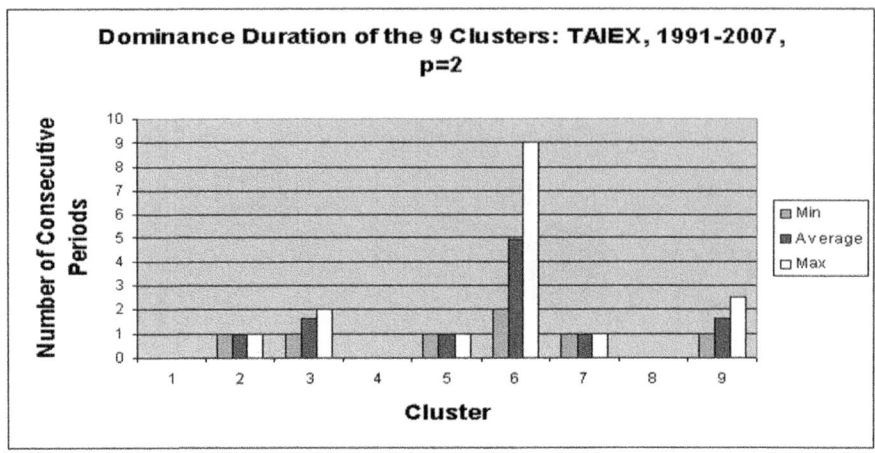

Fig. 5. Duration of Dominance ($p=2$)

can remain the dominant cluster. Figure 5 gives three statistics regarding duration, namely, minimum, average and maximum. For example, for Cluster Six, these three statistics are 1, 3 and 9, respectively. In other words, the maximum duration of dominance for Cluster Six is about nine periods, i.e., four and a half years. For other clusters, the longest duration is no more than three periods, i.e, one and half years. So, for most of the time, dominant clusters can hardly continue for long. Hence, we reach the conclusion that, regardless of the types of traders, we can rarely see the consecutive dominance. In this sense, our data lend support to the market fraction hypothesis in a weak sense.

3.2   Long-Term Distribution

The second hypothesis which we can form regarding the market fraction behavior is its *long-term distribution*. Many H-type agent-based financial models can show us that, under some proper parameter values, the long-term market fraction is *even*. In other words, if we have H types of traders, their long-term frequency of appearance should be close to $\frac{1}{H}$. Let $Card_{i,t}$ be the number (cardinality) of traders in Cluster i in time period t.

$$\sum_{i=1}^{H} Card_{i,t} = N, \quad \forall t. \tag{9}$$

In our current setting, N, the total number of traders, is 500. The long-term histogram can be derived by simply summing the number of traders over all periods and dividing it by a total of $N \times T$ (# of periods),

$$\omega_i = \frac{\sum_{t=1}^{T} Card_{i,t}}{N \times T}. \tag{10}$$

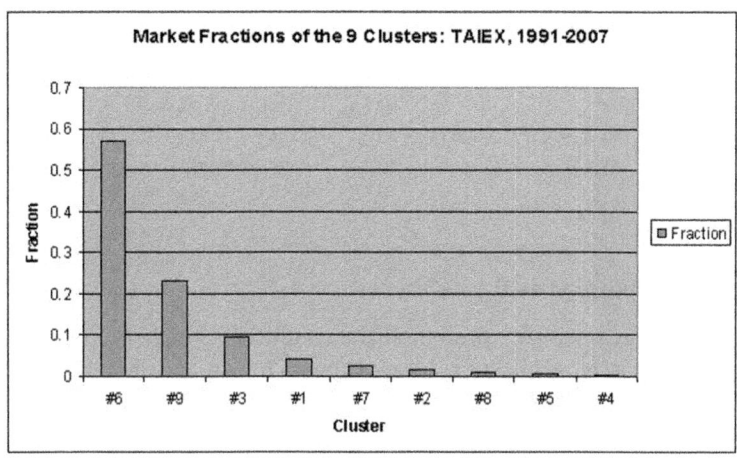

Fig. 6. Long-Term Histogram

Figure 6 gives the long-term histogram of these clusters, $\{\omega_i\}$. Obviously, they are not equal so that we present them in descending order from the left to the right. Cluster Six has the largest market fraction up to almost 60%, whereas Cluster 4 has the smallest market fraction, which is not even up to 1%.

Of course, this distribution is very different from the uniform one. In order to give a measure of how far it is from the uniform one, we use the familiar *entropy* as a metric. For the discrete random variable, the entropy is defined as

$$Entropy = -\sum_{i=1}^{H} p_i \ln p_i, \tag{11}$$

where p_i is the fraction of each cluster. Let us denote the empirical distribution presented in Figure 6 as f_X, and the uniform distribution as f_Y. By definition, $f_Y = \frac{1}{H}$, where H is the number of clusters, which in this case is 9. In order to measure how close f_X is to the uniform distribution f_Y, we calculate the entropy of both distributions. It is well known that for the uniform distribution $Entropy(Y) = \ln H$. When $H=9$, it is $\ln 9 \approx 2.2$. The closer $Entropy(X)$ is to 2.2, the closer X is to the uniform distribution. After calculating X's entropy, we find it equal to 1.3, which is only 59% of the entropy of the uniform distribution.

Summary. As we have seen in this section and the previous one, both the short-run and the long-run version of the market fraction hypothesis are not well supported. The short-run dynamics indicates the appearance of a long-lasting dominant cluster (up to a maximum of 9 periods). On the other hand, the long-run histogram is very far away from the uniform distribution.

Table 3. Summary Results over 10 runs, for a 3×3 SOM

	Short-Run	Long-Run	
	Mean	Max	E-Ratio
TAIEX (9 Clusters)	2.02	8.25	0.55
TAIEX (3 Clusters)	4.05	8.14	0.80

3.3 Results from Multiple Runs

However, so far we have only presented the results of a single run. To consolidate our results, we further replicate the experiments for an additional nine runs, and Table 3 gives the results for ten runs together.

The first two numeric columns are related to the short-run dynamics and present the averages over the 10 runs for both the average duration and the maximum duration of the 9 clusters. This result is not much different from our earlier single-run results. The mean dominance duration over these ten runs is just about 2 (one year). Nevertheless, the existence of few long-lasting dominant clusters is very evident with the mean maximum duration reaching as high as 8.25 periods (more than 4 years). Hence, the short-run version of the market fraction hypothesis is only weakly supported. The next column presents the ratio of the average realized entropy (over the 10 runs) relative to the base entropy under the null of the uniform distribution, which is 55%, and still quite far away from one. Therefore, the long-term version of the market fraction hypothesis is not well supported.

4 Does the Number of Types Matter?

The illustration presented above is based on a 3 by 3 SOM, which automatically generates nine clusters. This analysis has its limitations mainly because we do not know how many types of agents are really there in the market. In a rather theoretical analysis, [2] showed that it would be enough to characterize the market behavior by a few types, say two to three. Others are rather marginal[8]. Therefore, it would be interesting to investigate the microstructure dynamics based on a smaller SOM corresponding to the few-type agent-based financial models[9].

---

[8] Aoki [2] is probably the only paper known to us that deals with number of types of agents in the multi-agents system. Using the Ewens-Pitman-Zabell induction method, Aoki applies the result from the evolution of biological species and population genetics to determine the minimum number of types of behavior required to capture multi-agent economic systems. He showed that when agent behavior are positively correlated, two largest clusters are likely to develop to which most agents belong. This result, therefore, provides some justification for studying economic models composed of many interacting agents of two or three strategy types.

[9] Based on [5], the 2-type or the 3-type agent-based financial models are still the most popularly-used classes in the literature.

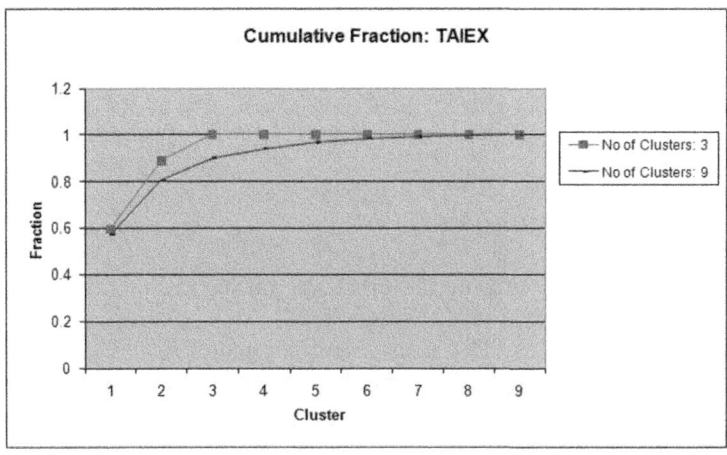

Fig. 7. Cumulative Fractions of 3 Clusters and 9 Clusters

In this section, we therefore repeat the above experiments by using a rather small 3×1 SOM. We then examine both its short-term dynamics and the long-term histogram. As before, we have 10 multiple runs. The results are shown in Table 3. In terms of duration behavior, we can see that there is no significant difference in the maximum duration between the 9-cluster case and the 3-cluster case, for here the mean maximum duration is consistently a little above eight (four years). However, a significant difference in mean duration does exist. What we find here is that when the number of clusters decreases, the mean duration increases from the original 2.02 periods (one year) to 4.05 periods (two years). Therefore, it seems that a smaller number of clusters really drives the short-run dynamics further away from the expectations of the market fraction hypothesis.

On the other hand, if we look at the long-term distribution behavior, we find that a smaller number of clusters does help the distribution (histogram) get closer to the uniform distribution. As shown in Table 3, the realized entropy ratio now increases up to 80% from the original 55%. Hence, the market fraction hypothesis is better supported from a long-term point of view.

Putting them together, what we have observed here is that, when the number of clusters gets smaller, the dominant cluster maintains its position longer, but a different cluster does take the lead in turn, and so, in the long run, they are better tied[10].

If the number of clusters does matter for the microstructure dynamics, then it is imperative to know how many clusters we need. To answer this question, Figure 7 presents the cumulative fraction sum from the largest cluster to the smallest cluster. For the 3-cluster case, when the number of clusters (the x axis)

---

[10] To see how significant or how interesting this pattern is, Monte Carlo simulation is conducted, and the patterns obtained are significantly different. Due to the size limit of the paper, details are not provided here, but are available in [13].

gets to 3, the cumulative fraction becomes one, and similarly for the 9-cluster case when the number of clusters gets to 9. However, what we can see here is that when coming to the first five clusters, there is already an accumulation of 96% of the market share. In fact, if we care only about 90% of the market fraction, then 3 clusters are sufficient.

5   Concluding Remarks

After a decade of development, the literature on agent-based financial models has successfully demonstrated the connection between microstructure dynamics and asset price dynamics. The next research agenda would be to gain more understanding of the empirical properties of this microstructure dynamics. In this paper we have shown that the number of types (clusters) of agents may be limited, but the duration of dominant groups are larger than what we may expect from, say, the adaptive market hypothesis [18]. The next step is to explore other financial markets and to see whether this is a universal phenomenon.

To achieve that purpose, it would be also our purpose to examine the sensitivity of our results to the tools used to process the data. Can any features which we obtained using genetic programming or self-organizing maps be valid if different rule-inference machines, clustering techniques, or simply just different settings of genetic programming (GP) or self-organizing maps (SOM) are employed? For example, the use of *standard hierarchical clustering* [22] or the growing hierarchical self-organizing map [8] can provide us a much finer details of the hierarchical structure of the market participants, which has not been well exploited in the literature yet.

Acknowledgements

The version has been revised in light of three anonymous referees' very helpful reviews, for which the authors are most grateful. The NSC grant 98-2410-H-004-045-MY3 is also gratefully acknowledged.

References

1. Allen, F., Karjalainen, R.: Using genetic algorithms to find technical trading rules. Journal of Financial Economics 51(2), 245–271 (1999)
2. Aoki, M.: Open models of share markets with two dominant types of participants. Journal of Economic Behavior and Organization 49(2), 199–216 (2002)
3. Backus, J.: The syntax and semantics of the proposed international algebraic language of Zurich. In: ICIP, Paris (1959)
4. Chen, S.-H., Yeh, C.-H.: Evolving traders and the business school with genetic programming: A new architecture of the agent-based artificial stock market. Journal of Economic Dynamics and Control 25, 363–394 (2001)
5. Chen, S.-H., Chang, C.-L., Du, Y.-R.: Agent-based economic models and econometrics. Knowledge Engineering Review (forthcoming)

6. Chen, S.-H., Kuo, T.-W., Hsu, K.-M.: Genetic programming and financial trading: How much about 'What we Know'? In: Zopounidis, C., Doumpos, M., Pardalos, P. (eds.) Handbook of Financial Engineering, pp. 99–154. Springer, Heidelberg (2008)
7. De Bondt, W., Thaler, R.: Does the stock market overreact? Journal of Finance 40(3), 793–808 (1985)
8. Dittenbach, M., Rauber, A., Merkl, D.: Recent advances with the growing hierarchical self-organizing map. In: Allinson, N., Yin, H., Allinson, L., Slack, J. (eds.) Advances in Self-Organizing Maps: Proceedings of the 3rd Workshop on Self-Organizing Maps. Springer, Heidelberg (2001)
9. Duffy, J., Engle-Warnick, J.: Using symbolic regression to infer strategies from experimental data. In: Chen, S. (ed.) Evolutionary Computation in Economics and Finance, pp. 61–82. Springer, Heidelberg (2002)
10. Forbes, W.: Picking winners? A Survey of the mean revision and overreaction of stock prices literature. Journal of Economic Surveys 10(2), 123–158 (1996)
11. Gigerenzer, G., Todd, P.: Fast and Frugal Heuristics: The Adaptive Toolbox. In: Gigerenzer, G., Todd, P., the ABC Research Group (eds.) Simple Heuristics That Make Us Smart, pp. 3–34. Oxford University Press, New York (1999)
12. Izumi, K., Ueda, K.: Using an artificial market approach to analyze exchange rate scenarios. In: Chen, S. (ed.) Evolutionary Computation in Economics and Finance, pp. 135–157. Springer, Heidelberg (2002)
13. Kampouridis, M., Chen, S.-H., Tsang, E.: Market fraction hypothesis: A proposed test. Working Paper, School of Computer Science and Electronic Engineering, University of Essex (2010)
14. Kirman, A.: Ants, rationality, and recruitment. Quarterly Journal of Economics 108, 137–156 (1993)
15. Kohonen, T.: Self-organized foundation of topologically correct feature maps. Biological Cybernetics 43, 59–69 (1982)
16. Koza, J.: Genetic Programming: On the Programming of Computers by Means of Natural Selection. MIT Press, Cambridge (1992)
17. Li, J.: FGP: A genetic programming based financial forecasting tool. PhD thesis, Department of Computer Science, University of Essex (2001)
18. Lo, A.: Reconciling efficient markets with behavioral finance: The adaptive market hypothesis. Journal of Investment Consulting 7(2), 21–44 (2005)
19. Neely, C., Weller, P., Dittmar, R.: Is technical analysis in the foreign exchange market profitable? A genetic programming approach. Journal of Financial and Quantitative Analysis 32(4), 405–426 (1997)
20. Provost, F., Kohavi, R.: Glossary of terms. Journal of Machine Learning 30(2-3), 271–274 (1998)
21. Simon, H.: Rational choice and the structure of environments. Psychological Review 63, 129–138 (1956)
22. Xu, R., Wunsch, D.: Clustering. Wiley-IEEE Press, Hokoben (2008)

Computational Modeling of Culture's Consequences

Gert Jan Hofstede[1,2], Catholijn M. Jonker[2], and Tim Verwaart[3]

[1] Wageningen University, Postbus 9109, 6700 HB Wageningen, The Netherlands
gertjan.hofstede@wur.nl
[2] Delft University of Technology, Mekelweg 4, 2628 CD Delft, The Netherlands
c.m.jonker@tudelft.nl
[3] LEI Wageningen UR, Postbus 29703, 2502 LS Den Haag, The Netherlands
tim.verwaart@wur.nl

Abstract. This paper presents an approach to formalize the influence of culture on the decision functions of agents in social simulations. The key components are (a) a definition of the domain of study in the form of a decision model, (b) knowledge acquisition based on a dimensional theory of culture, resulting in expert validated computational models of the influence of single dimensions, and (c) a technique for integrating the knowledge about individual dimensions. The approach is developed in a line of research that studies the influence of culture on trade processes. Trade is an excellent subject for this study of culture's consequences because it is ubiquitous, relevant both socially and economically, and often increasingly cross-cultural in a globalized world.

Keywords: dimensions of culture, computational model, social simulation.

1 Introduction

Being competent in trading depends on more than economic rationality. To model trade as it actually happens, creating agents that compute the most profitable deal is therefore not enough. The agents' incentives could be modeled using Williamson's framework [1] in which four time scales are used: resource allocation (for instance: trade) happens continuously, and is subject to governance rules that may change on a time scale of 1 to 10 years. These rules are themselves subject to institutional changes, e.g. new legislation, at a time scale of 10 to 100 years. Institutions in their turn are based on and attuned to the hidden rules of the game (culture) that are embedded in society and change on a time scale of 100 to 1000 years. So this model states that people involved in trade use governance rules, institutions and cultural values to guide their behavior, albeit unconsciously. The present article takes this position as a basis for modeling the effect of culture in agent-based social simulations.

Societies around the world differ greatly with respect to the value systems and ideas that govern patterns of human interaction. Hofstede [2], p.9, defines culture as *"the collective programming of the mind that distinguishes the members of one group of people from another"*. The behavior of people and their interpretation of the behavior of others are based on their norms for appropriate behavior. These norms vary from culture to culture.

T. Bosse, A. Geller, and C.M. Jonker (Eds.): MABS 2010, LNAI 6532, pp. 136–151, 2011.
© Springer-Verlag Berlin Heidelberg 2011

In different cultures, different norms may prevail for behavior in trade; e.g., trade partner selection, bargaining style, trust that has to be shown, favor that is given to in-group relations or high-ranked society members, and opportunistic advantage that may be taken from partners. Different systems may be viable in different societies. For example, [3] used multi-agent simulations to show that economic systems based on trust and systems based on opportunism may both be viable.

When traders operate in foreign cultures, the programming of their minds may not be efficient. This explains the existence of practical guides for business behavior in different countries, e.g. [4] and [5], and the extensive body of scientific literature that has been developed. The scientific literature ranges from business oriented stud-ies, e.g. Kumar [6], and cross-cultural surveys, e.g., Kersten et al. [7], to economic models, e.g., Guo [8] and Kónya [9].

The approach proposed in this paper aims to model culture at the mid-range level according to the classification by Gilbert [10], p.42. Mid-range models depend on a rich description of processes, but do not in facsimile model a particular situation. For mid-range models, observed trends should be similar to those observed in reality. This is important for our long-term research goal of improving the understanding of human decision-making in international supply chains with asymmetric information, see, for instance, [11]. The research method proposed in [11] combines multi-agent models with gaming simulation, but a general multi-agent-based model as proposed in [11] does not explain the cultural difference observed in the gaming simulations.

For the modeling of culture, one must lean on social sciences literature. Two main streams of research can be distinguished.

First, there is the anthropological approach of rich description, in which specific cultures are studied by detailed and close observation of behaviors during an exten-sive time-span. Examples are the works of Lévi-Strauss [12] and Geertz [13].

Second, there is the comparative approach that tries to identify dimensions on which different cultures can be ordered, aiming to develop a classification system in which cultures can be typed by a small number of qualifications. Examples are the models of culture by G. Hofstede [2], Schwarz [14], and Trompenaars and Hampden-Turner [15]. The approach of that type of research is to characterize cultures by their indices on a limited number of dimensions.

The dimensions and the indices of cultures are identified by factor analyzing massive surveys with standardized questionnaires in many countries. The value of such dimen-sions largely depends on the questionnaires used in combination with the sets of respon-dents that are required. Questionnaire studies will be more reliable predictors of behavior if respondent samples are well matched (e.g. do not compare industry x in one country with industry y in another), and the number of cases (cases are group averages, often country averages) should be considerable. Results tend to be more reliable if they are asked to a broad range of types of respondents as opposed to just one type (e.g., students or managers). The resulting models provide a linear ordering of cultures along each di-mension, where particular values and practices are hypothesized (based on empirical evidence) to be stronger or weaker or occur more frequently or less frequently according to the index on the dimension. For instance, in cultures on one extreme of a particular dimension concerned with asymmetry of power relations, the implicit norm is for parents to treat children as equals, while in cultures on the other end parents are supposed to teach children obedience. As authors of dimensional models stress, these same implicit norms carry over to all relationships in society that involve potential power differences, whether in school, in politics or in trade. In all social situations, they act as filters on perception and on action range. This means that there are no specific values for activity x, e.g. 'trade values', in a dimensional model. It also means that a dimensional model is suited for modeling any process that involves social intercourse, including trade and its sub-activities.

Cultural descriptions of the first type provide rich details about values, norms, symbols, beliefs, rituals, social structure, behavioral patterns etc. in a particular culture. These are useful for facsimile modeling of specific social systems. The model proposed in the present paper aims to compare the influence of a great diversity of cultures in the standardized environment of a gaming simulation which is by itself an abstraction of social life. For that purpose we need to posit the model at an impartial distance from any single culture. A dimensional model is more suited than a collection of incommensurable rich descriptions. Dimensional models are culture-level abstractions. They do not depict individuals, but average group characteristics, and therefore the agents in our simulation will be iconic for a culture (mid-range, in our term), not specific for any individual (facsimile, in our term).

Of the well-known dimensional models, the most widely used is Hofstede [2]. Hofstede's work is accessible, sparse, and based on a very large, very well stratified sample of questions, asked of people in all professions, that continues to give it great explanatory value. No other model matches society-level variables so well to date [16]. An overview of Hofstede's dimensions and their definitions is presented in Table 1.

Table 1. Hofstede's dimensions of culture [2]

Dimension	Definition
Power Distance	*"The extent to which the less powerful members of institutions and organizations within a country expect and accept that power is distributed unequally"* [2, p. 98]
Uncertainty Avoidance	*"The extent to which the members of a culture feel threatened by uncertain or unknown situations"* [2, p. 161]
Individualism and Collectivism	*"Individualism stands for a society in which the ties between individuals are loose: Everyone is expected to look after him/herself and her/his immediate family only. Collectivism stands for a society in which people from birth onward are integrated into strong, cohesive in-groups, which throughout people's lifetime continue to protect them in exchange for unquestioning loyalty"* [2, p. 255]
Masculinity and Femininity	*"Masculinity stands for a society in which social gender roles are clearly distinct: Men are assumed to be assertive, tough, and focused on material success; women are supposed to be more modest, tender and concerned with the quality of life. Femininity stands for a society in which gender roles overlap: Both men and women are supposed to be modest, tender and concerned with the quality of life."* [2, p. 297]
Long- Versus Short-Term Orientation	*"Long Term Orientation stands for the fostering of virtues oriented towards future rewards, in particular, perseverance and thrift. Its opposite pole, Short Term Orientation, stands for the fostering of virtues related to the past and the present, in particular, respect for tradition, preservation of 'face' and fulfilling social obligations"* [2, p. 359]

The hypothesis of the research reported in this paper is that computational models of culturally differentiated agents can be deduced from social scientific theories that differentiate cultures along a limited number of dimensions. An agent-based model can be developed to incorporate behavior and agent interactions which are realistically differentiated along each of the cultural dimensions. Note that the model based on the cultural indices may reliably reproduce general trends, but will not differentiate up to the detail of actual individuals. For the long term, a computational model based on a dimensional theory of culture in multi-agent-based simulations can provide insights into the functioning of social systems and institutions in different cultural contexts.

To develop computational models of culturally differentiated agents in a specific domain of application a general agent-based model for that domain of application can be taken as a point of departure. That general model should be based on a task, process, or activity analysis of the domain of application. A dimensional theory of culture can be used to determine the required adaptations to the model to reflect the way culture influences behavior trends. Such adaptations also pertain to the way the agents perceive their environment and the behavior of other agents. For instance, if the theory describes that in some cultures favor is to be shown to in-group customers, while in other cultures the norm is to treat all customers equally, the agents need a cognitive model in which they can be aware of what group they belong to and maintain models of other agents in which they maintain beliefs about other agents' group memberships (e.g., "I belong to group x and she does not belong to that group"). For each of the processes of the general model, an adaptation must be developed that models the adaptation of decisions by culture. This paper describes an approach to develop computational adaptations of the processes within the agent that are based on a dimensional model of culture, and expert knowledge about cultural effects on decisions and interpretation of behaviors.

The case for which the approach described in this paper has been developed is a simulation game of trade under asymmetric information [17]. A multi-agent-based simulation of this game has been developed [11], with two purposes: to test hypotheses about players' decision making and to design optimal configurations for human games. When playing the game with human participants, differences in outcomes were observed that were attributed to differences in cultural background [17]. The latter was the rationale for modeling culture into the artificial agents.

The process model for trading agents acting in the game is given in Fig. 1. First, agents determine a short-term trade goal (e.g., to buy or to sell? what type of product? top quality or basic quality?). Next, agents search for acceptable trade partners with complementary needs that are willing to negotiate. After negotiating a contract, it comes to delivery, where an agent may deliver according to contract or defect in some way. Partners have the choice to trust the other to comply with the contract, or to spend resources on monitoring and enforcing deliveries. Finally, after these trade interactions, the trading agents reflect upon the effectiveness of their trade, on the trustworthiness of their trade partners, and on their own decisions. On the basis of that reflection they update their beliefs.

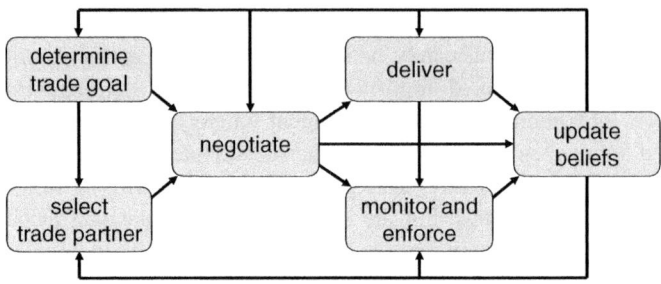

Fig. 1. Processes and internal information flows of trading agents (adapted from [18])

The plans that the agents execute for process fulfillment are based on validated models taken from literature on social sciences and artificial intelligence. The agent's decision models implemented in the plans were adapted to include effects of culture, based on Hofstede's [2] dimensional model. The present paper describes the approach taken to incorporate the dimensional model of culture into the decision functions. The paper is organized as follows. Section 2 presents an overview of the method that was followed in knowledge acquisition and model formulation. Section 3 formulates the computational model. A discussion of results concludes the paper.

2   Modeling Method

The exercise of modeling culture in trading agents could be carried out in a multitude of ways, using a variety of theories. The present article describes one such attempt. It also presents the choices and the line of reasoning behind this method. This could enable other researchers to choose which of the principles, choices and practices of this approach to adopt and from which ones to deviate.

In order to model cultural differentiation in agents the following steps were taken, once the domain to be modeled had been defined. Agent roles, possible actions and communications, agent network, the environment and entities in it, as well as their observable properties, were defined. For the agents, a process model had been established (see Fig. 1).

In each process the agents take decisions based on decision rules. For these rules, models were preferred that had in empirical research been validated to simulate actual human behavior. For instance, in the model of culture implemented by the authors, the ABMP (Agent-Based Market Place) negotiation architecture is applied to model the negotiation process. It has been validated in experiments with Dutch adolescents and adults [19].

For some processes, no validated model can be found in literature. In such a case a dedicated model had to be formulated based on empirical data or research. An example of such a model is the deceit model developed by the authors [20]. This model is applied in the decion rules for delivery process.

The decision models taken from literature can be implemented as a set of rules (the agent's knowledge base. Typically, the decision rules are parameterized. For instance, parameters in the rules of the ABMP negotiation strategy have names like *concession*

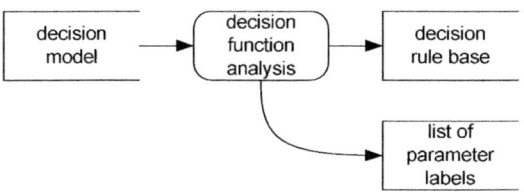

Fig. 2. Decision function analysis[1]

factor, negotiation speed, impatience. So, the decision model can be formulated as a set of parameterized rules, and the labels of the parameters can be listed. We refer to this modeling activity as "decision function analysis". The results are the decision rule base and a list of parameter labels (see Fig.2).

The decision rule parameters are the point of application for cultural differentiation. This assumes that the process model structure is universally valid, for instance the assumption for negotiation is that making concessions is a universal element of negotiation across cultures, but that acceptable speed and size of concessions depend on culture and relational context. Validations of behavior with subjects from one culture are no guarantee for the occurrence of similar behavior in other cultures. This is amply shown by a multitude of experimental studies published in journals such as the Journal of Cross-Cultural Psychology, and in review volumes such as [21]. This fact implies that further validations in other countries could yield results that necessitate structural revisions of the process models.

For the cultural differentiation Hofstede's five-dimensional model of national cultures [2] was selected. Two criteria were important in the selection. First, the model had to be applicable for the social processes to be simulated, based on the contexts in which it has been developed and validated, and the availability of research results that provide rules for decision parameter adaptation. As argued in section 1, this condition holds for the Hofstede framework. Second, the modelers had to have access to expertise on the cultural model to be applied, for knowledge acquisition and expert validation of results.

Knowledge about the influence of individual dimensions of culture on the decision functions of the process model was acquired, using the concept of Synthetic Cultures [22] complemented by an expert systems approach. Synthetic Cultures are scripts, created by experts on cross-cultural communication, that catch a single extreme of a single dimension of culture in rules of behavior. They have been created for use in training counselors [22] and later adapted for use in simulation gaming for a multitude of applications [23]. Synthetic Cultures lead to believable behavior by simulation participants, and to realistic cross-cultural miscommunication, even though the synthetic cultures themselves are obviously unrealistic. Since their publication, a number of simulations based on synthetic cultures were created, the synthetic cultures were refined based on experience [24] and they have become adopted by cross-cultural trainers around the world.

| represented knowledge |
| modeling activity |

[1] Legend of figures 2 to 5

Literature and expert knowledge are mostly based on differentiation along the dimensions. It is feasible to acquire knowledge on the differentiation along a single dimension, whereas it proved to be impossible in practice to interpret the joint influence of multiple dimensions on general rules. A classical knowledge acquisition approach was followed for each dimension: interview experts on the cultural theory, read literature, write narratives of expected system behavior, have experts validate the narratives, correct until the experts have confidence in the narratives. In addition to the narratives, the knowledge acquisition resulted in a list of relevant cultural factors[2] for each dimension. On the basis of the knowledge gained, the influence of the relevant factors for a single dimension on each parameterized decision rule can be formalized as a set of rules that modify the parameter values (see Fig. 3).

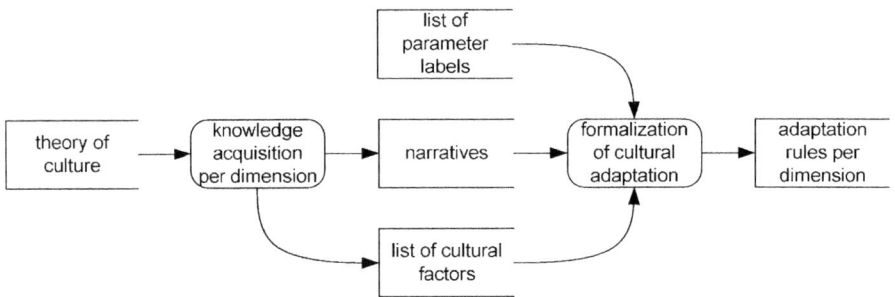

Fig. 3. Knowledge acquisition and formalization

The next activity in the modeling was to implement the adaptation rules in multi-agent-based models for each single dimension (Fig. 4). The step of the modeling per dimension is described for each of Hofstede's dimensions in [25], [26], [27], [28], and [29]. The results of these models can practically only be validated through expert validation, because they concern synthetic cultures, which work as a concept for reasoning about cultures, but have no examples in the real world. In reality, cultures are composites of all dimensions and only effects of interactions with the other dimensions can be observed.

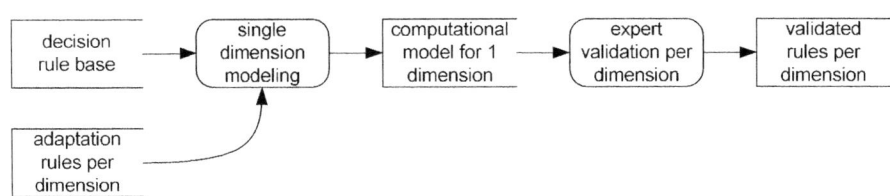

Fig. 4. Computational modeling and validation for a single dimension

---

[2] Some dimensions adapt the perceived relevance of certain relational attributes. For instance, the salience of common group membership (in-group versus out-group) is adapted by the dimension of individualism versus collectivism. Other such relational attributes are status difference and trust. 'Cultural factors' combine dimension scores and relational attributes.

Finally, the parameter adaptation rules of the individual dimensions were combined into an integrated set of rules, as the basis for a computational model of the simultaneous influence of all dimensions (Fig. 5). The integration technique used to integrate the adaptation rules is described in the next section. This technique has been applied in models for the agent's processes of partner selection [30], negotiation [31], and delivery, monitoring and enforcing, and belief update [20].

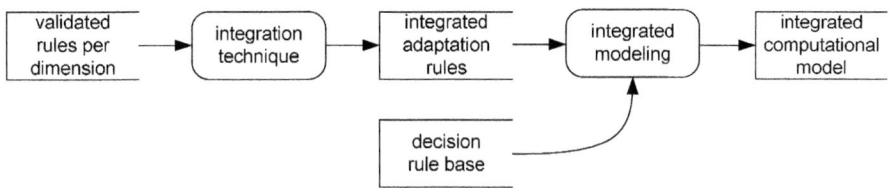

Fig. 5. Integration and computational modeling of joint dimensions

3   Integrated Computational Model

This section describes the approach taken to integrate the parameter adaptation rules for the single dimensions into an agent model that simulates a complete cultural "Gestalt". The approach has been applied to differentiate trading agents in a simulation game according to Hofstede's dimensions, but it is described in a more general way. The approach can also be applied when using other dimensional models or to other processes where the decisions can be described by parameterized rules and data or expertise is available to assess the effects of culture on the parameter values. From this general perspective, we formulate the approach as follows.

Assume for some domain of application that a set of adapted decision rules per dimension and accompanying sets of parameters and cultural factors are given (see Fig. 2 and Fig. 3). This section discusses an approach to integrating all this knowledge into one integrated computational model that reflects the influence of culture on decision making in the domain. The key concepts of the approach are described as follows (see Table 2 for an overview).

The m parameters used in the domain model are labeled p_1 through p_m, with associated default values x_1 through x_m, for some reference culture, and values adjusted for culture x_1' through x_m'. For instance, in the negotiation model applied in the trading agents, the i-th parameter may have label p_i="negotiation_speed" with an associated global default value x_i, equal for all agents for a particular type of trade; for each individual agent, the value is modified to its cultural adjusted value x_i', so x_i' may be different for agents having different cultural profiles.

For each culture dimension j, there is a range of q_j cultural factor labels l_{j1} through l_{jq_j} with associated values f_{j1} through f_{jq_j}. Variable i is consistently used in this paper to range over parameters (values or labels), whereas j ranges over dimensions, and k over cultural factors per dimension j. For each factor label l_{jk} and each parameter p_i, there is a function r_{ijk} that maps factor value f_{jk} and default value x_i to adjusted parameter value x_i'. Table 2 presents an overview of these key concepts.

Table 2. Overview of the key concepts

Dimensions	Cultural factors		Parameters ranging over $1 \leq i \leq m$			
ranging	Factor	Factor	Label set P:	p_1	...	p_m
over	label set	value set	default value:	x_1	...	x_m
$1 \leq j \leq n$	L	F	adjusted value:	x_1'	...	x_m'
1	l_{11}	f_{11}		r_{111}	...	r_{m11}
	...	...		...	...	...
	l_{1q_1}	f_{1q_1}		r_{11q_1}	...	r_{m1q_1}
...	...	...		...	...	...
n	l_{n1}	f_{n1}		r_{1n1}	...	r_{mn1}
	...	...		...	...	...
	l_{nq_n}	f_{nq_n}		r_{1nq_n}	...	r_{mnq_n}

The integrated effect of culture on agent behavior can be modeled as a function h that maps a vector of cultural factors $\vec{f}$ and a vector of default values of model parameters $\vec{x}$ to a vector of culturally adjusted parameters $\vec{x}'$:

$$h(\vec{f}, \vec{x}) = \vec{x}' . \tag{1}$$

The hypothesis of this work entails that, given the set of decision functions, a dimensional theory of culture can be used (a) to identify the cultural factors to be taken into account and (b) to define the mapping h. If this is possible, the agent modeling can benefit from vast bodies of social sciences literature that describe the differentiation of many behaviors along the dimensions of the cultural model. This literature can be used to define h for the wide range of behaviors, assuming that we can formulate parameterized decision functions governing the behaviors. The literature is the basis for finding the attributes of agents and their relations which are relevant for adaptation of the model parameters. This approach to integration of effects of cultural dimensions has been applied in [20], [30], [31]. In expert-systems based knowledge acquisition the effect of culture can be formulated in statements like: "*In hierarchical societies there are differences in selected trade strategy. The higher ranked prefer to trade high quality valuable commodities to underline their status that fits their position in life. They will not avoid deals where less powerful opponents technically have the opportunity to defect, because the higher ranked rely on their power to enforce cooperation*" [25].

This example refers to the effect of Hofstede's power distance dimension. It refers to multiple decision processes: partner selection, delivery, and monitoring and enforcing. It illustrates that research and experts can explain the differentiation of behaviors along a single dimension on the basis of dimensional theory. It also illustrates that it is hard to acquire knowledge about the processes in isolation. Therefore, the approach is taken to first model individual dimensions and then integrate the models process-by-process. The example also illustrates that not just the values of the dimensional indices are relevant for modeling the effect of culture. Relational attributes are relevant as well. In this example Hofstede's power distance index (PDI) is relevant. It orders countries on a scale with the most hierarchical culture at the high end and the most egalitarian country at the low end. Conditional upon the value of PDI, the status of the agent and its partner are relevant: *"The higher ranked"* refers to agents that have a high status s_a in society; *"less powerful opponents"* refers to opponents with which the status difference s_a–s_b , where s_b refers to opponent's status, is high. So, in order to model cultural effects on decisions, not just the indices on the dimensions have to be taken into account as factors, but also relational attributes if their effect is differentiated across cultures. Based upon the example given, one can identify PDI·s_a and PDI(s_a–s_b) as relevant factors in addition to PDI.

Based on the knowledge acquired for all individual dimensions, all relevant cultural, relational and situational factors can be identified. In the example of trade the following have been identified as relevant relational attributes: status, in-group versus out-group membership, and the trust relation between partners. For instance, the vector of cultural factors influencing the decisions to deceive and to trust identified by Jonker et al. [20] can be taken from the column labeled "Cultural factor" in Table 3.

Table 3. Relevant factors with respect to trust and deceit, adapted from [20]; PDI^*, UAI^*, IDV^*, MAS^*, and LTO^* represent Hofstede's indices of culture, s_a the agent's own status, s_b partner's perceived status, and d_b group distance between the agent and its partner; all variables were normalized to the interval [0,1]; + indicates an increasing effect on the parameter; − indicates a decreasing effect

Dimension index	Culture and relational characteristics	Cultural factor	Effect on			
			deceit threshold	inclination to trace	negative update factor	positive update factor
PDI	Large power distance	PDI^*				
	- with higher ranked partn.	$\max\{0,\text{PDI}^*(s_b{-}s_a)\}$	+	−		
	- with lower ranked partn.	$\max\{0,\text{PDI}^*(s_a{-}s_b)\}$		−		
	Small power distance	$1{-}\text{PDI}^*$				
UAI	Uncertainty avoiding	UAI^*			+	−
	- with stranger	$\text{UAI}^*{\cdot}d_b$	−	+		
	Uncertainty tolerant	$1{-}\text{UAI}^*$				
IDV	Individualistic	IDV^*				
	Collectivistic	$1{-}\text{IDV}^*$			+	
	- with in-group partner	$(1{-}\text{IDV}^*)(1{-}d_b)$		−		
	- with out-group partner	$(1{-}\text{IDV}^*)d_b$	−			
MAS	Masculine (competitive)	MAS^*	−	+	−	
	Feminine (cooperative)	$1{-}\text{MAS}^*$		−		
LTO	Long-term oriented	LTO^*	+	−	+	
	Short-term oriented	$1{-}\text{LTO}^*$				
	- with well-respected part.	$(1{-}\text{LTO}^*)s_b$	+	−		
	- with other partners	$(1{-}\text{LTO}^*)(1{-}s_b)$	−			

Such a table is constructed for each process or group of processes, in this case the trade processes of delivery, monitoring and enforcing, and belief update. It contains the expert knowledge for cultural adaptation of the agents' decision making. It contains the relevant cultural factors (on the rows) and the parameters or variables to be adapted (in the columns). The cells describe the effect of culture. The effect may be either increasing or decreasing. For instance, according to Table 3, the inclination to trace is to be reduced for agents with a collectivistic cultural background, when they trade with in-group partners.

Having identified $\vec{f}$ for a particular set of processes, and assuming that the vector of parameter values $\vec{x}$ follows from the chosen decision functions, it comes to the definition of the function h. h can be decomposed into a vector of functions g_i, i.e., one per parameter, that map h's arguments to the individual culturally adjusted parameter values x_i':

$$h(\vec{f},\vec{x}) = \left(g_1(\vec{f},\vec{x}),...,g_m(\vec{f},\vec{x})\right) = (g_1,...,g_m)(\vec{f},\vec{x}) = \vec{g}(\vec{f},\vec{x}) , \qquad (2)$$

so that

$$x_1' = g_1(\vec{f},\vec{x})$$
$$... \qquad\qquad (3)$$
$$x_m' = g_m(\vec{f},\vec{x})$$

The problem now is to find the functions g_i for $i = 1,...,m$. For this purpose the following hypothesis can be formulated: given that dimensional models of culture aim to provide for each dimension a linear ordering of the strength or frequency of occurrence of phenomena associated with that dimension, the effect of each cultural factor may be modeled as a strictly monotonic function r_{ijk} that adapts the i-th parameter to the k-th factor associated with the j-th dimension. r_{ijk} can be seen as a member of a set of functions r that can be indexed by the labels of cultural factors and parameters as arguments. r_{ijk} maps the value f_{jk} of the cultural factor with label l_{jk} into an effect e_{ijk} on the parameter with label p_i:

$$r_{ijk} : f_{jk} \times x_i \rightarrow e_{ijk} , \qquad (4)$$

$$r_{ijk} \equiv r(p_i, l_{jk}) , \qquad (5)$$

and

$$e_{ijk} = r_{ijk}(f_{jk}, x_i) = r(p_i, l_{jk})(f_{jk}, x_i) , \qquad (6)$$

where $p_i \in P$, the set of parameter labels, and $l_{jk} \in L$, the set of factor labels.

As the r_{ijk} are strictly monotonic, they can be classified as either increasing or decreasing. For each parameter label p_i its set of factors L_i^+ that have an increasing effect and its set of factors L_i^- that have a decreasing effect can be defined:

$$\forall p_i \in P: \quad L_i^+ \equiv \{l_{jk} \mid r_{ijk} \text{ is increasing}\}, \tag{7}$$

$$\forall p_i \in P: \quad L_i^- \equiv \{l_{jk} \mid r_{ijk} \text{ is decreasing}\}. \tag{8}$$

By the knowledge acquisition process taken, the increasing and decreasing effects of the cultural factors can be identified, as illustrated in Table 3 [20]: L_i^+ is the set of factor labels that have a + sign in the column associated with the parameter labeled p_i; L_i^- is the set of factor labels that have a minus sign in the column associated with p_i.

The next problem to solve is the combination of these influences into a single effect on each parameter, i.e. to identify the functions g_i that map the effects of culture onto the parameters. On the basis of expert knowledge the following rules can be formulated as hypotheses:

1. In g_i there is no interaction between the factors $\vec{f}$ and other parameters than x_i.
   This assumes that any decision model can be formulated in such a way that any parameter can be modified for culture without taking the values of the other parameters into account. For the models we have implemented so far ([20], [30], [31]) this assumption is valid.
2. The joint decreasing and the joint increasing effect can compensate for each other. This expertise is confirmed by expert statements, e.g. (in cultures with high power distance) "*The powerful dictate the conditions. The less powerful have to accept. In feminine or collectivist cultures the powerful may exercise restraint, ...*" [25].
3. For the increasing and for the decreasing effects, the effect with the maximal influence is dominant: influences in the same direction do not reinforce each other. According to expert knowledge, if several factors influence a parameter in the same direction, it is sufficient for one to be maximal in order to sort maximal effect (disjunctive factor influence, see e.g. "*feminine or collectivist*") under 2 above.
4. Cultural factors working in the same direction do not reinforce each other. This means that, for instance, in Table 3 three factors are identified to have increasing effect on deceit threshold. If two of the factors have effect 0.5 and one has effect 0.2, their joint effect is 0.5; not 0.4 (the average) or another linear combination (see 3 above); not 0.8 (probabilistic) or another product combination.

The first of these three hypotheses implies that the integration can be performed column-by-column using factor tables like Table 3, and we can write the functions as:

$$g_i(\vec{f}, \vec{x}) = g_i(\vec{f}, x_i). \tag{9}$$

The second hypothesis implies that the functions g_i can each be defined as the sum of x_i and a function $g_i^+ \geq 0$ that combines the increasing effects and a function $g_i^- \leq 0$ that combines the decreasing effects:

$$g_i(\vec{f}, x_i) \equiv x_i + g_i^+ \left(\{r_{ijk}(f_{jk}, x_i) \mid l_{jk} \in L_i^+ \} \right) + g_i^- \left(\{r_{ijk}(f_{jk}, x_i) \mid l_{jk} \in L_i^- \} \right). \tag{10}$$

For the functions g_i^+ and g_i^- a range of function types were experimented with (probabilistic and linear combinations, to name the most obvious). However, under the third and fourth hypotheses all except weak disjunction proved to be untenable[3]. We found that both g_i^+ and g_i^- can be written as a weak disjunction:

$$g_i^+\left(\left\{r_{ijk}\left(f_{jk},x_i\right)\mid l_{jk}\in L_i^+\right\}\right)=\max\left\{r_{ijk}\left(f_{jk},x_i\right)\mid l_{jk}\in L_i^+\right\}, \tag{11}$$

$$g_i^-\left(\left\{r_{ijk}\left(f_{jk},x_i\right)\mid l_{jk}\in L_i^-\right\}\right)=\min\left\{r_{ijk}\left(f_{jk},x_i\right)\mid l_{jk}\in L_i^-\right\}. \tag{12}$$

Equations (11) and (12) enable the integration of the computational models constructed for the single dimensions. For this the form of the functions $r_{ijk}\left(f_{jk},x_i\right)=r\left(p_i,l_{jk}\right)\left(f_{jk},x_i\right)$ has to be defined. All that is known so far about these functions is that they are strictly monotonic. As long as there is no further evidence, a first order approach can be taken, i.e., let r_{ijk} adjust x_i proportionally to f_{jk} from its default value in the direction of the extreme values $\varepsilon_{ijk}^+ > x_i$ and $\varepsilon_{ijk}^- < x_i$:

$$\forall i\mid p_i\in P:\quad \forall j\forall k\mid l_{jk}\in L_i^+:\quad r_{ijk}\left(f_{jk},x_i\right)=\left(\varepsilon_{ijk}^+-x_i\right)f_{jk}, \tag{13}$$

$$\forall i\mid p_i\in P:\quad \forall j\forall k\mid l_{jk}\in L_i^-:\quad r_{ijk}\left(f_{jk},x_i\right)=\left(\varepsilon_{ijk}^--x_i\right)f_{jk}. \tag{14}$$

Under this first order approach, using (11) and (12), (10) becomes:

$$g_i\left(\vec{f},x_i\right)=x_i+\max\left\{\left(\varepsilon_{ijk}^+-x_i\right)f_{jk}\mid l_{jk}\in L_i^+\right\}+\min\left\{\left(\varepsilon_{ijk}^--x_i\right)f_{jk}\mid l_{jk}\in L_i^-\right\}. \tag{15}$$

In practice, the values of ε_{ijk}^+ and ε_{ijk}^- are unknown. However, minimal and maximal values can be assumed not to depend on the cultural dimension j, and estimates $\hat\varepsilon_i^-$ and $\hat\varepsilon_i^+$ can be determined per model parameter. Under the assumptions

$$\forall i\mid p_i\in P:\quad \forall j\forall k\mid l_{jk}\in L_i^+:\quad \varepsilon_{ijk}^+=\hat\varepsilon_i^+, \tag{16}$$

$$\forall i\mid p_i\in P:\quad \forall j\forall k\mid l_{jk}\in L_i^-:\quad \varepsilon_{ijk}^-=\hat\varepsilon_i^-, \tag{17}$$

(15) can be written (N.B.: $\hat\varepsilon_i^+-x_i>0$ and $\hat\varepsilon_i^--x_i<0$):

$$g_i\left(\vec{f},x_i\right)=x_i+\left(\hat\varepsilon_i^+-x_i\right)\max\left\{f_{jk}\mid l_{jk}\in L_i^+\right\}+\left(\hat\varepsilon_i^--x_i\right)\max\left\{f_{jk}\mid l_{jk}\in L_i^-\right\}. \tag{18}$$

Concluding, given default values for a specific context, e.g. trade in biologically grown vegetables or trade in second hand cars, and realistic minimal and maximal

---

[3] Weak disjunction is consistent with the hypotheses 3 and 4 above. Any linear or product combination of cultural factor is not.

values for each parameter, using knowledge represented as in Table 3, the function in equation (18) can be used to estimate parameter values x_i' that are adjusted for culture.

4 Conclusion

This paper presents an approach to model cultural differentiation in multi-agent based simulations. It argues that a dimensional theory of culture is a good basis for middle-range agent-based models that simulate differentiation over a broad range of cultures. In the case where a specific culture were to be modeled, an ethnographic type "thick description" could offer a better basis for modeling of culture-specific processes, but where a model aims for differentiation of particular behaviors across many cultures, combining a dimensional theory with expert-knowledge about the differentiation is a practicable approach.

The decomposition of cultural phenomena into a set of linear orderings on a limited number of dimensions enables dimension-by-dimension modeling of cultural effects. The concept of Synthetic Cultures [22, 23, 24], which is well tested in practice, shows that dimension-by-dimension scripts give rise to believable, if unrealistic, behavior. As the dimensions provide a linear ordering, it is reasonable to assume that each dimension (and relational attributes relevant for differentiation of behavior associated with it) has a strictly monotonic effect on decision rule parameters, if all other factors are kept constant.

This paper has proposed a technique to integrate the effects of individual dimensions. The assumptions underlying the integration technique are the following:

1. It is possible to formulate universally valid, parameterized, process models with default values for typical, minimal, and maximal values of the parameters.
2. Effects of culture on parameters are independent: culture's effect on a parameter does not depend on the value of any other parameter.
3. Relevant cultural factors can be modeled as either the relative positions on a dimension, or as the product of such a score with the score on a relational aspect (e.g. status, group distance, trust).
4. For each parameter, an expert can identify a (possibly empty) set of factors having an increasing effect and a (possibly empty) set of factors having a decreasing effect.
5. The joint effect of each set is the effect of the dominant cultural factor, i.e. the factor having the maximal value.
6. The joint decreasing effect may compensate for the joint increasing effect, vice versa.

On the basis of these assumptions, expert knowledge can be used to identify a function h that adapts the global default values of model parameters to culture-specific values according to the indices of a dimensional model of culture. It follows from the assumed independence of parameters that the function h can be decomposed into a set of m functions g_i, $i = 1\ldots m$, where each g_i adapts the default value x_i of a parameter p_i independently of the values of other parameters. The expert knowledge concerning relevant cultural factors and their effects on model parameters can be summarized in tables of the form of Table 3. In a first order approach, the functions g_i follow from these tables, applying equation (18).

The validity of the approach depends on whether the above-mentioned assumptions are reasonable for the domain of application. For the application of Hofstede's model to trade, the validity of the approach is supported by several simulations of trade processes. In these simulations, the approach has shown to produce realistic tendencies across cultures in expert validations [20, 30, 31, 32].

An approach as followed in this paper aims to reproduce general tendencies of behavioral differentiations across cultures at an aggregated level. It can be used as a research instrument to generate hypotheses about behavioral differentiation that can be validated in experiments, or to validate theories induced from experimental results. As a mid-range model, it cannot be used to predict effects of culture in actual situations or at the individual level.

The approach has been applied to simulations of trade processes, on the basis of Hofstede's five-dimensional theory of culture (e.g. [23]), but it is not specific for this domain and this theory of culture. It could also be applied to other domains, using other theories of culture, provided that parameterized decision models are available that may be expected to have general validity across cultures, and that sufficient knowledge for cultural adaptation can be acquired from social sciences literature and experts.

References

1. Williamson, O.E.: The New Institutional Economics: Taking Stock, Looking Ahead. Journal of Economic Literature 38, 595–613 (2000)
2. Hofstede, G.: Culture's Consequences, 2nd edn. Sage Publications, Thousand Oaks (2001)
3. Gorobets, A., Nooteboom, B.: Agent Based modeling of Trust Between Firms in Markets. In: Advances in Artificial Economics. LNEMS, vol. 584, pp. 121–132. Springer, Heidelberg (2006)
4. Acuff, F.L.: How to negotiate anything with anyone anywhere around the world. Amacom, New York (1997)
5. Olofsson, G.: When in Rome or Rio or Riyadh: Cultural Q&A's for successful business behavior around the world. Intercultural Press, Yarmouth Maine (2004)
6. Kumar, R.: Brahmanical Idealism, Anarchical Individualism, and the Dynamics of Indian Negotiation Behavior. International Journal of Cross Cultural Management 4(1), 39–58 (2004)
7. Kersten, G.E., Köszegi, S.T., Vetschera, R.: The Effects of Culture in Anonymous Negotiations: Experiment in Four Countries. In: Procs. of the 35th HICSS, pp. 418–427 (2002)
8. Guo, R.: How culture influences foreign trade: evidence from the U.S. and China. Journal of Socio-Economics 33, 785–812 (2004)
9. Kónya, I.: Modeling Cultural Barriers in International Trade. Review of International Economics 14(3), 494–507 (2006)
10. Gilbert, N.: Agent-Based Models. Sage Publications, Los Angeles (2008)
11. Tykhonov, D., Jonker, C., Meijer, S., Verwaart, T.: Agent-Based Simulation of the Trust and Tracing Game for Supply Chains and Networks. Journal of Artificial Societies and Social Simulation 11(3), 1 (2008),
http://jasss.soc.surrey.ac.uk/11/3/1.html
12. Lévi-Strauss, C.: Tristes Tropiques (originally in French, 1955). Penguin Books, New York (1992)

13. Geertz, C.: The interpretation of cultures. Basic Books, New York (1973)
14. Schwarz, S.H.: Culture Matters: National value cultures, Sources, and Consequences. In: Wyer, R.S., Chiu, C.Y., Hong, Y.Y. (eds.) Understanding Culture. Psychology Press, New York (2009)
15. Trompenaars, F., Hampden-Turner, C.: Riding the waves of culture: understanding cultural diversity in business, 2nd edn. Economist Books, London (1993)
16. Smith, P.: Nations, Cultures, and Individuals: New Perspectives and Old Dilemmas. J. of Cross-cultural Psychology 35(1), 50–61 (2004)
17. Meijer, S., Hofstede, G.J., Beers, G., Omta, S.W.F.: Trust and Tracing game: learning about transactions and embeddedness in a trade network. Production Planning and Control 17, 569–583 (2006)
18. Meijer, S., Verwaart, T.: Feasibility of Multi-agent Simulation for the Trust and Tracing Game. In: Ali, M., Esposito, F. (eds.) IEA/AIE 2005. LNCS (LNAI), vol. 3533, pp. 14–154. Springer, Heidelberg (2005)
19. Bosse, T., Jonker, C.M., Treur, J.: Experiments in Human Multi-Issue Negotiation: Analysis and Support. In: Proceedings of the Third International Joint Conference on Autonomous Agents and Multi-Agent Systems, pp. 672–679 (2004)
20. Hofstede, G.J., Jonker, C.M., Verwaart, T.: A Multi-agent Model of Deceit and Trust in Intercultural Trade. In: Nguyen, N.T., Kowalczyk, R., Chen, S.-M. (eds.) ICCCI 2009. LNCS, vol. 5796, pp. 205–216. Springer, Heidelberg (2009)
21. Smith, P., Bond, M.H., Kagitçibasi, C.: Understanding Social Psychology across Cultures. Sage Publications, Thousand Oaks (2006)
22. Pedersen, P.B., Ivey, A.E.: Culture-Centered Counseling and Interviewing Skills: A Practical Guide. Greenwood Press, Westport (1993)
23. Hofstede, G.J., Pedersen, P.B.: Synthetic Cultures: Intercultural Learning Through Simulation Gaming. Simulation & Gaming 30, 415–440 (1999)
24. Hofstede, G.J., Pedersen, P.B., Hofstede, G.: Exploring Culture: Exercise, Stories and Synthetic Cultures. Intercultural Press, Yarmouth (2002)
25. Hofstede, G.J., Jonker, C.M., Verwaart, T.: Modeling Power Distance in Trade. In: David, N., Sichman, J.S. (eds.) MABS 2008. LNCS, vol. 5269, pp. 1–16. Springer, Heidelberg (2009)
26. Hofstede, G.J., Jonker, C.M., Verwaart, T.: Modeling Culture in Trade: Uncertainty Avoidance. In: 2008 Agent-Directed Simulation Symposium (ADSS 2008), Spring Simulation Multiconference 2008, pp. 143–150. SCS, San Diego (2008)
27. Hofstede, G.J., Jonker, C.M., Verwaart, T.: Individualism and Collectivism in Trade Agents. In: Nguyen, N.T., Borzemski, L., Grzech, A., Ali, M. (eds.) IEA/AIE 2008. LNCS (LNAI), vol. 5027, pp. 492–501. Springer, Heidelberg (2008)
28. Hofstede, G.J., Jonker, C.M., Meijer, S., Verwaart, T.: Modeling Trade and Trust across Cultures. In: Stølen, K., Winsborough, W.H., Martinelli, F., Massacci, F. (eds.) iTrust 2006. LNCS, vol. 3986, pp. 120–134. Springer, Heidelberg (2006)
29. Hofstede, G.J., Jonker, C.M., Verwaart, T.: Long-term Orientation in Trade. In: Schredelseker, K., Hauser, F. (eds.) Complexity and Artificial Markets, pp. 107–118. Springer, Heidelberg (2008)
30. Hofstede, G.J., Jonker, C.M., Verwaart, T.: Simulation of Effects of Culture on Trade Partner Selection. In: Hernández, C., et al. (eds.) Artificial Economics: The Generative Method in Economics, pp. 257–268. Springer, Heidelberg (2009)
31. Hofstede, G.J., Jonker, C.M., Verwaart, T.: Cultural Differentiation of Negotiating Agents. Group Decis Negot (2010), doi: 10.1007/s10726-010-9190-x
32. Hofstede, G.J., Jonker, C.M., Verwaart, T.: The Influence of Culture on ABMP Negotiation Parameters. In: Ito, T., et al. (eds.) Innovations in Agent-based Complex Automated Negotiations. Springer, Heidelberg (2010)

Agent-Based Simulation Modelling of Housing Choice and Urban Regeneration Policy

René Jordan[*], Mark Birkin, and Andrew Evans

Centre for Spatial Analysis and Policy
School of Geography, University of Leeds
Leeds, LS2 9JT, UK
r.j.jordan@leeds.ac.uk

Abstract. Phenomena in the housing market can be recreated and analysed using the technique of agent-based modelling. Housing policies introduced as part of urban regeneration often seek to address problems of deprivation in segregated communities by introducing the concept of mixed communities, that is, communities mixed by housing tenure and housing type. In this paper, a framework for the creation of a model of housing choice and regeneration policy is presented.

Keywords: agent-based modelling, housing choice, urban regeneration policy.

1 Introduction

Housing Policy is one of the instruments used by government to manage the housing sector and includes, as a part of its remit, attempts to improve the dwelling conditions of those unable to provide suitable homes for themselves. Deprivation and the state of the poor have played instrumental roles in the direction of these policies. Housing policies are often presented under the umbrella of Urban Regeneration. As defined by Bramley *et al.* [1], regeneration is the process of recovering and renewing lost vitality to the physical and social landscape. Hull [2] argues, however, that despite the physical changes in the urban mosaic of most regenerated cities, urban regeneration has not been effective in narrowing the gap between the disadvantaged and those of higher social standing. On the contrary, Hull [2] calls the associated suite of policies a failure.

In the UK and elsewhere, the relatively limited success of regeneration policy raises many questions. Explicit in the UK government's plans for urban regeneration is the new goal of equipping the less advantaged with the tools to seek market provisions Questions can be raised to challenge this new goal; is it likely to yield successful results? What are the likely results of the recent housing-led regeneration policies and will these results fall in line with the goals envisioned by government? In this paper, we suggest that agent-based modelling (ABM) is a technique which can illuminate the problems associated with urban regeneration.

---

[*] Corresponding author.

T. Bosse, A. Geller, and C.M. Jonker (Eds.): MABS 2010, LNAI 6532, pp. 152–166, 2011.

Housing market models in the realm of social simulation are discussed as a precursor for the introduction of a new housing market model. An original modelling framework is presented which refines conventional notions of preference to include a broad range of socio-demographic, economic and geographical variables. The importance of model testing and validation in specific local contexts will be emphasized, and an empirical application for the area of East and South-East Leeds (EASEL), England, will be developed.

2 Urban Regeneration Policy and EASEL

With a population of over 700,000 residents, Leeds is one of the largest metropolitan districts in England. The city is characterised by a booming financial sector and a large student population. Despite this view of the city, it contains some of the most deprived communities in the United Kingdom [3]. At least 46,000 Leeds residents live in areas rated amongst the 3% most deprived in England [4]. Most of these residents live within the EASEL area.

The EASEL area is resident to more than 36,000 households. According to the EASEL Aspiration Needs and Housing Study 2007 [5], 85% of the Super Output Areas (SOAs) in EASEL fall within the top 10% most deprived in England while 91% fall within the top 20% in England. (A SOA is a neighbourhood with approximately 300 households.) Issues of deprivation and social disadvantage, high unemployment, and above average rates of crime plague these communities.

Of primary interest to this research is the role of housing in the regeneration scheme. In the UK context, housing tenure can be largely divided into two categories: social housing – houses owned and or administered by the Local Council, and private housing. In general these two housing categories are geographically separate. However, a central policy objective is the creation of sustainable communities, a term strongly linked in the UK to mixed communities. Leeds City Council [4] believes that the success of this goal hinges on the creation of a stable housing market. The council intends to introduce a greater mix of housing tenures in council owned areas by introducing private housing. This, it argues, reduces movement turnover in communities thus providing a gateway for creating sustainable communities. In order to facilitate this, an estimated 7,800 new homes are to be built to create these new mixed communities – mixed by tenure. Note that mixed communities are communities diversified by socioeconomic status *and* housing tenure.

Proponents for this form of tenure diversification argue that mixed communities can contribute to a smaller concentration of unemployed people by attracting economically active households to previously deprived neighbourhoods [6]. Others claim, however, that though this can thin out the problem of deprivation, it still does not solve the problem of social disadvantage [7], [8].

Whether the policy of creating mixed communities will yield the required results is questionable - there are not sufficient results on which to base an informed judgement. What is known, however, illustrates that the theory overshadows the practicality of the results. Through computational modelling, the validity of these hypotheses can be tested.

3   Social Simulations in the Housing Market

Approaches to housing market modelling are not new to the field of computer simulation, however, realistic models of the system that are spatially explicit at a local level are few. There are great difficulties involved: the dynamics of this market are intricately woven into the complex system of the world in which we live. Its volatility can be seen as house prices fluctuate due to activity in the financial market, affecting terms of lending, interest rates and general attitudes towards risk, among others. Nevertheless merging these factors with discriminatory individual behaviour creates an environment ripe with modelling opportunities.

Existing research on the dynamics of the housing market is extensive. Ethnic segregation is a topic which has attracted enduring attention in relation to both the processes of dispersion [9], [10] and the resulting spatial patterns [11], [12]. Other questions such as residential preferences and mobility [13], housing choices and the impact of government policy [14], continue to generate interest. Through computer models and simulation, the intricacies of this dynamic market can be explored.

The work of Thomas Schelling is noted to be one of the first agent-based models of its kind to replicate segregation from individual level behaviour [15]. Schelling [16], [17] examined the role of ethnic preferences in an artificially created community and illustrates how individual behaviour can create significant collective results not directly intended by the individual [16]. Schelling proved that even with slight preferences, total segregation can be effected if these preferences are exercised.

Schelling's work, though simple, forms the basis for much research on individual choice, segregation and integration. Work by Pancs and Vriend [18] examined the role of preferences in relation to integration policy. They concluded that even when individuals preferred integrated neighbourhoods, the impact of preferences led to segregated communities. Furthermore, when public policies were enacted to heighten tolerance levels, individuals still gravitated towards others like themselves. In a similar way, Zhang [19], [20], in his mathematical model, concludes that even in areas where pure integration is preferred, segregation is likely.

Aguilera and Ugalde [21] attached house prices to each space on a lattice grid. Individuals were rated by socioeconomic status and income and moved to match their status with the price of their house. In this case, segregation was observed. Yin [22] increased the dynamics in his model by devising a social simulation to examine the issue of race, social class and residential segregation. He illustrates that factors such as race and economic constraints, when exercised as a part of the housing choice process, can cause segregation of varying degrees at the aggregate level. However, Yin illustrated that when housing policies were implemented this segregation could be reduced once racial sensitivity was low. Therefore, integration seems possible if people are educated to favour it and/or housing policies are implemented to create integrated societies. However, if communities are left to form naturally with limited interference where policy is concerned, segregation is likely to occur.

Models like these tackle various aspects of the problem of segregation and integration as they relate to activity in the housing market. The model outlined in this paper encapsulates the design noted in previous, similar social simulations while extending the design further to mirror conditions and trends in the EASEL area more closely. Such a real world application is aimed at refining Schelling's notion of preferences to include not only ethnicity but also preferences pertaining to the family life cycle; tenure type; accommodation type; distance to city; accessibility of transport routes; distance to schools; cost of housing and knowledge of the new neighbourhood. These preferences interact with policy directives and environmental conditions such as changes in interest rates, in/out migration and the presence of new facilities such as schools. Not only is there no record of this being done but applying such a model to an existing project such as EASEL provides the opportunity to test model outcomes against actual outcomes as time progresses.

Research such as this challenges our understanding of causal relationships in the housing market and more specifically in the EASEL area. At the aggregate level, policy makers are able to gauge how population profiles change over time, raising a need for more services such as schools and healthcare facilities. In a similar way, such research could point out where services are not used sufficiently and lead to reassessment of resource planning. This is important when asset management is considered, especially amidst the reality of difficult economic times. Also, having never been implemented in the EASEL area, regeneration policies do not have a proven track record. A model such as this can provide a platform for scenarios to be created and tested in an effort to speculate on their performance.

Other modelling techniques, such as microsimulation [23] and spatial interaction modeling [24], are well established in the housing market domain. Spatial interaction models represent transitions in the market as aggregate flows by groups of individuals from place to place. Microsimulation models facilitate the representation of households and their constituent individuals, but movement between states is mediated through deterministic and relatively inflexible transition rules. An agent-based modeling approach allows for the recreation of a market environment in which the search for housing reflects heterogeneous preferences of different household units. Furthermore it emphasises interdependence as households not only compete with one another for limited housing stock, but their actions create dynamic feedbacks between the decision-making process and the residential environment. For example, decision-makers may have a preference for areas with a profile matching their own ethnic background. The preference to move into such areas could give rise to positive feedback by which areas would tend to become progressively more segregated. Agent-based systems therefore have the potential to recreate events in ways more similar to activities in the real world. They are dynamic in nature as agent states continue to change due to their interaction with other agents and interaction with the environment in which they exist. Collective resultant behaviour possibly characterised by emergence may provide further useful insights beyond conventional results [25]. Building on this premise, the framework for the EASEL Housing Simulation model is discussed.

4   The Model Defined

As a replica of activity in the EASEL area, the EASEL Housing Simulation uses a formulation in which individual households are represented as agents. For the purpose of this project, a household is used to represent a collection of residents living together. Details of the household representative person were derived from the UK

Census Household Sample of Anonymised Records and this record is used to represent the entire household. Such a record is deemed sufficient in representing the unit as it contains details on the number of residents living with the household representative, including the number of children.

In the model, each household resides in a house for an undetermined time period until some push factor influences the decision to move. These push factors may range from changes in household size, to changes in disposable income or forced moves of council tenants as initiated by the City Council. In general, household agents are entered into the simulation and initially assigned to houses. As the model advances from one time step to the other, environmental variables are updated to simulate changing economic and social conditions in the market. While this happens, households wishing to move are identified and attempts to find a suitable new dwelling are made.

The underlying framework of this model is presented in the sections to follow. We examine the key stages in the modelling process, beginning with the derivation of the input data, and the assignment of households to housing. Time stepping in the model and the determination of movers is explained. Then the location decisions of households are examined along with the background modelling of environmental variables.

4.1 Derivation of the Input Data

In demographic terms, the starting point for the simulation is a complete representation of households in the EASEL area. As individual-level records are not available for the UK, they have to be simulated. Starting with a large anonymised sample from the UK population, households are selected to match the census characteristics of EASEL (for example, high levels of council-owned housing, significant deprivation) using a reweighting process which is well-known in the spatial microsimulation literature [26]. Household data is generated from the Household Sample of Anonymised Records (SAR) for England and Wales (www.ccsr.ac.uk), and output area data is from the Census Area Statistics. This method provides a complete simulation for individual households of attributes collected in the UK Census, including ethnicity, age, family composition, health status, accommodation type and housing tenure. This range of attributes provides the basis for implementing a rich set of rules for household movement and destination choice. Shapefiles representing houses and roads are derived from data provided through the Ordnance Survey, while Output Area boundaries are downloaded through Edina UK Borders (www.edina.ac.uk).

4.2 Assignment of Households to Houses

Attached to each Output Area (OA) is a set of attributes describing it. Crime rates, house quality, access to healthcare, etc are encapsulated in the UK's Index of Multiple Deprivation data. The Index of Multiple Deprivation rates the level of deprivation for each Output Area. Better areas are characterised by lower IMD figures. When households are initially read into the model, each household is assigned to a house using the OA field in the household record. This matching of OA and households ensures that households are placed in areas which match their socioeconomic status. Note that this process is necessary as data produced during the microsimulation only contains OA references and not exact house codes. This is important in order to ensure that actual individuals cannot be identified in the Census data.

4.3 Time-Stepping

The technique of time-stepping is used in the simulation project to recreate an environment where events are measured in actual time. In this way, the simulation can mimic time-driven events in the real world. We choose to increment the time step counter on a yearly basis as immigration rates can be monitored at this level.

4.4 Determination of Household Movers

The probability that a household wishes to move in a specific time interval is derived through an analysis of the Household SAR, which includes the variable 'moved in the last year' alongside other social, demographic and household characteristics. In order to determine different movement probabilities for different socio-demographic groups, we built a decision-tree using the SPSS AnswerTree extension (www.spss.org). The Household SAR contains several categorical variables, AnswerTree allows for the manipulation of categorical variables through the use of chi-square analysis.

It was discovered that age and household composition, housing tenure, house size, accommodation type, and housing requirements, crowding and socioeconomic status are all important drivers of the movement process. *Age* is divided into four categories (16-24, 25-44, 45-64 and over 65), and *household composition* (also household comp or hh comp) is divided into single individuals, couples, families, lone parents and others. *Housing requirements* are divided according to the number of rooms which a household is seeking (0-5, 6-10, 11 or more) as opposed to the *house size* that it currently occupies (0-5, 6-10, 11 or more). *Accommodation type* may be a flat, terraced house or detached house, and *tenure* may be either owner-occupied, privately rented or council rented. *Crowding* can be high or low density according to the number of homes per square kilometer in the location, and *socioeconomic status* is either high status (working in a professional or managerial occupation) or low status (working in a clerical or manual occupation).

The decision tree is shown schematically in Figure 1. At each level in the tree, a household attribute is identified which differentiates by movership. For example, at the first level in the tree, Branch 1 represents household heads aged 25-44 (high movement), branch 2 is ages 45-64 (moderate movement), and branch 4 is ages 65+ (low movement). Branch 3 represents young adults (under the age of 25), with very high levels of movement. At the next level of the tree, each branch is further sub-divided by the next differentiating attribute. In the case of branch 1 (ages 25-44) there is a further three-way split which is based on housing tenure (e.g. private renters have the highest rates of movement). The process continues for as long as significant factors can be identified to differentiate migration probabilities between households.

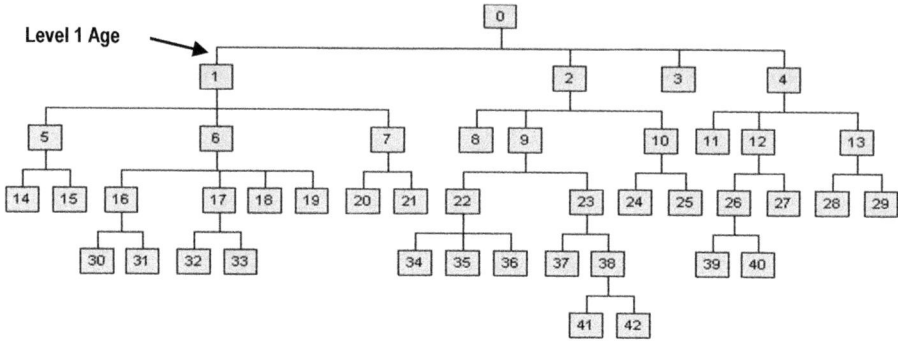

Fig. 1. Decision Tree

Table 1. Tabular list of decision tree clusters

Cluster code	Node	Level 1	Level 2	Level 3	Level 4
		Age of Head	Tenure	Housing reqd	
1a1	14	•Adults 25-44	•Private rented	•<6 rooms	xxxxxxxx
1a2	15			•>5 rooms	xxxxxxxx
				Household comp.	
1b1	18			•Single	xxxxxxxx
1b2	19		•Owner-occ	•Couple	xxxxxxxx
					Crowding
1b3i	30			•Family	•Low density
1b3ii	31				•High density
					Socio-economic status
1b4i	32			•Lone parents	•Low status
1b4ii	33				•High status
				Household comp.	
1c1	20		•Council rented	•Lone parent	xxxxxxxx
1c2	21			•Single/couple/family	xxxxxxxx
			Tenure		
2a	8	•Adults 45-64	•Private rented	xxxxxxxx	xxxxxxxx
				Housing reqd.	House size
2b1i	34		•Owner occupied	•Rooms required 0-10	•Rooms occupied 1-5
2b1ii	35				•Rooms occupied 6-10
2b1iii	36				•Rooms occupied 11+
					•Household comp.
2b2i	41			•Rooms required 11+	•Family
2b2ii	42				•Other hh comp
3	3	•Adults 16-24	xxxxxxxx	xxxxxxxx	xxxxxxxx
			Accom. Type		
4a	11	•Adults 65+	•Flat	xxxxxxxx	xxxxxxxx
				Household comp.	
4b1	39		•Terrace	•Couple/family	xxxxxxxx
4b2	40			•Other hh comp	xxxxxxxx
4c1	28		•Detached house	•Couple/family	xxxxxxxx
4c2	29			•Other hh comp	xxxxxxxx

At the bottom of the tree this leads to clusters of households with discrete characteristics and an associated probability of movement. When the simulation is implemented, the characteristics of a household are parsed in order to allocate the household to an appropriate cluster. Thus a household with a head aged between 25 and 44, renting privately with less than 6 rooms would be allocated to cluster 14, with a migration probability of 0.53. A random number is generated in the simulation, and if that number is lower than 0.53 then this household will be directed to the movement pool in the simulation.

A full list of 22 clusters from the decision tree is shown in Table 1. Observe that notable attributes such as *ethnicity* (and others) were considered in the decision tree but not found to be significant. We conclude that any variations in movement between ethnic groups are proxied by other variables such as household size and tenure, but also note that ethnicity can still be important in the choice of destination, which is a separate process (see below). Note that, a variable is classified as significant when there are at least 1000 cases available for examination in the entire dataset. Branches are therefore terminated when this condition is not met.

4.5 Selection of Destinations

When it is determined that a household will move, a new home must be found. Existing research examines the type of behaviours contributing to residential segregation as a consequence of selecting a location at which to live [10], [13], [14]. Segregation is often attributed to issues such as culture, religion, language, ethnicity groups, economic advantage and school searches [14]. Forces for segregation and dispersal are complex, dynamic and contextual in that they are experienced in different ways in different places by different types of households [14].

The choice of where to move is a combination of dwelling alternatives. One of the most important factors in this decision is the financial budget of the household [27], [28]. This is integral to the decision to be made, as across the housing market houses are grouped according to price. Even when limited by a budget, neighbourhood characteristics are important factors as they still influence where a household moves. The physical conditions of the neighbourhood, amenities such as shops, school quality, security and transport connections are characteristics which can determine whether a household chooses to live in an area or not.

In a similar way, dwelling characteristics are important. Dwelling characteristics such as dwelling size, type, age and quality must be included because at various stages of the family life cycle there are different dwelling requirements [29]. The choice to live in a house as opposed to a flat could be the result of a household with children desiring a garden for children to play. Similarly, the number of rooms may be linked to the size of the family.

We opt to implement seven main rules to represent the process adopted by households when choosing a new dwelling. The rules have been derived from the existing literature as well as information given during informal talks with personnel from the Leeds City Council and will be implemented individually in the first instance in order to reduce the complexity of interpreting the results. Following this, rules will be weighted in combination according to the scenarios chosen, for example, a poor household, facing unemployment is likely to sacrifice living in or near to a community where 'better' schools can be found. Thus, in this case the weighting for Rule 6 would be relatively low.

The rules are as follows:

1. Households first tend to look for a new house within known areas [30].
2. Households will move to houses where the size of the house is adequate [30].
3. Households will move to houses where the tenure type of the house is desired [29].
4. Households will move to areas where the ethnic makeup is tolerable [10], [13], [14], [15], [31].
5. Households will move to areas where transport routes are accessible [29], [32].
6. Households containing school-aged children will try to move to areas where better schools are accessible [35], [36], [37].
7. Households will move to houses where the neighbourhood quality is better. [30]

4.6   What Are the Environmental Variables?

As in the real world, the dynamics of the housing market continually change; interest rates, monetary policies, mortality and fertility rates vary continually. Each of these variables has an effect on residential mobility. Changes in interest rates affect house prices in the form of increased or decreased mortgage rates and or rental rates. Such changes may cause the household to find a cheaper home or it may encourage the household to move opportunistically to a better home. Each of these factors can encourage or discourage a household choice of a new home.

5   Results

In order to generate initial results, five experiments centred on ethnicity were created and executed. The experiments are presented below with an overview of the method and a brief presentation of the results associated with the other rulesets. A view of the way forward is presented in Section 5.2.

5.1   Brief Review and Discussion of Results

Experiments were generated in the following way. First a sample population of 559 households and 606 houses is distributed across 6 Output Area (OA) zones. Each individual in the sample dataset has the characteristics described in Section 4.1, thus age, ethnicity, accommodation type and so on. The number of houses is greater than the number of households to provide vacancies in the housing market. The sample populations are generated to match the known demographic characteristics of the OAs.

At every iteration of the model, households are shuffled into a random order for consideration. Each household needs to "decide" whether or not it wishes to move, and if so then it needs to select a vacant house to occupy. The newly occupied house is removed from the stock of vacant housing, and the newly vacated property is added to the stock of vacant housing. Movement probabilities are annualized, and thus each iteration of the model approximates to a single year of elapsed time.

The movement model takes one of two forms. In the 'random model', each household has an equal probability of moving. In the 'mover model', a probability is applied according to the characteristics of the household using the decision tree which was described in Section 4.4. For each household type corresponding to the leaves of the tree a different probability is applied. These probabilities are derived from the source data in the Household Sample of Anonymised Records.

To find a new house, each mover tests all of the available destinations and then selects the one which best meets its requirements. The suitability of each vacant house is assessed in relation to one or more of the seven movement rules. For example, in the "ethnic pull" model the suitability of the vacant property is evaluated in relation to the ethnic composition of the area surrounding the destination property. Each of the experiments described here represents a single model run from the same initial conditions.

Table 2. Description of Experiments

Exp#	Description	Assumptions	# Moves	Time Elapsed	Equilibrium	Clustering
1	Pure Schelling	Random movers	9	45	Yes	Strong
		Ethnic push				
2	Ethnic 1	Random movers	10	70	Yes	Strong
		Ethnic push				
		Ethnic pull				
		(Rule 4; Section 4.5)				
3	Ethnic 2	Mover model	15	900	Limited	Weak
		Ethnic pull				
		(Rule 4; Section 4.5)				
4	Ethnic 3	Mover model	7	450	Yes	Strong
		Ethnic push				
		Ethnic pull				
		(Rule 4; Section 4.5)				
5	Housing	Mover model	1	20	Very Limited	Very Weak
		Ethnic push				
		Housing pull				
		(Rule 2; Section 4.5)				

Experiment #1 is our starting point and represents the original Schelling model. Here an ethnic push is assumed; individuals are motivated to move based on a dislike for the current ethnic mix in their community and opt to move to any other vacant home. Clustering and equilibrium are realised very quickly with the average number of moves per household recorded at 9. Note that equilibrium refers to a stable state where a negligible number of households are observed to be moving. We refer to clustering as 'strong' in that ethnic concentration between areas is qualitatively similar to the actual data.

Experiment #2 is an augmentation of Experiment #1. Both an ethnic push and ethnic pull are assumed here; households leave neighbourhoods where the ethnic mixed is not tolerable and find homes in areas where the ethnic mix is tolerable (Section 4.5; Rule 6). Again segregation is realised though after almost twice the amount of processing time as previous due to the ethnic pull constraint.

Experiment #3, Experiment #4 and Experiment #5 adopt the mover model as discussed in Section 4.4. In Experiment #3, the combination of the mover model as the push factor and ethnic tolerance as the pull factor resulted in limited segregation. We refer to clustering here as 'weak' because although there is segregation it is much less pronounced than in the actual data. Adding ethnicity to the push factors result in strong clustering after ~450 processing units as observed in Experiment #4. Experiment #5 extended from Experiment #4 by searching for houses with the required number of rooms (Rule 2, Section 4.5). As Table 2 notes, equilibrium is limited with hardly any discernible clusters, which we therefore characterise as 'very weak'.

These observations highlight the contributions of the mover model in limiting the number of times households move but also point out the importance of coupling this model with more subjective preferences such as ethnicity. Though the ethnicity attribute was not highlighted in the model of the probability of movement, these experiments show that it is important that provisions be made for its inclusion in the full model. Given strong clustering in the real world, it seems the results in Experiment #4 appear to be closer to reality.

Adding more pull factors, as in Experiment #5, appears to grind the model to a halt very quickly while a negligible number of clusters appear. It seems likely that this is due to the limited availability of the required house size, tenure type etc. in the market. This is similar to reality as oftentimes a household may compromise on their housing requirements because of limitations in the available housing stock; future work will concentrate on building more compromise into the decision making mechanisms of the agents.

Other rules can also be run in isolation to study the reasonableness of their results using the mover model to govern the selection of households wanting to move. The known area rule results in households moving short distances. The IMD rule recognises deprived areas being vacated. With regards to the transport routes and schools rule, households without cars and households with dependent children are seen gravitating closer to these respective resources. In the case of the rooms and socioeconomic status rules, households strongly limit their selection of a new house to their preference for a specific number of rooms and housing tenure respectively. Finally, we can alter these experiments by coupling the mover model with the full complement of rules. This means that each of the seven rules must be satisfied in order for a household to move to a new home. Such a simulation results in limited movement because of the rigidity of the conditions.

5.2 Where to Next?

In reality households are known to compromise on some preferences once the decision to move has be made. It seems likely that as an initial compromise each household type will have a different combination of rules that is likely to be more applicable. For example, ethnic minority groups in the EASEL area are known to cluster together strongly and often do not display wealth by way of housing tenure [15]. For such a group, the ethnicity rule would be very important while the socioeconomic rule may be ignored. In a similar way, for young students, though small dwellings may be required, because of the availability of house shares they may choose to live in larger houses than necessary. Here the rooms rule is compromised.

In the simulations discussed in Section 5.1 above we have described a set of experiments in which the outcome of certain behavioural rules derived from the literature are tested. Future work will concentrate on the process of calibration, by which rule sets can be created which mirror the behaviours of each type of household. de Smith *et al.* [38] define calibration as the process of ensuring that the model parameters match the parameters used in the real world to effect real world results. It is the process of refining the behaviour of the model to ensure that the model replicates behaviours in the real world. The model is executed with various combinations of rules; the results generated are compared to known results for the EASEL area to test the level of accuracy. Once this process is complete, a collection of rule sets for each household type should be identifiable leading to the generation of final model results.

Data rich sources such as the National Shoppers' Survey and the Pupil Level Annual School's Census (PLASC) will be used in the process of calibration to assess the extent to which the model is able to recreate reality. The National Shoppers' Survey contains demographic details and preference data of householders while the PLASC contains demographic details on school children. Counts of households by ethnicity, age, etc. will be compared and the goodness of fit indicator, the Index of Heterogeneity will be used to assess the level of heterogeneity in each Output Area. Blau [39] uses the following notation to describe the index:

$$ H = 1 - \sum_i P_i^2 $$

Where P is the proportion of a particular group in each area i. The Index of Heterogeneity returns a value between 0 and 1 and is defined at the Output Area level for our model. A value closer to 0 denotes a high level of segregation while a value closer to 1 denotes a high level of diversity. Values generated from our model can be compared to values generated from the real data. Strategies for validation of the model could include the analysis of model performance and behavior at a different time period to that in which the model was calibrated, or an extension of the model to different geographical contexts.

With this framework in place, the model can then be used to run scenarios in which the background landscape to the model may be varied, for example new houses can be added to the EASEL area, schools may be moved and or houses demolished to examine the likely effects of Regeneration Policy. Other data sources such as the British Household Panel Survey (BHPS) may also be used to assist in updating the demographic variables of the model. Such a dataset is similar to the Household SAR in that it is devoid of spatial references but rich in information.

Finally, the model in its present state may be described as closed; households neither move beyond the boundaries of EASEL nor enter from outside this area. The homogeneity of the present market makes this an acceptable first-sweep for the current population. However, for scenario runs, new, external, populations may be needed to meet the objective of modeling more mixed communities. Scaling up the model to represent Leeds is one option, though the computational requirements for such a venture may outstrip the capacity of the available systems.

6   Conclusion

The housing market is stratified, so without policies which support mixed communities, households will cluster according to socioeconomic status and ethnicity. In this paper, we have established a policy framework for housing market behaviour with urban regeneration. A rich basis for the creation of agents and their movement patterns has been introduced. We set out rules for location decisions based on a diverse set of characteristics and migration behaviours. From our early experiments to explore the effect of agent rules, further results and policy simulations are now awaited which can begin to support the policy process and provide real insights into the establishment and maintenance of socially mixed communities.

Acknowledgements

Census output is Crown copyright and is reproduced with the permission of the Controller of HMSO and the Queen's Printer for Scotland.

References

1. Bramley, G., Pawson, H., Munro, M.: Key Issues in Housing: Policies and Markets in 21st Century Britain. Palgrave Macmillan, Britain (2004)
2. Hull, A.: Neighbourhood Renewal: A toolkit for regeneration. GeoJournal 51(4), 301–310 (2000)
3. Unsworth, R., Stillwell, J.: Twenty-First Century Leeds: Geographies of a Regional City (Revised Edition). PLACE Research Centre, York (2004)
4. Leeds City Council. East and South East Leeds Area Action Plan. Leeds Local Development Framework (2007)
5. Leeds City Council. EASEL Aspiration Needs and Housing Study 2007 (2007)
6. Beekman, T., Lyons, F., Scott, J.: Improving the understanding of the influence of owner occupiers in mixed tenure neighbourhoods. ODS Ltd. for Scottish Homes, Edinburgh (2001)
7. Kleinhans, R.: Social implications of housing diversification in urban renewal: A review of recent literature. Journal of Housing and the Built Environment 19(4), 367–390 (2004)
8. Kintrea, K.J., Atkinson, R.: Owner-occupation, social mix and neighbourhood impacts. Policy & Politics 28(1), 93–108 (2000)

9. Phillips, D.: Black Minority Ethnic Concentration, Segregation and Dispersal in Britain. Urban Studies 35(10), 1681–1702 (1998)
10. Phillips, D.: Ethnic and Racial Segregation: a critical perspective. Geography Compass 1(5), 1138–1159 (2007)
11. Johnston, R.J., Poulsen, M.F., Forrest, J.: Are There Ethnic Enclaves/Ghettos in English Cities? Urban Studies 39, 591–618 (2002)
12. Peach, C.: London and New York: contrasts in British and American models of segregation. International Journal of Population Geography 5, 319–351 (1999)
13. Gilbert, A.: A home is forever? Residential mobility and homeownership in self-help settlements. Environment and Planning A 31(6), 1073–1091 (1991)
14. Kim, J., Pagliara, F., Preston, J.: The Intention to Move and Residential Location Choice Behaviour. Urban Studies 42(9), 1621–1636 (2005)
15. Macy, M.W., Willer, R.: From factors to actors: computational sociology and agent-based modeling. Annual Review of Sociology 28 (2002)
16. Schelling, T.: Models of Segregation. The American Economic Review 59(2), 488–493 (1969)
17. Schelling, T.: Dynamic models of segregation. Journal of Mathematical Sociology 1(2), 143–186 (1971)
18. Pancs, R., Vriend, N.: Schelling's Spatial Proximity Model of Segregation Revisited. Journal of Public Economics 91, 1–24 (2007)
19. Zhang, J.: A Dynamic Model of Residential Segregation. The Journal of Mathematical Sociology 28(3), 147–170 (2004)
20. Zhang, J.: Residential segregation in an all-integrationist world. Journal of Economic Behavior & Organization 54(2004), 533–550 (2004)
21. Aguilera, A., Ugalde, E.: A Spatially Extended Model for Residential Segregation. Discrete Dynamics in Nature and Society. Article ID 48589, 20 pages (2007)
22. Yin, L.: The Dynamics of Residential Segregation in Buffalo: An Agent-based Simulation. Urban Studies 46(13), 2749–2770 (2009)
23. Miller, E., Hunt, H., Abraham, J., Salvini, P.: Microsimulating urban systems. Computers, Environment and Urban Systems 28, 9–44 (2004)
24. Leishman, C., Bramley, G.: A local housing market model with spatial interaction (2005)
25. Epstein, J.M.: Agent-based computational models and generative social science. Complexity 4(5), 41–60 (1999)
26. Williamson, P., Birkin, M., Rees, P.H.: The estimation of population microdata using data from small area statistics and samples of anonymised records. Environment and Planning A 30, 785–816 (1998)
27. Tu, Y., Goldfinch, J.: A Two-stage Housing Choice Forecasting Model. Urban Studies 33(3), 517–537 (1996)
28. Boehm, T.: A Hierarchical Model of Housing Choice. Urban Studies 19(1), 17–31 (1982)
29. Dieleman, F.: Modelling residential mobility; a review of recent trends in research. Journal of Housing and the Built Environment 16(3), 249–265 (2001)
30. Cho, Y.: Who moves and where? A comparison of housing association tenants in London and northern regions. Housing Corporation London and Sector Study, vol. 40. Housing Corporation, London (2004)
31. van Kempen, R., Özüekren, A.: Ethnic segregation in cities: new forms and explanations in a dynamic world. Urban Studies 35, 1631–1656 (1998)
32. Forrest, R.: Spatial Mobility, tenure mobility, and emerging social divisions in the UK housing market. Environment and Planning A 19, 1611–1630 (1987)

33. Cho, Y., Lyall Grant, F., Whitehead, C.: Affordable housing in London: who expects to move and where? Housing Corporation Sector Studies: Sector Study, vol. 39. Housing Corporation, London (2004)
34. Böheim, R., Taylor, M.P.: Residential Mobility, Housing Tenure and the Labour Market in Britain. ILR working papers 035. Institute for Labour Research (1999)
35. Gibbons, S., Machin, S.: Valuing English Primary Schools'. Journal of Urban Economics 53, 197–219 (2003)
36. Black, S.: Do Better Schools Matter? Parental Valuation of Elementary Education. Quarterly Journal of Economics, 578–599 (1999)
37. Strand, S.: Pupil Mobility, Attainment and Progress in Key Stage 1: A Study in Cautious Interpretation. British Education Research Journal 28, 63–78 (2002)
38. de Smith, M., Goodchild, M., Longley, P.: Geospatial Analysis. Mathador, United Kingdom (2009)
39. Blau, P.: Inequality and Heterogeneity: A Primitive Theory of Social Structure. Free Press, New York (1977)

Author Index

Aleman, Florian   1

Birkin, Mark   152

Caminada, Martin   76
Chen, Shu-Heng   121

Dupont, Daniel   16

Evans, Andrew   152

Ferber, Jacques   1

Hofstede, Gert Jan   136

Jonker, Catholijn M.   136
Jordan, René   152

Kampouridis, Michael   121

Laur, Pierre-Alain   1

Michel, Fabien   1
Morvan, Gildas   16

North, Michael J.   108

Parunak, H. Van Dyke   44
Purvis, Martin   93
Purvis, Maryam   93

Sallach, David L.   108
Salvit, Jordan   28
Savarimuthu, Bastin Tony Roy   93
Savarimuthu, Sharmila   93
Sklar, Elizabeth   28
Staab, Eugen   76
Stonedahl, Forrest   61

Tatara, Eric   108
Tsang, Edward   121

Veremme, Alexandre   16
Verwaart, Tim   136

Wilensky, Uri   61